HOW BIG THINGS GET DONE

HOW BIG THINGS GET DONE

HOW BIG THINGS GET DONE

THE SURPRISING FACTORS
THAT DETERMINE THE FATE OF EVERY PROJECT,
FROM HOME RENOVATIONS TO SPACE EXPLORATION
AND EVERYTHING IN BETWEEN

BENT FLYVBJERG
and DAN GARDNER

CROWN CURRENCY
NEW YORK

Copyright © 2023 by Connaught Street Inc. and Bent Flyvbjerg

All rights reserved.

Published in the United States by Crown Currency, an imprint of Random House, a division of Penguin Random House LLC, New York.

CROWN is a registered trademark and CROWN CURRENCY and colophon are trademarks of Penguin Random House LLC.

Library of Congress Cataloging-in-Publication Data
Names: Flyvbjerg, Bent, author. | Gardner, Dan, author.
Title: How big things get done / Bent Flyvbjerg and Dan Gardner.
Identifiers: LCCN 2022036817 (print) | LCCN 2022036818 (ebook) | ISBN 9780593239513 (hardcover) | ISBN 9780593239520 (ebook)
Subjects: LCSH: Project management.
Classification: LCC HD69.P75 F58 2023 (print) | LCC HD69.P75 (ebook) | DDC 658.404—dc23/eng/20220830
LC record available at https://lccn.loc.gov/2022036817
LC ebook record available at https://lccn.loc.gov/2022036818

ISBN 978-0-593-23951-3
Ebook ISBN 978-0-593-23952-0
Export edition ISBN 978-0-593-79901-7

Printed in the United States of America on acid-free paper

currencybooks.com

2 4 6 8 9 7 5 3

First Export Edition

Book design by Fritz Metsch

To Carissa, in awe, with gratitude

CONTENTS

Introduction: California Dreamin'. ix

1. Think Slow, Act Fast 3
   The record of big projects is even worse than it seems.

2. The Commitment Fallacy 22
   You need to commit, but not in the way you think.

3. Think from Right to Left 43
   Start with the most basic question of all: Why?

4. Pixar Planning 60
   Plan like Pixar and Frank Gehry do.

5. Are You Experienced? 80
   Experience is often misunderstood and marginalized.

6. So You Think Your Project Is Unique? 97
   Think again. Your project is "one of those."

7. Can Ignorance Be Your Friend? 127
   Planning ruins projects, some say. But is it true?

8. A Single, Determined Organism 143
   Everyone must row in the same direction: toward delivery.

9. What's Your Lego? 157
   Modularity is the key to building at world-transforming scale.

Coda: Eleven Heuristics for Better Project Leadership 185

Appendix A: Base Rates for Cost Risk 191

Appendix B: Further Readings by Bent Flyvbjerg 193

Acknowledgments 197

Notes 203

Bibliography 239

Index 275

INTRODUCTION: CALIFORNIA DREAMIN'

How is a vision turned into a plan that becomes a triumphant new reality?

Let me tell you a story. You may have heard about it, particularly if you live in California. If you do, you're paying for it.

In 2008, Golden State voters were asked to imagine themselves at Union Station in downtown Los Angeles, on board a sleek silver train. Departing the station, the train slips quietly through the urban sprawl and endless traffic jams and accelerates as it enters the open spaces of the Central Valley, until the countryside is racing by in a blur. Breakfast is served. By the time attendants clear coffee cups and plates, the train slows and glides into another station. This is downtown San Francisco. The whole trip took two and a half hours, not much more than the time it would take the average Los Angeleno to drive to the airport, clear security, and get on a plane to queue on the tarmac, waiting for departure. The cost of the train ticket was $86.

The project was called California High-Speed Rail. It would connect two of the world's great cities, along with Silicon Valley, the global capital of high technology. Words such as *visionary* are used too liberally, but this really was visionary. And for a total cost of $33 billion it would be ready to roll by 2020.[1] In a statewide referendum, Californians approved. Work began.

As I write, it is now fourteen years later. Much about the project remains uncertain, but we can be sure that the end result will not be what was promised.

After voters approved the project, construction started at various points along the route, but the project was hit with constant delays. Plans were changed repeatedly. Cost estimates soared, to $43 billion, $68 billion, $77 billion, then almost $83 billion. As I write, the current highest estimate is $100 billion.[2] But the truth is that nobody knows what the full, final cost will be.

In 2019, California's governor announced that the state would complete only part of the route: the 171-mile section between the towns of Merced and Bakersfield, in California's Central Valley, at an estimated cost of $23 billion. But when that inland section is completed, the project will stop. It will be up to some future governor to decide whether to launch the project again and, if so, figure out how to get the roughly $80 billion—or whatever the number will be by then—to extend the tracks and finally connect Los Angeles and San Francisco.[3]

For perspective, consider that the cost of the line between only Merced and Bakersfield is the same as or more than the annual gross domestic product of Honduras, Iceland, and about a hundred other countries. And that money will build the most sophisticated rail line in North America between two towns most people outside California have never heard of. It will be—as critics put it—the "bullet train to nowhere."

How do visions become plans that deliver successful projects? Not like this. An ambitious vision is a wonderful thing. California was bold. It dreamed big. But even with buckets of money, a vision is not enough.

Let me tell you another story. This one is unknown, but I think it gets us closer to the answers we need.

In the early 1990s, Danish officials had an idea. Denmark is a small country with a population less than New York City's, but it is rich and gives a lot of money in foreign aid and wants that money to do good. Few things do more good than education. The Danish officials got together with colleagues from other governments and agreed to fund a school system for the Himalayan nation of Nepal. Twenty thousand schools and classrooms would be built, most of them in the poorest and most remote regions. Work would begin in 1992. It would take twenty years.[4]

The history of foreign aid is littered with boondoggles, and this project could easily have added to the mess. Yet it finished on budget in 2004—eight years ahead of schedule. In the years that followed, educational levels rose across the country, with a long list of positive consequences, particularly a jump in the number of girls in classrooms. The schools even saved lives: When a massive earthquake struck Nepal in 2015, almost nine thousand people died, with many being crushed to death in collapsing buildings. But the schools had been designed to be earthquake proof, as a first. They stood. Today, the Bill & Melinda Gates Foundation uses the project as an exemplar of how to improve health by increasing enrollment in schools, particularly for girls.[5]

I was the planner on that project.[6] At the time, I was pleased with how it turned out, but I didn't think much about it. It was my first big project, and, after all, we only did what we had said we would do: turn a vision into a plan that was delivered as promised.

However, in addition to being a planner, I am an academic, and the more I studied how big projects come together—or fail to—the more I understood that my experience in Nepal was not normal. In fact, it was not remotely normal. As we'll see, the data show that big projects that deliver as promised are rare. Normal looks a lot more like California High-Speed Rail. Average practice is a disaster, best practice an outlier, as I would later point out in my findings about megaproject management.[7]

Why is the track record of big projects so bad? Even more important, what about the rare, tantalizing exceptions? Why do they succeed where so many others fail? Had we just been lucky delivering the schools in Nepal? Or could we do it again? As a professor of planning and management, I've spent many years answering those questions.

As a consultant, I've spent many years putting my answers into practice. In this book, I'm putting them into print.

The focus of my work is megaprojects—*very* big projects—and lots of things about that category are special. Navigation of national politics and global bond markets, for example, is not something the average home remodeler has to contend with. But that stuff is for another book. What I'm interested in here are the drivers of project failure and success that are universal. That explains the title. *How Big Things Get Done* is a nod to my expertise in megaprojects, which are big by anyone's standards. But "big" is relative. For average homeowners, a home remodeling can easily be one of the most expensive, complex, challenging projects they ever tackle. Getting it right means as much or more to them as the fate of megaprojects means to corporations and governments. It is absolutely a "big thing."

So what are the universal drivers that make the difference between success and failure?

PSYCHOLOGY AND POWER

One driver is psychology. In any big project—meaning a project that is considered big, complex, ambitious, and risky by those in charge—people think, make judgments, and make decisions. And where there are thinking, judgment, and decisions, psychology is at play; for instance, in the guise of optimism.

Another driver is power. In any big project people and organizations compete for resources and jockey for position. Where there are competition and jockeying, there is power; for instance, that of a CEO or politician pushing through a pet project.

Psychology and power drive projects at all scales, from skyscrapers to kitchen renovations. They are present in projects made of bricks and mortar, bits and bytes, or any other medium. They are found whenever someone is excited by a vision and wants to turn it into a plan and make that plan a reality—whether the vision is to place another jewel in the Manhattan skyline or launch a new business, go to Mars, invent a new product, change an organization, design a program, convene a conference, write a book, host a family wedding, or renovate and transform a home.

With universal drivers at work, we can expect there to be patterns in how projects of all types unfold. And there are. The most common is perfectly illustrated by California's bullet train to nowhere.

The project was approved, and work began in a rush of excitement. But problems soon proliferated. Progress slowed. More problems arose. Things slowed further. The project dragged on and on. I call this pattern "Think fast, act slow," for reasons I'll explain later. It is a hallmark of failed projects.

Successful projects, by contrast, tend to follow the opposite pattern and advance quickly to the finish line. That's how the Nepal schools project unfolded. So did the Hoover Dam, which was completed a little under budget in fewer than five years—two ahead of schedule.[8] Boeing took twenty-eight months to design and build the first of its iconic 747s.[9] Apple hired the first employee to work on what would become the legendary iPod in late January 2001, the project was formally approved in March 2001, and the first iPod was shipped to customers in November 2001.[10] Amazon Prime, the online retailer's enormously successful membership and free shipping program, went from a vague idea to a public announcement between October 2004 and February 2005.[11] The first SMS texting app was developed in just a few weeks.

Then there's the Empire State Building.

A NEW YORK SUCCESS STORY

The vision that became arguably the world's most legendary skyscraper started with a pencil. Who held the pencil depends on which version of the story you trust. In one, it was the architect, William Lamb. In another, it was John J. Raskob, a financial wizard and former General Motors executive. In either case, a pencil was taken from a desk and held vertically, point up. That's what the Empire State Building would be: slim, straight, and stretching higher into the sky than any other building on the planet.[12]

The idea to erect a tower probably came early in 1929 from Al Smith. A lifelong New Yorker and former New York governor, Smith had been the Democratic presidential candidate in the 1928 election. Like most New Yorkers, Smith opposed Prohibition. Most Americans disagreed, and Smith lost to Herbert Hoover. Unemployed, Smith needed a new challenge. He took his idea to Raskob, and they formed Empire State Inc., with Smith acting as the president and face of the corporation and Raskob as its moneyman. They settled on a location—the site of the original Waldorf-Astoria hotel, once the pinnacle of Manhattan luxury—set the parameters of the project, and developed the business plan. They fixed the total budget, including the purchase and demolition of the Waldorf-Astoria, at $50 million ($820 million in 2021 dollars), and scheduled the grand opening for May 1, 1931. They hired Lamb's firm. Someone held up a pencil. At that point, they had eighteen months to go from first sketch to last rivet.

They moved fast because the moment was right. In the late 1920s, New York had overtaken London as the world's most populous metropolis, jazz was hot, stocks were soaring, the economy was booming, and skyscrapers—the thrilling new symbol of prosperous Machine Age America—were leaping up all over Manhattan. Financiers were looking for new projects to back, the more ambitious the better. The Chrysler Building would soon become the tallest of the titans, garnering all the prestige and rental income that went with the title. Raskob, Smith, and Lamb were determined to have their pencil top them all.

In planning the building, Lamb's focus was intensely practical. "The day that [the architect] could sit before his drawing board and make pretty sketches of decidedly uneconomic monuments to himself has gone," he wrote in January 1931. "His scorn of things 'practical' has been replaced by an intense earnestness to make practical necessities the armature upon which he moulds the form of his idea."

Working closely with the project's builders and engineers, Lamb developed designs shaped by the site and the need to stay on budget and schedule. "The adaptation of the design to conditions of use, construction and speed of erection has been kept to the fore throughout the development of the drawings of the Empire State," he wrote. The designs were rigorously tested to ensure that they would work. "Hardly a detail was issued without having been thoroughly analyzed by the builders and their experts and adjusted and changed to meet every foreseen delay."[13]

In a 1931 publication, the corporation boasted that before any work had been done on the construction site "the architects knew exactly how many beams and of what lengths, even how many rivets and bolts would be needed. They knew how many windows Empire State would have, how many blocks of limestone, and of what shapes and sizes, how many tons of aluminum and stainless steel, tons of cement, tons of mortar. Even before it was begun, Empire State was finished entirely—on paper."[14]

The first steam shovel clawed into the Manhattan dirt on March 17, 1930. More than three thousand workers swarmed the site, and construction advanced rapidly, beginning with the steel skeleton thrusting upward, followed by the completed first story. Then the second story. The third. The fourth. Newspapers reported on the skyscraper's rise as if it were a Yankees playoff run.

As workers learned and processes smoothed, progress accelerated. Up went three stories in one week. Four. Four and a half. At the height of construction, the pace hit a story a day.[15] And a little more.

"When we were in full swing going up the main tower," Lamb's partner Richmond Shreve recalled, "things clicked with such precision that once we erected fourteen and a half floors in ten working days—steel, concrete, stone and all."[16] That was an era when people marveled at the efficiency of factories churning out cars, and the Empire State designers were inspired to imagine their process as a vertical assembly line—except that "the assembly line did the moving," Shreve explained, while "the finished product stayed in place."[17]

By the time the Empire State Building was officially opened by President Herbert Hoover—exactly as scheduled, on May 1, 1931—it was already a local and national celebrity. Its height was daunting. The efficiency of its construction was legendary. And even though practicality had been at the front of Lamb's mind, the building was unmistakably beautiful. Lamb's drive for efficiency had created a lean, elegant design, and the New York chapter of the American Institute of Architects awarded it the 1931 Medal of Honor.[18] Then, in 1933, King Kong climbed the building on the silver screen while clutching the glamorous Fay Wray, and the Empire State Building became a global star.

The Empire State Building had been estimated to cost $50 million. It acually cost $41 million ($679 million in 2021). That's 17 percent under budget, or $141 million in 2021 dollars. Construction finished several weeks before the opening ceremony.

I call the pattern followed by the Empire State Building and other successful projects "Think slow, act fast."

At the start, I asked how a vision is turned into a plan that becomes a triumphant new reality. As we will see, that is the answer: Think slow, act fast.

HOW BIG THINGS GET DONE

HOW BIG THINGS GET DONE

1

THINK SLOW, ACT FAST

The record of big projects is even worse than it seems. But there is a solution: Speed up by slowing down.

Denmark is a peninsula with islands scattered along its east coast. Danes therefore long ago became experts at operating ferries and building bridges. So it was no surprise, in the late 1980s, when the government announced the Great Belt project. It comprised two bridges, one of which would be the world's longest suspension bridge, to connect two of the bigger islands, including the one with Copenhagen on it. There would also be an underwater tunnel for trains—the second longest in Europe—which would be built by a Danish-led contractor. That was interesting because Danes had little experience boring tunnels. I watched the announcement on the news with my father, who worked in bridge and tunnel construction. "Bad idea," he grumbled. "If I were digging a hole that big, I would hire someone who had done it before."

Things went wrong from the start. First there was a yearlong delay in delivering four giant tunnel-boring machines. Then, as soon as the machines were in the ground, they proved to be flawed and needed redesign, delaying work another five months. Finally, the big machines started slowly chewing their way under the ocean floor.

Up above, the bridge builders brought in a massive oceangoing dredger to prepare their worksite.[1] To do its work, the dredger stabilized itself by lowering giant support legs into the seafloor. When the work was done, the legs were lifted, leaving deep holes. By accident, one of the holes happened to be on the projected path of the tunnel. Neither the bridge builders nor the tunnelers saw the danger.

One day, after a few weeks of boring, one of the four machines was stopped for maintenance. It was about 250 meters (820 feet) out to sea and an assumed 10 meters (33 feet) under the seafloor. Water was seeping into the maintenance area in front of the machine, and a contractor unfamiliar with tunneling hooked up a pump to get the water out. The cables of the pump were trailed through a manhole into the boring machine. Suddenly water started pouring in at a speed indicating a breach of the tunnel. Evacuation was immediate—with no time to remove the pump and cables and close the manhole.

The machine and the whole tunnel flooded. So did a parallel tunnel and the boring machine within it.

Luckily, no one was injured or killed. But the salt water in the tunnel was like acid to its metal and electronics. Engineers on the project told me at the time that it would be cheaper to abandon the tunnel and start again rather than pull out the borers, drain the tunnel, and repair it. But politicians overrode them because an abandoned tunnel would be too embarrassing. Inevitably, the whole project came in very late and way over budget.

This story isn't all that unusual. There are lots more like it in the annals of big projects. But it was that project that nudged me to start a big project of my own—a database of big projects. It continues to grow. In fact, it is now the world's largest of its kind.

And it has a great deal to teach us about what works, what doesn't, and how to do better.

HONEST NUMBERS

After the accident, the recovery, and the eventual completion of the Great Belt bridges and tunnel, everyone agreed that the project had gone badly over budget. But by how much? Management said 29 percent for the whole project. I dug into the data, did my own analysis, and discovered that their number was, shall we say, optimistic. The actual overrun was 55 percent, and 120 percent for the tunnel alone (in real terms, measured from the final investment decision). Still, management kept repeating their number in public, and I kept correcting them, until they did a public opinion poll that showed that the public sided with me. Then they gave up. Later, an official national audit confirmed my numbers, and the case was closed.[2]

That experience taught me that megaproject management may not be a field of what University of Washington public affairs professor Walter Williams called "honest numbers."[3] As simple as it should be in theory to judge projects, in practice it's anything but. In every big project, there are blizzards of numbers generated at different stages by different parties. Finding the right ones—those that are valid and reliable—takes skill and work. Even trained scholars get it wrong.[4] And it doesn't help that big projects involve money, reputations, and politics. Those who have much to lose will spin the numbers, so you cannot trust them. That's not fraud. Or rather, it's not usually fraud; it's human nature. And with so many numbers to choose from, spinning is a lot easier than finding the truth.

This is a serious problem. Projects are promised to be completed by a certain time, at a certain cost, with certain benefits produced as a result—benefits being things such as revenues, savings, passengers moved, or megawatts of electricity generated. So how often do projects deliver as promised? That is the most straightforward question anyone could ask. But when I started to look around in the 1990s, I was stunned to discover that no one could answer it. The data simply hadn't been collected and analyzed. That made no sense when *trillions* of dollars had been spent on the giant projects increasingly being called megaprojects—projects with budgets in excess of $1 billion.

Our database started with transportation projects: the Holland

Tunnel in New York; the BART system in San Francisco; the Channel Tunnel in Europe; bridges, tunnels, highways, and railways built throughout the twentieth century. It took five years, but with my team I got 258 projects into the database, making it the biggest of its kind at the time.[5] When we finally began publishing the numbers in 2002, it made waves because nothing like it had been done before.[6] Also, the picture that emerged wasn't pretty.

"Project estimates between 1910 and 1998 were short of the final costs an average of 28 percent," according to *The New York Times*, summarizing our findings. "The biggest errors were in rail projects, which ran, on average, 45 percent over estimated costs [in inflation-adjusted dollars]. Bridges and tunnels were 34 percent over; roads, 20 percent. Nine of 10 estimates were low, the study said."[7] The results for time and benefits were similarly bad.

And these are conservative readings of the data. Measured differently—from an earlier date and including inflation—the numbers are *much* worse.[8]

The global consultancy McKinsey got in touch with me and proposed that we do joint research. Its researchers had started investigating major information technology projects—the biggest of which cost more than $10 billion—and their preliminary numbers were so dismal that they said it would take a big improvement for IT projects to rise to the level of awfulness of transportation projects. I laughed. It seemed impossible that IT could be that bad. But I worked with McKinsey, and indeed we found that IT disasters were even worse than transportation disasters. But otherwise it was a broadly similar story of cost and schedule overruns and benefit shortfalls.[9]

That was startling. Think of a bridge or a tunnel. Now picture the US government's HealthCare.gov website, which was a mess when it first opened as the "Obamacare" enrollment portal. Or imagine the information system used by the National Health Service in the United Kingdom. These IT projects are made of code, not steel and concrete. They would seem to be different from transportation infrastructure in every possible way. So why would their outcomes be statistically so similar, with consistent cost and schedule overruns and benefit shortfalls?

We shifted our research to mega-events such as the Olympic Games and got the same result. Big dams? Same again. Rockets? Defense? Nuclear power? The same. Oil and gas projects? Mining? Same. Even something as common as building museums, concert halls, and skyscrapers fit the pattern. I was astonished.[10]

And the problem wasn't limited to any country or region; we found the same pattern all over the world.[11] The famously efficient Germans have some remarkable examples of bloat and waste, including Berlin's new Brandenburg Airport, which was years delayed and billions of euros over budget, hovering on the verge of bankruptcy only a year after opening in October 2020.[12]

Even Switzerland, the nation of precise clocks and punctual trains, has its share of embarrassing projects; for instance, the Lötschberg Base Tunnel, which was completed late and with a cost overrun of 100 percent.

OVER BUDGET, OVER TIME, OVER AND OVER AGAIN

The pattern was so clear that I started calling it the "Iron Law of Megaprojects": over budget, over time, under benefits, over and over again.[13]

The Iron Law is not a "law" like in Newtonian physics, meaning something that invariably produces the same outcome. I study people. In the social sciences, "laws" are probabilistic (they are in natural science, too, but Isaac Newton didn't pay much attention to that). And the probability that any big project will blow its budget and schedule and deliver disappointing benefits is very high and very reliable.

The database that started with 258 projects now contains more than 16,000 projects from 20-plus different fields in 136 countries on all continents except Antarctica, and it continues to grow. There are some recent and important wrinkles in the numbers, which I'll discuss later, but the general story remains the same: In total, only 8.5 percent of projects hit the mark on both cost and time. And a minuscule 0.5 percent nail cost, time, and benefits. Or to put that another way, 91.5 percent of projects go over budget, over schedule, or both. And 99.5 percent of projects go over budget, over schedule, under benefits, or some combination of these. Doing what you said you would do should be routine, or at least common. But it almost never happens.

Graphically, the Iron Law looks like this:

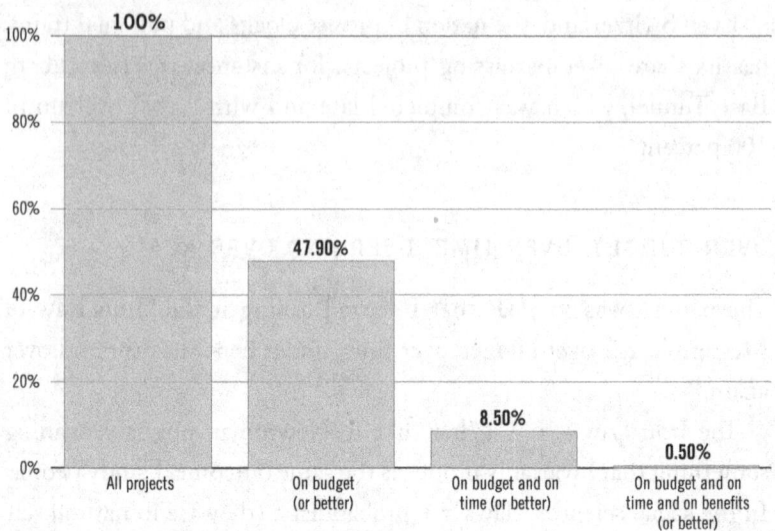

THE IRON LAW OF PROJECT MANAGEMENT:
"Over Budget, Over Time, Under Benefits, Over and Over Again"

Tellingly, the 0.5 percent of projects that are on budget, time, and benefits are nearly invisible to the naked eye. It's hard to overstate how bad that record is. For anyone contemplating a big project, it is truly depressing. But as grim as those numbers are, they don't tell the full truth—which is *much* worse.

From experience, I know that most people are aware that cost and time overruns are common. They don't know *how* common—they are usually shocked when I show them my numbers—but they definitely know that if they lead a big project, they should consider and protect themselves against overruns, particularly cost overruns. The obvious way to do that is to build a buffer into the budget. You hope it won't be needed, but you'll be covered just in case. How big should that buffer be? Typically, people make it 10 percent or 15 percent.

But let's say you are an unusually cautious person and you are planning the construction of a large building. You put a 20 percent buffer into the budget and think you are now well protected. But then you come across my research and discover that the actual mean cost overrun of a major building project is 62 percent. That is heart-stopping. It may also be project-stopping. But let's say you are the very rare planner who can get your financial backers to cover that risk and still go ahead with the project. You now have an extraordinary 62 percent buffer built into your budget. In the real world, that almost never happens. But you're one of the fortunate few. Are you at last protected? No. In fact, you have *still* drastically underestimated the danger.

That's because you have assumed that if you are hit with a cost overrun, it will be somewhere around the mean—or 62 percent. Why did you assume that? Because it would be true if the cost overruns followed what statisticians call a "normal distribution." That's the famous bell curve, which looks like a bell when graphed. Much of statistics is built upon bell curves—sampling, averages, standard deviations, the law of large numbers, regression to the mean, statistical tests—and it has filtered into the culture and into the popular imagination, where it fits well with how we intuitively grasp risk. In a normal distribution, results are overwhelmingly lumped in the middle and there are very few or no extreme observations at either end—the so-called tails of the distribution. These tails are therefore said to be *thin*.

Height is normally distributed. Depending on where you live, most adult males are around five feet, nine inches (1.75 meters) tall, and the tallest person in the world is only about 1.6 times taller than that.[14]

But the "normal" distribution isn't the only sort of distribution that exists—or even the most common one. So it is not normal in that sense of the word. There are other distributions that are called "fat-tailed" because, compared with normal distributions, they contain far more extreme outcomes in their tails.

Wealth, for example, is fat-tailed. At the time of writing, the wealthiest person in the world is 3,134,707 times wealthier than the average person. If human height followed the same distribution as human wealth, the tallest person in the world would not be 1.6 times taller than the average person; he would be 3,311 miles (5,329 kilometers) tall, meaning that his head would be thirteen times farther into outer space than the International Space Station.[15]

So the critical question is this: Are project outcomes distributed "normally," or do they have fat tails? My database revealed that information technology projects have fat tails. To illustrate, 18 percent of IT projects have cost overruns above 50 percent in real terms. And for those projects the average overrun is 447 percent! That's the *average* in the tail, meaning that many IT projects in the tail have even higher overruns than this. Information technology is *truly* fat-tailed![16] So are nuclear storage projects. And the Olympic Games. And nuclear power plants. And big hydroelectric dams. As are airports, defense projects, big buildings, aerospace projects, tunnels, mining projects, high-speed rail, urban rail, conventional rail, bridges, oil projects, gas projects, and water projects. (See Appendix A.)

In fact, most project types have fat tails. How "fat" their tails are—how many projects fall into the extremes and how extreme those extremes are—does vary. I've cited them in order, from fattest to least fat (but still fat)—or, if you prefer, from most at risk of terrifying overruns to less at risk (but still very much at risk).[17]

There *are* a few project types that do not have fat tails. That's important. I'll explain why, and how we can all make use of this fact, in the last chapter.

But for now the lesson is simple, clear, and scary: Most big projects are not merely at risk of not delivering as promised. Nor are they only at risk of going seriously wrong. They are at risk of going *disastrously* wrong because their risk is fat-tailed. Against that background, it is interesting to note that the project management literature almost completely ignores systematic study of the fat-tailedness of project risk.

What do fat-tailed outcomes look like? Boston's "Big Dig"—replacing an elevated highway with a tunnel, with construction started in 1991—put the city through the wringer for sixteen years and cost more than *triple* what it was supposed to. NASA's James Webb Space Telescope, which is now almost a million miles from Earth, was forecast to take twelve years but required nineteen to complete, while its final cost of $8.8 billion was an astronomical—forgive me—450 percent over budget. Canada's firearms registry, an IT project, went 590 percent over budget. And then there is Scotland's Parliament Building. When it opened in 2004, it was three years late and a bagpipe-exploding 978 percent over budget.

Nassim Nicholas Taleb famously dubbed low-probability, high-consequence events "black swans." Disastrous project outcomes such as these can end careers, sink companies, and inflict a variety of other carnage. They definitely qualify as black swans.

Just look at what a black swan outcome did to Kmart: Responding to competitive pressure from Walmart and Target, it launched two enormous IT projects in 2000. Costs exploded, contributing directly to the company's decision to file for bankruptcy in 2002.[18] Or consider what another IT blowout did to the legendary jeans maker Levi

Strauss: Originally forecast to cost $5 million, the project forced the company to take a $200 million loss and show its CIO the door.[19]

There are worse fates for executives. When a troubled nuclear power plant project in South Carolina fell badly behind schedule, the CEO of the company in charge withheld that information from regulators "in an effort to keep the project going," noted a 2021 US Department of Justice press release, which also announced that the executive had been sentenced to two years in federal prison and forced to pay $5.2 million in forfeitures and fines.[20] Black swan outcomes do indeed have consequences for projects and those who lead them.

If you are not a corporate executive or government official, and if the ambitious project you are contemplating is on a much smaller scale than these giants, it may be tempting to think that none of this applies to you. Resist that temptation. My data show that smaller projects are susceptible to fat tails, too. Moreover, fat-tailed distributions, not normal distributions, are typical within complex systems, both natural and human, and we all live and work within increasingly complex systems, which means increasingly interdependent systems. Cities and towns are complex systems. Markets are complex systems. Energy production and distribution are complex systems. Manufacturing and transportation are complex systems. Debt is a complex system. So are viruses. And climate change. And globalization. On and on the list goes. If your project is ambitious and depends on other people and many parts, it is all but certain that your project is embedded in complex systems.

That describes projects of all types and scales, all the way down to home renovations. A few years ago, in a BBC show about renovating historic British properties, one episode featured a London couple who bought a run-down house in the countryside and got a builder to estimate the cost of a complete renovation. He pegged it at $260,000. Eighteen months later, the project was far from done and the couple had already spent $1.3 million.[21] That is the sort of overrun we would expect to find in a fat-tailed distribution. And it is certainly not unique. Later in the book, we'll witness a home renovation in Brooklyn spin wildly out of control and inflict an equally devastating overrun on the unfortunate and unexpecting homeowners.

That London couple were apparently wealthy enough to keep funding the renovation. Similarly, major corporations on the hook for runaway projects may be able to keep things going by borrowing more and more money. Governments can also pile up debt. Or raise taxes. But most ordinary folks and small businesses cannot draw on a big stockpile of wealth, run up debt, or raise taxes. If they start a project that hurtles toward the fat tail of the distribution, they will simply be wiped out, giving them even more reason than a corporate executive or government official to take the danger seriously.

And that starts by understanding what causes project failure.

THE WINDOW OF DOOM

The patterns I mentioned earlier, confirmed by my data, are strong clues: Projects that fail tend to drag on, while those that succeed zip along and finish.

Why is that? Think of the duration of a project as an open window. The longer the duration, the more open the window. The more open the window, the more opportunity for something to crash through and cause trouble, including a big, bad black swan.

What could that black swan be? Almost anything. It could be something dramatic, like an election upset, a stock market collapse, or a pandemic. After Covid-19 emerged in January 2020, projects all over the world—from the 2020 Tokyo Olympics to the release of the James Bond movie *No Time to Die*—were delayed, postponed, or scrapped altogether. Events such as these may be extremely unlikely on any given day, month, or year. But the more time that passes from the decision to do a project to its delivery, the greater their probability.

Notice that these big, dramatic events, which are easily capable of damaging a project so badly that it delivers a black swan outcome, are themselves low probability and high consequence. That is, they are black swans. So a black swan crashing through the window of vulnerability may itself cause a black swan outcome.

But drama isn't necessary for change to batter and bury projects. Even mundane change can do that. Journalists who write biographies of up-and-coming politicians know, for example, that the market for their books depends on the politician continuing to be on the rise when the book is released. Any number of events can change that: a scandal, a lost election; an illness; a death. Even something as simple as the politician getting bored with politics and taking another job would ruin the project. Again, the more time that passes from decision to delivery, the greater the probability of one or more of these events happening. It's even possible that trivial events, in just the wrong circumstances, can have devastating consequences.

It's hard to think of anything more trivial to most people around the world than gusts of wind in the Egyptian desert. Yet on March 23, 2021, it was just such gusts, at just the wrong moment, that pushed the bow of *Ever Given*, a giant container ship, into a bank of the Suez Canal. The ship got stuck and couldn't be budged for six days, blocking the canal, halting hundreds of ships, freezing an estimated $10 billion in trade each day, and sending shocks rippling through global supply chains.[22] The people and projects who suffered as a result of those supply-chain troubles may never have realized it, but the cause of their trouble was ultimately strong winds in a faraway desert.[23]

A complex systems theorist might describe what happened by saying that the dynamic interdependencies among the parts of the system—the wind, the canal, the ship, and supply chains—created strong nonlinear responses and amplification. In plain English, minor changes combined in a way to produce a disaster. In complex systems, that happens so often that the Yale sociologist Charles Perrow called such events "normal accidents."[24]

Growing complexity and interdependency may make such outcomes more likely in today's world, but they are hardly a new phenomenon. A proverb that originated in the Middle Ages and comes in many forms tells us, "For want of a nail, the shoe was lost. For want of a shoe, the horse was lost. For want of a horse, the rider was lost. For want of a rider, the battle was lost. For want of a battle, the kingdom was lost." This version was published by Benjamin Franklin in 1758, and he introduced it with the warning that "a little neglect may breed great mischief." The key word is *may*. Most nails can be lost without anything bad happening at all. A few such losses will have consequences, but they will be minor, like the loss of one horse or one rider. But sometimes a lost nail may cause something truly terrible.

From the dramatic to the mundane to the trivial, change can rattle or ruin a project—if it occurs during the window of time when the project is ongoing.

Solution? Close the window.

Of course, a project can't be completed instantly, so we can't close the window entirely. But we can make the opening radically smaller by speeding up the project and bringing it to a conclusion faster. That is a main means of reducing risk on any project.

In sum, keep it short!

THE NEED FOR SPEED

How do we get a project done as quickly as possible? The obvious answer—and certainly the most common one—is to set severe timelines, get started right away, and demand that everyone involved work at a furious pace. Drive and ambition are key, goes the conventional wisdom. If experienced observers think a project will take two years, say you will do it in one. Commit to the project, heart and soul, and charge ahead. And in managing others, be fierce. Demand that everything be done yesterday. Like the drummer on a Roman galley preparing to ram a ship, beat the drum at a furious pace.

This thinking is as misguided as it is common. There is a monument to it in Copenhagen.

The Copenhagen Opera House, the home of the Royal Danish Opera, was the vision of Arnold Maersk Mc-Kinney Møller, the CEO and chairman of Maersk, the Danish shipping giant. In the late 1990s, Møller, who was then in his late eighties, decided he wanted a grand building situated prominently at the harborside as his very visible and permanent legacy. And he wanted it designed and built quickly. The queen of Denmark would attend the opening, and Møller had no intention of missing his big night. When Møller asked the architect, Henning Larsen, how long it would take, Larsen said five years. "You'll get four!" Møller curtly responded.[25] With much beating of galley drums, the deadline was met, and Møller and the queen opened the opera house together on January 15, 2005.

But the cost of that haste was terrible, and not only in terms of cost overruns. Larsen was so appalled by the completed building that he wrote a whole book to clear his reputation and explain the confused structure, which he called a "mausoleum."

Haste makes waste.

Even that cost is mild compared to what rushing projects this way can do. In 2021, after an overpass collapsed beneath a metro train in Mexico City, three independent investigations concluded that rushed, shoddy work was to blame. A Norwegian firm hired by the city to conduct an investigation concluded that the tragedy had been caused by "deficiencies in the construction process," as did a later report released by the attorney general of Mexico City.[26] *The New York Times* did its own investigation and concluded that the city's insistence that construction be completed before the city's powerful mayor was due to leave office had been a key contributing cause of the collapse. "The scramble led to a frenzied construction process that began before a master plan had been finalized and produced a metro line with defects from the start," the *Times* concluded.[27] The collapse of the overpass killed twenty-six people. Haste makes not only waste but tragedy.

MAKE HASTE—SLOWLY

To understand the right way to get a project done quickly, it's useful to think of a project as being divided into two phases. This is a simplification, but it works: first, planning; second, delivery. The terminology varies by industry—in movies, it's "development and production"; in architecture, "design and construction"—but the basic idea is the same everywhere: Think first, then do.

A project begins with a vision that is, at best, a vague image of the glorious thing the project will become. Planning is pushing the vision to the point where it is sufficiently researched, analyzed, tested, and detailed that we can be confident we have a reliable road map of the way forward.

Most planning is done with computers, paper, and physical models, meaning that planning is relatively cheap and safe. Barring other time pressures, it's fine for planning to be slow. Delivery is another matter. Delivery is when serious money is spent and the project becomes vulnerable as a consequence.

Consider a Hollywood director working on a live-action movie project in February 2020. The Covid pandemic is about to arrive. How badly will that hurt the project? The answer depends on what stage the project is in. If the director and her team are writing scripts, drawing storyboards, and scheduling location shoots—if they are planning, in other words—it's a problem but not a disaster. In fact, a lot of the work will probably continue despite the pandemic. But what if, when the pandemic arrives, the director is filming in the streets of New York with a crew of two hundred plus a handful of very expensive movie stars? Or what if the movie is finished but still a month away from its release in theaters that are about to close indefinitely? That's not a problem; it's a disaster.

Planning is a safe harbor. Delivery is venturing across the storm-tossed seas. This is a major reason why, at Pixar—the legendary studio that created *Toy Story, Finding Nemo, The Incredibles, Soul*, and so many other era-defining animated movies—"directors are allowed to spend years in the development phase of a movie," noted Ed Catmull, a co-founder of Pixar. There is a cost associated with exploring ideas, writing scripts, storyboarding images, and doing it all over and over again. But "the costs of iterations are relatively low."[28] And all that good work produces a rich, detailed, tested, and proven plan. When the project moves into the production phase, it will, as a consequence of all that work, be relatively smooth and quick. That's essential, Catmull noted, because production "is where costs explode."

Not only is it safer for planning to be slow, it is *good* for planning to be slow, as the directors at Pixar well know. After all, cultivating ideas and innovations takes time. Spotting the implications of different options and approaches takes more time. Puzzling through complex problems, coming up with solutions, and putting them to the test take still more time. Planning requires thinking—and creative, critical, careful thinking is slow.

Abraham Lincoln is reputed to have said that if he had five minutes to chop down a tree, he'd spend the first three sharpening the ax.[29] That's exactly the right approach for big projects: Put enormous care and effort into planning to ensure that delivery is smooth and swift.

Think slow, act fast: That's the secret of success.

"Think slow, act fast" may not be a new idea. It was on grand display back in 1931, after all, when the Empire State Building raced to the sky. You could even say that the idea goes at least as far back as

Rome's first emperor, the mighty Caesar Augustus, whose personal motto was "*Festina lente,*" or "Make haste slowly."

But "Think slow, act fast" is not how big projects are typically done. "Think fast, act slow" is. The track record of big projects unequivocally shows that.

PROJECTS DON'T *GO* WRONG, THEY *START* WRONG

Look at California High-Speed Rail. When it was approved by voters and construction started, there were lots of documents and numbers that may have superficially resembled a plan. But there was no carefully detailed, deeply researched, and thoroughly tested program, which is to say that there was no real plan. Louis Thompson, an expert on transportation projects who chairs the California High-Speed Rail Peer Review Group convened by the California State Legislature, says that what California had in hand when the project got under way could at best be described as a "vision" or an "aspiration."[30] It's no wonder that problems started multiplying and progress slowed to a crawl soon after delivery began.

That is, sadly, typical. On project after project, rushed, superficial planning is followed by a quick start that makes everybody happy because shovels are in the ground. But inevitably, the project crashes into problems that were overlooked or not seriously analyzed and dealt with in planning. People run around trying to fix things. More stuff breaks. There is more running around. I call this the "break-fix cycle." A project that enters it is like a mammoth stuck in a tar pit.

People say that projects "go wrong," which they all too often do. But phrasing it that way is misleading; projects don't *go* wrong so much as they *start* wrong.

This raises an urgent question: If "Think slow, act fast" is the wise approach, why do leaders of big projects so often do the opposite? I'll answer that question in chapter 2.

In chapter 3, I'll look at how to start a project without stumbling into the "Think fast, act slow" tar pit.

People often think that planning is about filling in flowcharts. And too often, it is. But it shouldn't be. In chapter 4, I'll take a close look at what I call "Pixar planning," how the movie studio and others use simulation and iteration to produce a plan that is creative, rigorous, detailed, and reliable—and highly likely to make delivery smooth and swift. I'll use "Pixar planning" as a name and a model for planning, not just at Pixar but for any planning that develops a tested and tried plan; that is, a plan worthy of its name.

In chapter 5, I'll examine the invaluable role of experience in both planning and delivery of big projects—or rather, the invaluable role it could play if it were not so often marginalized, misunderstood, or simply ignored.

In chapter 6, it's on to forecasting. How long will the project take? How much will it cost? Setting the wrong expectations at the start can set you up for failure before you've even started. Fortunately, there is a fix. More fortunately, it's surprisingly easy.

Some people will object to all this emphasis on planning. They believe that big projects, particularly creative projects such as movies, signature architecture, or innovative software, get better results when people take a leap of faith, get started right away, and rely on ingenuity to see them through. In chapter 7, I'll examine this argument in its strongest form—and present the data to prove that it's dead wrong.

But even the best plan won't succeed if it doesn't have a solid team delivering it. So in chapter 8, I'll look at how one giant project successfully drew together thousands of people from hundreds of different organizations with different interests and turned them into a united, determined, effective team that delivered the planned benefits on time and on budget.

In the final chapter, I'll draw on the themes of the previous chapters to explore a concept that brings them all together: modularity. Its potential is huge. Not only can it cut costs, boost quality, and speed things up for a vast array of projects from wedding cakes to subways, it can transform how we build infrastructure—and even help save the world from climate change.

But first we have to answer that question about why projects so often start prematurely. Let me tell you the story of a man in a hurry—and how he almost ruined one of the most beautiful places in the United States.

2

THE COMMITMENT FALLACY

If "Think slow, act fast" is the wise approach to big projects, why do so many people do the exact opposite? Because they rush to commit. You do need to commit. But not in the way you think.

In July 1941, the United States was the last major power sitting out World War II. Few expected that to last. President Franklin Delano Roosevelt had declared a national emergency and was rapidly expanding the country's tiny peacetime military into a giant capable of fighting fascism in Europe and the Pacific.

The government's War Department, scattered around Washington, DC, in a number of small office buildings, urgently needed a proper headquarters. It would have to be huge. And it would have to be built quickly. That was the conclusion of Brigadier General Brehon B. Somervell, the chief of the army's Construction Division. And when Brehon Somervell decided to do something, it usually got done. He was an engineer with a record of building big things—most recently New York's LaGuardia Airport—faster than anyone had thought possible. "He drove his staff relentlessly, seven days a week, leaving officers exhausted," wrote Steve Vogel, the author of *The Pentagon: A History*, a superb chronicle of the building's construction.[1]

THE MISSHAPEN PENTAGON

On the evening of July 17, a Thursday, Somervell gave his staff their marching orders: Draft a plan for an office building of five hundred thousand square feet, twice as much as in the Empire State Building. But it can't be a skyscraper; that would take too much steel at a time when steel is needed for ships and tanks. And it can't be in the District of Columbia; there is no room. It has to be across the Potomac River in Virginia, on the site of a recently abandoned airfield. Half the building will be finished and operating in six months, Somervell told them. The whole thing will be fully open in a year. Have the plan on my desk Monday morning, the general said, ending his instructions.

Somervell's staff quickly realized that the selected site was a marshy floodplain unsuitable for construction. They scrambled to find another site and came up with one half a mile upriver on a plateau between Arlington National Cemetery and the Potomac. The new site was called "Arlington Farm." Somervell approved the switch.

Arlington Farm was bounded on five sides by roads, giving it an irregular shape. To make the building as big as it needed to be, Somervell's staff designed it to fill most of the land within the five sides. The result was a misshapen pentagon. It was downright ugly, a draftsman recalled later, but "it fit."[2]

On Monday morning, the plan was on Somervell's desk. He approved it, took it to the secretary of war, praised it, and got the secretary's sign-off. Then he took the plan to a congressional subcommittee, praised it some more, and got the subcommittee's unanimous support. The secretary of war then took the plan to the cabinet, where President Roosevelt nodded his personal approval. The entire process took exactly one week.

Reading this so many decades later, you may think you know how the story ends. The Pentagon was indeed built, it played a critical role during the Second World War, and it became one of the most famous buildings in the world. So maybe this is a model of how to quickly plan and deliver a big project? But no. Notice that the pentagon described here is "misshapen." The Pentagon that we know today is not. It is symmetrical. And it is *not* the product of Somervell's original plan, which was never used. Because the plan was terrible.

To see why, you need to follow the millions of tourists who annually cross the Potomac River to stand at the heart of Arlington National Cemetery. You're on a high bluff. In the distance, you can see the Capitol dome, the Washington Monument, and all the other grand buildings and monuments of Washington, DC. The gentle slopes of the bluff are green and covered with long, straight lines of headstones marking the last resting places of Americans who died in combat or served their country in uniform as far back as the Civil War. Prominent among them is the grave of John F. Kennedy.

And right there, smack in the middle of that beautiful and bittersweet vista, is the site once known as Arlington Farm, the place where Brehon Somervell wanted to build the world's biggest and ugliest office building. Imagine building a ring of banal skyscrapers around the Eiffel Tower. That's how bad Somervell's plan was. "The unparalleled view of Washington from the heights of Arlington Cemetery would be distorted by acres upon acres of ugly flat roofs," a newspaper editorialist moaned in 1941 after Somervell's plan was made public. It "would be an act of vandalism."[3]

In Somervell's defense, the United States was facing a global emergency, so you might think that aesthetic and cultural concerns had to be thrown overboard. His staff had no choice.

Except they did. Less than a mile south of the Arlington Farm site and just outside Arlington Cemetery's spectacular vista lay the "Quartermaster Depot" site. It met all the technical requirements. Somervell's critics identified the site and fought to move the project there. Eventually, they won. That's where the Pentagon is today. Not only did that site leave the view from Arlington Cemetery unsullied; the size of the site allowed the architects to even up the sides of the building and make it symmetrical. That made the building more functional, cheaper to build, and a lot less ugly.

So why didn't Somervell realize that there was a much better site available before he sought and got approval for the original design? Why didn't any of those who approved the plan spot the flaw? Because Somervell's plan was so absurdly rushed and superficial that no one had even looked for other sites, much less considered their relative merits carefully. They had all treated the first suitable site identified as the *only* suitable site and hurried to get construction going as quickly as possible. Such limited vision is rooted deep in our psychology, as we will see later. That doesn't make it any the wiser for big projects.

Harold Ickes, Roosevelt's long-serving secretary of the interior, was appalled when the president gave quick approval to Somervell's original plan. "Here was another example of acting before thinking," he wrote in his diary—words that can be applied with depressing frequency to big projects.[4]

THE RUSH TO COMMIT

Brehon Somervell was anything but a foolish or incompetent person. The same was true of Franklin Delano Roosevelt and the other highly accomplished people who approved Somervell's plan. Yet in this case, they proceeded in a way that is self-evidently foolish and incompetent. It seems hard to fathom. But fathom it we must, because although the details of this story may be extreme—particularly the speed—it is fundamentally typical of how big projects come together. Purposes and goals are *not* carefully considered. Alternatives are *not* explored. Difficulties and risks are *not* investigated. Solutions are *not* found. Instead, shallow analysis is followed by quick lock-in to a decision that sweeps aside all the other forms the project could take.

"Lock-in," as scholars refer to it, is the notion that although there may be alternatives, most people and organizations behave as if they have no choice but to push on, even past the point where they put themselves at more cost or risk than they would have accepted at the start. This is followed by action. And usually, sometime after that, by trouble; for instance, in the guise of the "break-fix cycle" mentioned in chapter 1.

I call such premature lock-in the "commitment fallacy." It is a behavioral bias on a par with the other biases identified by behavioral science.

The only thing that is truly unusual about the Pentagon story is that a group of politically connected critics managed to expose the flaws in Somervell's plan after it had been approved and get the project moved to another site—the one where the Pentagon is today. Happy endings are rare when projects start in a rush based on the commitment fallacy.

It is not exactly a secret that careful thinking about what a project is trying to achieve and how best to bring it about is more likely to lead to a positive outcome than a rushed commitment is. "Act in haste, repent at leisure" is a centuries-old chestnut. One variation of that saying replaces "act" with "marry." And in the novel *Infinite Jest*, David Foster Wallace observed that this old advice seems "custom-designed for the case of tattoos." Tattoos, marriages, big projects: In every case, we know we really should think it through carefully, so why do we so often fail to do so?

I can't help with tattoos and marriages, but when it comes to big projects, there are several explanations.

One is what I call "strategic misrepresentation," the tendency to deliberately and systematically distort or misstate information for strategic purposes.[5] If you want to win a contract or get a project approved, superficial planning is handy because it glosses over major challenges, which keeps the estimated cost and time down, which wins contracts and gets projects approved. But as certain as the law of gravity, challenges ignored during planning will eventually boomerang back as delays and cost overruns during delivery. By then the project will be too far along to turn back. Getting to that point of no return is the real goal of strategic misrepresentation. It is politics, resulting in failure by design.

A second is psychology. In 2003, I had a spirited debate with Daniel Kahneman, a Nobel laureate and arguably the most influential living psychologist, in the pages of the *Harvard Business Review* after he co-wrote an article pinning responsibility for bad decisions on psychology. I agreed, of course, that psychology was at work. The question was how much it was to blame relative to politics.[6]

After debating in print, Kahneman invited me to meet and discuss matters further. I also arranged for him to visit megaproject planners so he could study their experiences firsthand. Eventually each of us came to accept the other's position: psychology for me and politics for Kahneman.[7] Which factor is most important depends on the character of decisions and projects. In Kahneman's laboratory experiments, the stakes are low. There is typically no jockeying for position, no competition for scarce resources, no powerful individuals or organizations, no politics of any kind. The closer a project is to that situation, the more individual psychology will dominate, which is what Kahneman, Amos Tversky, and other behavioral scientists have found. But as projects get bigger and decisions more consequential, the influence of money and power grows. Powerful individuals and organizations make the decisions, the number of stakeholders increases, they lobby for their specific interests, and the name of the game is *politics*. And the balance shifts from psychology to strategic misrepresentation.[8]

That said, the common denominator of any project is that people are making the decisions about it. And wherever there are people, there are psychology and power.

Let's start with psychology.

YOU WANT THE FLIGHT ATTENDANT, NOT THE PILOT, TO BE AN OPTIMIST

We are a deeply optimistic species. That makes us an overconfident species.[9] The large majority of car drivers say that their driving skills are above average.[10] Most small-business owners are confident that their new business will succeed even though most small businesses fail.[11] Smokers believe that they are at less risk of lung cancer than other smokers.[12] There are countless more illustrations like these in the psychological literature.

The sheer pervasiveness of optimism and overconfidence suggests that they are useful for us, individually and collectively, and there's plenty of research and experience to support that conclusion. We definitely need optimism and a can-do attitude to inspire big projects and see them through. Or to get married and have kids. Or to get up in the morning. But if while boarding a plane you overhear the pilot say, "I'm optimistic about the fuel situation," get off immediately, because this is neither the time nor the place for optimism. My key heuristic for managing optimism on projects is "You want the flight attendant, not the pilot, to be an optimist." What you need from your pilot, and must insist on, is hard-nosed analysis that sees reality as clearly as possible. The same holds for optimism about budgets and schedules on big projects, which are their "fuel readings." Unchecked, optimism leads to unrealistic forecasts, poorly defined goals, better options ignored, problems not spotted and dealt with, and no contingencies to counteract the inevitable surprises. Yet, as we will see in later chapters, optimism routinely displaces hard-nosed analysis in big projects, as in so much else people do.

"Optimism is widespread, stubborn, and costly," observed Kahneman. His work with Tversky helped explain why.[13]

One of the basic insights of modern psychology is that quick and intuitive "snap judgments" are the default operating system of human decision making—"System One," to use the term coined by the psychologists Keith Stanovich and Richard West and made famous by Kahneman. Conscious reasoning is a different system: System Two.[14] A key difference between Systems One and Two is speed. System One is fast, so it always delivers first. System Two is slow; it can get involved only after System One delivers. Both systems may be right or wrong.

To generate snap judgments, the brain can't be overly demanding about information. Instead, it proceeds on the basis of what Kahneman calls "WYSIATI" (What You See Is All There Is), meaning an assumption that whatever information we have on hand is all the information available to make the decision.

After a quick and intuitive judgment is delivered by System One, we can think about the problem slowly and carefully, if we have time, using System Two, the conscious mind, and adjust the snap judgment or entirely override it. But another basic insight of psychology is that when we have a strong intuitive judgment we seldom subject it to slow, careful, critical scrutiny. We just go with it, spontaneously settling for whatever System One decided.

It's important to distinguish intuitive judgments from emotions such as anger, fear, love, or sadness. They, too, may inspire rash conclusions. We all know—at least when we're thinking coolly—that strong emotions are not necessarily logical or supported by evidence and are therefore an unreliable basis for judgment. Any reasonable boss who experiences a surge of anger toward an employee knows she should wait a day and calm down before deciding whether to fire him or her. But the intuitive judgments generated by System One are not experienced as emotions. They simply "feel" true. With the truth in hand, it seems perfectly reasonable to act on it. As Kahneman wrote, System One is "a machine for jumping to conclusions."

This is what makes optimism bias so potent. Small-business owners who are sure they will avoid the fate of most small-business owners—bankruptcy—would be offended if you told them that their belief comes less from a rational assessment of the evidence and more from a psychological bias. That doesn't *feel* true. What feels true is that their business will succeed.

Although much of Kahneman and Tversky's work focuses on how decision making dominated by System One can fail, it's important to recognize that quick, intuitive judgment often works remarkably well. That's *why* it is our default, as argued by the German psychologist Gerd Gigerenzer.[15] Decades ago, when Gary Klein, yet another psychologist, started studying how people make decisions at work and at home, he quickly realized that the classical decision theory he had been taught in university—that people identify the available set of options, carefully weigh them, and choose the best—wasn't remotely how they operate in real life. We typically don't engage in such careful calculation even when we are deciding whether to take a job offer or make some other highly consequential decision.[16] Instead, as Klein demonstrated, people ordinarily take the first option that occurs to them and quickly run it through a mental simulation. If it seems to work, they go with that option. If it doesn't, they search for another and repeat the process. This method tends to work well for familiar decisions, especially when there is little time to make them, and it can work brilliantly when done by an expert, as we will see later. But in the wrong circumstances, it's a mistake.

Look at how Brehon Somervell decided where to put the Pentagon. The first site he thought of was the abandoned airfield. At a glance, it seemed to work, so he told his staff to plan the building for that site. His staff discovered that the site was unsuitable and identified another, Arlington Farm, that seemed to work. So Somervell went with that, again without asking if there might be other, better sites. He was applying the standard decision process under the wrong circumstances. It was far from a familiar problem, and he could certainly have afforded the few days it would have taken to look around and compare sites. Although he had loads of other experience, he had never planned and built a massive office building and never worked in the District of Columbia or Virginia. To an extent, at least in the planning stages of the project, he was a rookie.

This is typical of the planning of big projects. It's just not suitable for the sort of quick-and-intuitive decision making that comes naturally to us. But all too often we apply it anyway—because it comes naturally to us. If we are routinely biased toward snap judgments and unrealistic optimism and these methods fail to deliver, we will suffer. Shouldn't we learn from those painful experiences? We should indeed. But to do that, we must pay attention to experience. And unfortunately, too often we do not.

HOFSTADTER'S LAW

Forty years ago, Kahneman and Tversky showed that people commonly underestimate the time required to complete tasks even when there is information available that suggests the estimate is unreasonable. They called this the "planning fallacy," a term that with Harvard law professor Cass Sunstein I have also applied to underestimates of cost and overestimates of benefits.[17] The physicist and writer Douglas Hofstadter mockingly dubbed it "Hofstadter's Law": "It always takes longer than you expect, even when you take into account Hofstadter's Law."[18]

Research documents that the planning fallacy is pervasive, but we need only look at ourselves and the people around us to know that. You expect to get downtown on a Saturday night within twenty minutes, but it takes forty minutes instead and now you're late—just like last time and the time before that. You think you'll have your toddler asleep after fifteen minutes of bedtime stories, but it takes half an hour—as usual. You're sure you will submit your term paper a few days early this time, but you end up pulling an all-nighter and make the deadline with a minute to spare—as always.

These aren't intentional miscalculations. Much of the voluminous research on the subject involves people who are not trying to win a contract, get financing for a project, or build a monument to themselves, so they have no reason to lowball their estimates. But still the estimates are much too rosy. In one study, researchers asked students to estimate how long it would take them to finish various academic and personal tasks and then asked them to break down their estimates by confidence level—meaning that someone might say she was 50 percent confident of finishing in a week, 60 percent confident of being done in two weeks, and so on, all the way up to 99 percent confidence. Incredibly, when people said there was a 99 percent probability that they would be done—that it was virtually certain—only 45 percent actually finished by that time.[19]

For us to be so consistently wrong, we must consistently ignore experience. And we do, for various reasons. When we think of the future, the past may simply not come to mind and we may not think to dig it up because it's the present and future we are interested in. If it does surface, we may think "This time is different" and dismiss it (an option that's always available because, in a sense, every moment in life is unique). Or we may just be a little lazy and prefer not to bother, a preference well documented in Kahneman's work. We all do this. Think of taking work home on the weekend. It's a safe bet that what you will get done is less than what you planned. And not once; repeatedly. That's you ignoring your experience when making an estimate.

So what *does* inform the estimate? You generate a mental image of working at home. From this scenario, a sense of how much work you can do on the weekend quickly and intuitively emerges. It feels true, so you go with it. Yet that judgment is very likely wrong. That's because, in constructing the scenario, you only imagine yourself working. That narrow focus excludes all the people and things around you that could intrude on your work time. In other words, you are imagining a "best-case" scenario. That's typical. When people are asked to make a "best-guess" scenario—the scenario most likely to occur—what they come up with is generally indistinguishable from what they settle on when asked for a "best-case" scenario.[20]

Using a best-case scenario as the basis for an estimate is a really bad idea because the best case is seldom the most likely way the future will unfold. It's often not even probable. There is an almost infinite number of things that could pop up during the weekend and eat into your work time: illness, an accident, insomnia, a phone call from an old friend, a family emergency, broken plumbing, and on down the list. This means that the number of possible futures that could unfold on the weekend is vast but in only one, the best-case scenario, are there no complications cutting into your work time. So you shouldn't be surprised when Monday morning comes and you didn't get as much done as you expected. But you probably will be anyway.

If this sort of casual forecasting seems miles removed from the cost and time estimates of big projects, think again. It's common for such estimates to be made by breaking a project down into tasks, estimating the time and cost of each task, then adding up the totals. Experience—in the shape of past outcomes of similar projects—is often ignored, and little or no careful consideration is given to the many ways the forecasts could be knocked off-kilter. These are effectively forecasts based on best-case scenarios—and they are about as likely as your top-of-mind guess to prove accurate.

A BIAS AGAINST THINKING

A preference for doing over talking—sometimes distilled into the phrase "bias for action"—is an idea as common in business as it is necessary. Wasted time can be dangerous. "Speed matters in business," notes one of Amazon's famous leadership principles, written by Jeff Bezos.[21] "Many decisions and actions are reversible and do not need extensive study. We value calculated risk taking." Notice, however, that Bezos carefully limited the bias for action to decisions that are "reversible." Don't spend lots of time ruminating on those sorts of decisions, he advises. Try something. If it doesn't work, reverse it, and try something else. That's perfectly reasonable. It is also inapplicable to many decisions on big projects because they are so difficult or expensive to reverse that they are effectively irreversible: You can't build the Pentagon, then knock it down and build it elsewhere after you discover that it ruins the view.

When this bias for action is generalized into the culture of an organization, the reversibility caveat is usually lost. What's left is a slogan—"Just do it!"—that is seemingly applicable in all situations. "When we surveyed participants in our executive education classes, we found that managers feel more productive executing tasks than planning them," observed business professors Francesca Gino and Bradley Staats. "Especially when under time pressure, they perceive planning to be wasted effort."[22] To put that in more general behavioral terms, people in power, which includes executives deciding about big projects, prefer to go with the quick flow of availability bias, as opposed to the slow effort of planning.[23] Executives everywhere will recognize that attitude. It isn't the bias *for* action promoted by Jeff Bezos; it's a bias *against* thinking.

When laid out like that, it's obviously a bad idea. But remember that it emerges from a desire to get going on a project, to see work happening, to have tangible evidence of progress. That's good. Everyone involved in a project should have that desire. It becomes trouble only when we belittle planning as the annoying stuff we have to deal with before we *really* get going on the project.

Planning *is* working on the project. Progress in planning *is* progress on the project, often the most cost-effective progress you can achieve. We lose sight of these facts at our peril. Let's see why.

STRATEGIC MISREPRESENTATION

The French architect Jean Nouvel, a winner of the Pritzker Architecture Prize, architecture's Nobel, was blunt about the purpose of most cost estimates for signature architecture. "In France, there is often a theoretical budget that is given because it is the sum that politically has been released to do something. In three out of four cases this sum does not correspond to anything in technical terms. This is a budget that was made because it could be accepted politically. The real price comes later. The politicians make the real price public where they want and when they want."[24] That's a long way of saying that estimates aren't intended to be accurate; they are intended to sell the project. In a word, they are lies—or spin, to use more polite language.

An American politician said the quiet part out loud in a 2013 column for the *San Francisco Chronicle* about transportation infrastructure in the Bay Area. "News that the Transbay Terminal is something like $300 million over budget should not come as a shock to anyone," wrote Willie Brown, a former San Francisco mayor and California state assemblyman. "We always knew the initial estimate was under the real cost. Just like we never had a real cost for the Central Subway or the Bay Bridge or any other massive construction project. So get off it. In the world of civic projects, *the first budget is really just a down payment.* If people knew the real cost from the start, nothing would ever be approved" (italics added).[25] Needless to say, Brown was retired from politics when he wrote that.

A senior transportation consultant once confided to me that oft-touted "feasibility studies" serve more as cover for engineers than as even-handed analysis. "In virtually all cases it was clear that the engineers simply wanted to justify the project and were looking to the traffic forecasts to help in the process." The only goal was to get the project going. "I once asked an engineer why their cost estimates were invariably underestimated and he simply answered, 'if we gave the true expected outcome costs nothing would be built.'"[26] It is not a coincidence that that engineer's words were remarkably similar to Brown's.

I've had executives from many different fields tell me about strategic misrepresentation, but mostly in private conversation. The editor of a major US architecture and design magazine even rejected an article I pitched about strategic misrepresentation on the grounds that lying about projects is so routine that his readers take it for granted, and thus the article wouldn't be newsworthy. "Our country is littered with big projects that fit your description," he wrote to me.[27] But that's in private. In public, it's rare that people say it so baldly.

Rushed, superficial planning is no problem for the creation of a lowball estimate. In fact, it can be enormously helpful. Problems and challenges overlooked are problems and challenges that won't increase the estimate.

It also helps to express ironclad confidence in estimates, as Montreal mayor Jean Drapeau did when he promised that the 1976 Olympic Games would cost no more than what was budgeted. "The Montreal Olympics can no more have a deficit than a man can have a baby," he said.[28] Future embarrassment awaits when you talk like that. But that's for later. After you get what you want. And maybe after you've retired.

"START DIGGING A HOLE"

With contracts signed, the next step is to get shovels in the ground. Fast. "The idea is to get going," concluded Willie Brown. "Start digging a hole and make it so big, there's no alternative to coming up with the money to fill it in."²⁹

It's a story at least as old as Hollywood. "My tactic was familiar to directors who make films off the common path," wrote the film director Elia Kazan—then retired, naturally—when he explained how he had gotten Columbia Pictures to fund a movie he wanted to make in the late 1940s. "Get the work rolling, involve actors contractually, build sets, collect props and costumes, expose negative, and so get the studio in deep. Once money in some significant amount had been spent, it would be difficult for Harry [Cohn, president of Columbia Pictures] to do anything except scream and holler. If he suspended a film that had been shooting for weeks, he'd be in for an irretrievable loss, not only of money but of 'face.' The thing to do was to get the film going."³⁰

That type of behavior did in the legendary studio United Artists. In the late 1970s, the red-hot young director Michael Cimino wanted to make *Heaven's Gate*, an epic western, like *Lawrence of Arabia* set in Wyoming. It would cost $7.5 million (about $30 million in 2021 dollars), at the high end of what movies cost in that era but reasonable for an epic. United Artists asked him if he could meet a proposed delivery schedule. He said he could. The studio signed the contracts.

Production started. In the first six days of shooting, the project fell five days behind schedule. Cimino burned through sixty thousand feet of film, which cost roughly $900,000 to develop, and for that he had produced "approximately a minute and a half of usable material," observed Steven Bach, the United Artists executive responsible for the picture, in his book *Final Cut: Art, Money, and Ego in the Making of* Heaven's Gate, *the Film That Sank United Artists,* which is one of the most detailed and startling looks at a Hollywood production ever written.³¹ That should have set off alarm bells at United Artists. To be so far off track a mere week into production strongly suggests that the original estimates weren't worth the paper they were written on.

But things only got worse. Time dragged on. Costs exploded. Studio executives finally demanded that Cimino streamline the production—and he told them to get lost. He would do things his way, he said, and the executives would shut up and pay the bills. If they didn't like it, they could tear up the contracts and he would take the project to another studio. The executives backed down. They were furious and terrified that the film was turning into a fiasco, but they were in too deep to walk away. Cimino had them in the vise Kazan describes above.

Today, *Heaven's Gate* is famous in Hollywood, but not in a good way. It ultimately cost five times the initial estimate and opened a year late. The critical reaction was so savage that Cimino withdrew the film, reedited it, and released it again six months later. It bombed at the box office. And United Artists was wiped out.

Cimino's star plunged as a result of the failure of *Heaven's Gate*, but often the costs of out-of-control projects do not fall on those who bring them about. When the Montreal Olympics went a spectacular 720 percent over budget, a cartoonist gleefully drew a heavily pregnant Mayor Drapeau. But so what? Drapeau got his Olympics. And although it took more than thirty years for Montreal to pay off the mountain of debt, the onus was on the taxpayers of Montreal and Quebec. Drapeau wasn't even voted out of office; he retired in 1986.[32]

DRIVING INTO THE BLIZZARD

Yet there remains a nagging question about why strategic misrepresentation works. Willie Brown wasn't strictly correct when he wrote that once a hole is dug "there's no alternative" but to keep paying for the project. In theory, the project could be scrapped and the construction site sold. In theory, United Artists could have written off *Heaven's Gate* and walked away when spending got out of control. But in practice, Brown is right. Again scholars call this phenomenon "lock-in" or "escalation of commitment."[33] If escalation of commitment comes after the commitment fallacy, there is overcommitment to the second degree. This typically spells disaster, or at least a result vastly inferior to what could have been achieved with a more thoughtful approach.

Why people spiral downward this way is an immensely important question that psychologists, economists, political scientists, and sociologists have studied for decades. A 2012 meta-analysis of the literature included 120 citations even after excluding the many non-quantitative analyses.[34] Not surprisingly, there is no simple explanation. But one element that is central to any account is the "sunk cost fallacy."

Money, time, and effort previously spent to advance a project are lost in the past. You can't get them back. They are "sunk." Logically, when you decide whether to pour more resources into a project, you should consider only whether doing so makes sense *now*. Sunk costs should not be a factor in your thinking—but they probably will be because most people find it incredibly hard to push them out of their minds. And so people commonly "throw good money after bad," to use the old phrase.

Consider two friends with tickets for a professional basketball game a long drive from where they live. On the day of the game, there is a big snowstorm. The higher the price the friends paid for the tickets—their sunk costs—the more likely they are to brave the blizzard and attempt driving to the game, investing more time, money, and risk. In contrast, the rational approach would be to disregard what they have already invested and stay home. The sunk-cost fallacy applies to individuals, groups, and whole organizations.[35]

"Driving into the blizzard" is particularly common in politics. Sometimes that's because politicians themselves fall for it. But even politicians who know better understand that the public is likely to be swayed by sunk costs, so sticking with a fallacy is politically safer than making a logical decision. It's a safe bet that when California governor Gavin Newsom decided not to scrap the California High-Speed Rail project, only curtail it, he and his aides were thinking very carefully about how sunk costs would weigh on the public mind, and they knew that scrapping the project would be interpreted by the public as "throwing away" the billions of dollars already spent. As a result, the state's taxpayers were led to continue to escalate their commitment and spend billions more on a shrunken version of the project they would never have approved had it been put before them in the first place.

I expect that California's "bullet train to nowhere" will one day be the standard textbook illustration of the sunk-cost fallacy and escalation of commitment.

SOMERVELL'S SPIRAL

We can't know for sure which force—psychology or politics—led Brehon Somervell to rush the planning of the Pentagon. But as usual with big projects, there's reason to think that both played a role.

Like Willie Brown, Somervell was politically astute. He often "adjusted" his plan, reducing the expected cost, number of floors, or square footage, to suit what powerful people wanted to hear to give him the approval he needed to get going. That would inevitably produce large gaps between what was said and what was done, but "Somervell was little concerned with cost overruns," as Steve Vogel noted.[36] And like Willie Brown, Somervell was determined to "start digging a hole," knowing that the existence of a big enough hole would ensure his project's future. Somervell was also steeped in a "can-do" army engineering culture that prized System One decisiveness and getting stuff done above all else.

We should be careful not to see psychology and politics as separate forces; they can be mutually reinforcing and typically are in big projects.³⁷ When they align in favor of a superficial plan and a quick start, that's probably what will occur—with predictable consequences.

When a group of determined critics of Somervell's plan pressed to move the project to the superior Quartermaster Depot site, Somervell fought back. He criticized the critics and insisted that only the Arlington Farm site was suitable. As he drove his staff even harder to start digging a hole at Arlington Farm, the critics urged the president to intervene. He did, telling Somervell to switch sites. Incredibly, Somervell still wouldn't quit. In a car with the president on the way to visit the Quartermaster Depot site, he doggedly insisted that only the Arlington Farm location was suitable and the president should change his mind. "My dear general," Roosevelt finally said, "I'm still commander-in-chief of the Army." In case that wasn't clear enough, he wrapped up the visit by pointing to the Quartermaster site and saying, "We're going to locate the War Department building over there."³⁸ That finally settled it. Somervell sucked it up and accepted the inevitable.

In fairness, the fault for the botched initial plan did not lie entirely with the general. Or perhaps even mostly. In that first, almost comically rushed week, Somervell presented his plan to the secretary of war, a congressional subcommittee, and the White House cabinet, including the president. Each time, so few probing questions were asked that the blatant flaws in the plan were not revealed. And each time, the plan was quickly approved. Somervell's superiors simply didn't do their jobs. The fact that the flaw was eventually exposed and the plan stopped—in part because one of the determined critics of the plan happened to be the president's uncle—only underscores their dereliction of duty and the arbitrariness of the decision.

Such flaws in decision making are unfortunately not unique to the Pentagon. Superficial planning is common and will be exposed only if those with the authority to supervise and approve plans—including the general public when it comes to government projects—exercise that power properly by subjecting plans to serious questioning. Too often, they don't, preferring instead to accept a glib story and "drive into the blizzard" as Somervell did. It's a lot easier. And it may serve their individual interests. But the result will speak for itself in its inferiority to what could have been achieved.

COMMIT TO NOT COMMIT

But let's set aside history and generals. The lesson for us is as simple as Somervell's initial mistake: Don't assume you know all there is to know. If you're a project leader and people on your team make this assumption—which is common—educate them or shift them out of the team. Don't let yourself or them draw what appear to be obvious conclusions. That sort of premature commitment puts you at risk of missing not only glaring flaws but also opportunities that could make your project much better than what you have in mind now.

In the next chapter, we'll turn from megaprojects to a home project and see how another premature conclusion turned a simple kitchen renovation into a disaster and years of misery for the family involved—and how one of the world's most famous and successful buildings started with an open mind, curiosity, and questions.

The process I lay out is anti-Somervell. It finds the flaws and the opportunities. If you feel the urge to commit—and you probably will—commit to completing that process before you draw conclusions about your big project.[39] At first, commit to having an open mind; that is, commit to not committing.

3

THINK FROM RIGHT TO LEFT

Projects are often started by jumping straight to a solution, even a specific technology. That's the wrong place to begin. You want to start by asking questions and considering alternatives. At the outset, always assume that there is more to learn. Start with the most basic question of all: Why?

David and Deborah's big project was to renovate their kitchen. As small as that sounds, the kitchen was even smaller.

David and Deborah live on the first two floors of a four-story, nineteenth-century brick town house in Cobble Hill, a charming Brooklyn neighborhood that looks like the set of every movie ever filmed in New York. The town houses in Cobble Hill are tall but cramped, with narrow stairways and small rooms. David and Deborah's whole apartment was 1,200 square feet, and the kitchen was so tiny it could be a sailboat's galley. Renovating it hardly seemed a challenge in the same league as constructing the Empire State Building. Yet, unlike the Empire State Building, David and Deborah's modest project came in late and over budget. And not by a little; it was eighteen months late—and more than half a million dollars over budget.

The root cause of that astonishing result was not a hurry to get work under way. In fact, David and Deborah did the opposite of Brehon Somervell's mad rush. Starting around 2011, they spent years musing about renovating the kitchen. When they finally decided to get started, they did not swing sledgehammers; they hired an experienced architect. The architect suggested that they knock out a wall between the kitchen and a small room to double the size of the kitchen. They agreed to the modest expansion. The architect then spent months preparing detailed drawings before he finally revealed the plans. "He had a big roll of drawings," David recalled, "and painstakingly he would take us through eight iterations of possible designs, talking us through each one at great length and then explaining why, however, this one isn't quite the right approach, so he would take out the next sheet and show us a different design and conclude, 'But really, this isn't the perfect solution, either, so let me show you another version.'"

The total estimated cost of the carefully detailed project was $170,000. That's a lot, but everything in New York is expensive, so David and Deborah decided to go ahead. They moved out, expecting to return in three months.

"The project began to morph and unravel right at the beginning," David recalled with a sigh. Standing in the kitchen, the contractor bounced up and down to test the floorboards. He didn't like what he felt. When he tore out the old kitchen and got a look at what was underneath, he saw why: "Because of shoddy construction in the 1840s and no one ever fixing it, there was not enough structural support to hold up this building." The entire floor would have to be removed and steel beams and supports installed in the basement.

When they were over the shock, David and Deborah thought about the existing wooden floorboards. They were old and ugly. If they had to be removed anyway, perhaps they should replace them rather than put them back? The kitchen floor had to go regardless, "and what are you going to do, have new wood on one half of the floor and not the other?" They agreed to replace all the floorboards. David and Deborah also thought about the living room's brick fireplace. It was an ugly, modern DIY job. Why not take this chance to replace it?

And the fireplace wasn't the worst feature of the living room. There was a tiny powder room under the stairs directly beside the living room. David's mother said it was "vulgar." It would be great to move that, David and Deborah thought, and easy to do while the floor was out. "So the architect went back and redrew everything," David recalled.

And since there would be work done in the basement, why not reroute the cellar stairs to create a small room for a washer and dryer? "So that is more design, more architectural drawings, more delays." Each new plan also had to be filed with New York's notoriously byzantine bureaucracy.

There was nothing extravagant or whimsical about any of the changes. Each was reasonable. Each led to the next. Besides, property values in the neighborhood had soared, so they would get back at least some of the money they had put into the apartment when they sold.

In that piecemeal way, the project expanded outward from the kitchen until the first floor was entirely gutted, redesigned, and refiled.

But the project didn't stop there. The main bathroom on the second floor was hideous and moldy. If you've moved out and got contractors working on-site, David's mother said, why not fix that now so you don't have to go through this again sometime down the road? Another reasonable argument. And again, that change led to others. Which led to others. Until the second floor was also entirely gutted, redesigned, and refiled.

"The $170,000 became $400,000, then $600,000 and $700,000." David pegs the final total at roughly $800,000. It's a bill so large that David will probably have to postpone his retirement. And that figure doesn't account for the dislocation of their lives. Instead of the three months' wait they had expected, David and Deborah moved back in a year and a half after they'd left.

When the job was finally done, everyone agreed the fully renovated apartment was quite lovely. But that was small consolation. If the project had been planned from the start as the bottom-to-top renovation it became, there would have been one plan, one filing with the city, and the contractor could have tackled the work in the most efficient order. The cost—in dollars, time, and aggravation—would have been much lower than what David and Deborah paid. No matter how you look at it, the project was a disaster.

WHY?

David's thinking was indisputably slow, and the architect's work was painstaking. Yet the plan—I'll be polite—was not good. This underscores a critical point about my advice to "think slow."

Slow isn't good in itself. Like David and Deborah, people can spend years daydreaming about a project but have nothing more than daydreams to show for it, just as organizations can burn enormous amounts of time holding meetings filled with meandering discussions that never go anywhere. Moreover, careful analysis like that done by David's architect can be laborious and take ages, but if it is too narrowly focused, it won't reveal fundamental flaws in the plan or gaps, much less correct them. And by its impressive detail, it may give the false idea that the overall plan is stronger than it is, like a beautiful facade with no structure behind it. Governments and bureaucratic corporations are good at churning out this sort of analysis. It is a major reason why the California High-Speed Rail project was able to spend more than a decade "in planning" before construction began, producing impressive quantities of paper and numbers without delivering a plan worthy of the name.

In contrast, good planning explores, imagines, analyzes, tests, and iterates. That takes time. Thus, slow is a consequence of doing planning right, not a cause. The cause of good planning is the range and depth of the questions it asks and the imagination and the rigor of the answers it delivers. Notice that I put "questions" before "answers." It's self-evident that questions come before answers. Or rather, it *should* be self-evident. Unfortunately, it's not. Projects routinely start with answers, not questions.

David and Deborah's project started with "renovate the kitchen." That's an answer, not a question. As so often happens with projects, the goal of the project seemed obvious, a given. The only question was when to go ahead with the project, and once that was decided, it was time to get into detailed planning. The failure to ask questions about the goal of the project was the root cause of its failure.

Frank Gehry, arguably the world's most acclaimed architect, never starts with answers. "I grew up with the Talmud," he told me when I interviewed him in 2021, "and the Talmud starts with a question." That's typical of Judaism, he says. "Jews question everything."[1]

What Gehry means by questioning isn't doubting or criticizing, much less attacking or tearing down. He means asking questions with an open-minded desire to learn. It is, in a word, exploration. "You're being curious," he says. That's the opposite of the natural inclination to think that What You See Is All There Is (WYSIATI), the fallacy we saw in the previous chapter. In contrast, Gehry assumes that there *must* be more to learn. By making that assumption, he avoids the trap of the fallacy.

In this frame of mind, the first thing Gehry does when he meets with potential clients is engage in long conversations. This isn't chit-chat or Gehry being personable, and it doesn't involve his delivering lectures about architectural theory or dwelling on the visions bubbling in his imagination. Instead, he asks questions. With no motive but curiosity, he explores the client's needs, aspirations, fears, and everything else that has brought them to his door. The whole conversation starts with a simple question: "Why are you doing this project?"

Few projects start this way. All should.

THE BOX ON THE RIGHT

Frank Gehry's most celebrated building—the one that elevated him from the ranks of rising stars to the pinnacle of the architecture world—is the Guggenheim Museum Bilbao. A gallery of contemporary art in Bilbao, Spain, it is a spectacular, glowing building unlike anything seen before, as much of an artwork as those on display inside.

Understandably, the Guggenheim Bilbao is often portrayed as the product of nothing more than the architect's imagination and genius. More cynical observers see it as an example of the "starchitect" phenomenon, in which architects give free rein to their inflated egos and idiosyncrasies. Both depictions are wrong.

When Gehry was first approached in the 1990s to consider the project, he flew to Bilbao and met with officials from the government of the Basque Country, an autonomous region in northern Spain. The government was the would-be client, having created a plan that would see it pay the Solomon R. Guggenheim Foundation to create and run a Guggenheim Museum in Bilbao, the Basque Country's largest city. Officials had selected an elegant but abandoned building, originally built in 1909 as a wine warehouse, to be the future home of the museum. Would Gehry consider doing the renovation?

Another architect might have simply said "No, thanks" and walked away. Or "Yes" and gotten to work—just as David and Deborah's architect did. Not Gehry; he asked questions, starting with the fundamental one: "Why are you doing this project?"

The Basque Country was once a hub of heavy industry and shipping, he was told. But that was in the past. "Bilbao was, like, not quite as bad as Detroit but almost," he recalled years later. "Steel industry gone. Shipping industry gone. It looked pretty sad."[2] Bilbao was rusting and remote, and few foreigners had even heard of it, so it didn't benefit from the enormous flow of tourists that annually flooded southern Spain and Madrid. A Guggenheim, officials hoped, would draw visitors to Bilbao and invigorate the economy. The officials told Gehry that they wanted a building that could do for Bilbao and the Basque Country what the Sydney Opera House had done for Sydney and Australia: put them on the map and bring back growth.[3]

Gehry inspected the old warehouse. He liked the building, but not for a project with that goal. The building would have to be torn down and replaced, he said. And that would be a shame when it could be put to good use some other way.

Gehry had another idea, however. He had spotted a derelict industrial site on the riverfront that had good sight lines in many directions. Forget the renovation, he said. Build a new, dazzling museum on that riverfront site.[4]

The officials agreed. And for good reason; their goal of boosting the economy was ambitious, requiring an increase in tourism. A new Guggenheim in a renovated building could perhaps deliver that in theory. But how likely was that? Has any renovation, however brilliant, ever created a global splash that drew people in large numbers from all over the world? It's hard to think of one. But dramatic new buildings in impressive locations can and do attract global attention. A few have even drawn visitors in major numbers, such as the Sydney Opera House. It would still be an enormous challenge, but that approach seemed more likely to deliver what the Basques wanted, or so Gehry argued.

The resulting building thrilled architecture critics and ordinary people alike, and the Guggenheim Bilbao was an overnight sensation. Tourists flooded the city. And they brought money. In the first three years of operation, almost 4 million people visited the once obscure corner of Spain, injecting a little less than $1 billion (in 2021 dollars) into the region.[5]

Frank Gehry's imagination, genius, and ego were certainly involved in the creation of the Guggenheim Bilbao. But the building was fundamentally shaped by the project's goal. As Gehry's record shows, he is perfectly capable of designing buildings that are modest and understated relative to what he did in Bilbao. In fact, he even did an understated museum renovation in Philadelphia, years later.[6] But what the client wanted to achieve in Bilbao called for much more than that, so he put the museum where it is and made it the way it is because that would best achieve the project's goal.

Projects are not goals in themselves. Projects are how goals are achieved. People don't build skyscrapers, hold conferences, develop products, or write books for their own sakes. They do these things in order to accomplish other things.

That's a simple and self-evident idea, but it is easily and commonly forgotten when the WYSIATI fallacy from chapter 2 rushes us to a conclusion that seems so obvious it's not even worth discussing. If I had asked David and Deborah at the start of their project what their goal was, they likely would have shrugged and said something like "To have a nice kitchen." That is what people say when they confuse means and ends.

At the beginning of a project, we need to disrupt the psychology-driven dash to a premature conclusion by disentangling means and ends and thinking carefully about what exactly we want to accomplish. Frank Gehry's question, "Why are you doing this project?," does that.

Picture politicians who want to connect an island to the mainland. How much would a bridge cost? Where should it be located? How long would it take to build? If they discuss all this in detail, they are likely to feel they have done excellent planning when, in fact, they started with an answer—a bridge is the best solution—and proceeded from there. If they instead explored *why* they want to connect the island to the mainland—to reduce commuting time, to increase tourism, to provide faster access to emergency healthcare, whatever—they would focus first on the *ends* and only then shift to discussing the *means* for achieving those ends, which would be the right order of things. That's how new ideas surface: What about a tunnel? Ferries? A helipad? There are lots of ways to connect an island with the mainland and meet a need. Depending on the goal, it may not even have to be a physical connection. Excellent broadband service may do what is required, and more, at a fraction of the cost. "Connecting" the island might not even be necessary or advisable. If access to emergency healthcare is the concern, for example, the best option may be installing that service on the island. But none of this will come to light if the discussion starts with an answer.

Developing a clear, informed understanding of what the goal is and why—and never losing sight of it from beginning to end—is the foundation of a successful project.

In project planning, a standard tool is a flowchart that lays out, from left to right, what needs to be done and when, with the project concluding when the goal is achieved in the final box on the right. That simple concept is also valuable in the initial planning stages because it can help us visualize a project not as an end in itself but as a means to an end: The goal is the box on the right. That's where project planning must begin by asking Frank Gehry's question and thoughtfully exploring what should go in that box. Once that is settled, you can shift to considering what should go into the boxes on the left—the means that will best get you to your goal.

I call this "thinking from right to left." But many other people working in different fields have identified similar notions and used different language to describe what is fundamentally the same idea.

"Backcasting" is used in urban and environmental planning. Originally developed by University of Toronto professor John B. Robinson to deal with energy problems, backcasting starts by developing a detailed description of a desirable future state; then you work backwards to tease out what needs to happen for that imagined future to become reality.[7] One backcasting exercise that looked at California's water needs started by imagining an ideal California twenty-five years in the future, then asked what would have to happen—to supply, consumption rates, conservation, and so on—to make that happy outcome real.[8]

"Theory of change" is a similar process often used by government agencies and nongovernmental organizations (NGOs) that seek social change, such as boosting literacy rates, improving sanitation, or better protecting human rights. Again, it starts by defining the goal and only then considers courses of action that could produce that outcome.

Silicon Valley is far removed from these worlds, yet the same basic idea is widely used in technology circles. "You've got to start with the customer experience and work backwards to the technology," Steve Jobs told the audience at Apple's 1997 Worldwide Developers Conference. "You can't start with the technology and try to figure out how you're going to try to sell it. I made this mistake probably more than anybody in this room, and I've got the scar tissue to prove it."[9] Today, "work backwards" is a mantra in Silicon Valley.

LOSING SIGHT OF THE RIGHT

The most common way in which thinking from right to left fails is losing sight of the right, the goal. Even Steve Jobs committed this error after insisting on the opposite: that projects have to start with the customer experience and work backwards to the technology. The most notorious example was Apple's Power Mac G4 Cube computer. Released in 2000, the G4 was a translucent cube that even today looks gorgeously futuristic. It had no power switch. You just waved your hand, and it turned on. So cool. So Steve Jobs. And that was the problem. The G4 had not been designed by looking at who Apple's customers were and what would serve them best. Its combination of cost, capabilities, and aesthetics was molded by Steve Jobs's passions, and impressive as the machine was, it was an awkward fit for customers. The G4 flopped, and Apple scrapped it a year later at great cost.[10]

But "work backwards" also fails when planners aren't compelled to nail down what's in that final flowchart box on the right and forced to think from right to left. Without that, it's easy to get consumed by the blizzard of details and difficulties that arise during the planning of any project, while the goal, which was only vaguely understood to begin with, fades from view. Then the project can veer off in unpredictable directions, as David and Deborah's kitchen renovation did so spectacularly.

Jeff Bezos was well aware of that danger, and he came up with an elegant way to keep Amazon focused on customers, which is the company's primary creed. Bezos noted that when a project is successfully completed and it's ready to be publicly announced, the conventional last step is to have the communications department write two documents. One is a very short press release (PR) that summarizes what the new product or service is and why it is valuable for customers. The other is a "frequently asked questions" (FAQ) document with more details about costs, functionality, and other concerns. Bezos's brainstorm was to make that *last* step in a conventional project the *first* step in Amazon projects.[11]

To pitch a new project at Amazon, you must first write a PR and FAQ, putting the goal smack in the opening sentences of the press release. Everything that happens subsequently is working backwards from the PR/FAQ, as it is called at Amazon. Critically, the language of both documents must be plain. "I called it 'Oprah-speak,'" says Ian McAllister, a former Amazon executive who wrote multiple PR/FAQs for Jeff Bezos.[12] "You know, Oprah would have someone on her show who would say something, and Oprah would turn to her audience and explain it in a very simple way that anyone can understand." With language like that, flaws can't be hidden behind jargon, slogans, or technical terms. Thinking is laid bare. If a thought is fuzzy, ill considered, or illogical, or if it is based on unsupported assumptions, a careful reader will see it.

Projects are pitched in a one-hour meeting with top executives. Amazon forbids PowerPoint presentations and all the usual tools of the corporate world, so copies of the PR/FAQ are handed around the table and everyone reads it, slowly and carefully, in silence. Then they share their initial thoughts, with the most senior people speaking last to avoid prematurely influencing others. Finally, the writer goes through the documents line by line, with anyone free to speak up at any time. "This discussion of the details is the critical part of the meeting," wrote Colin Bryar and Bill Carr, two former Amazon executives. "People ask hard questions. They engage in intense debate and discussion of the key ideas and the way they are expressed."[13]

The writer of the PR/FAQ then takes the feedback into account, writes another draft, and brings it back to the group. The same process unfolds again. And again. And again. Everything about the proposal is tested and strengthened through multiple iterations. And because it's a participatory process with the relevant people deeply involved from the beginning, it ensures that the concept that finally emerges is seen with equal clarity in the minds of everyone from the person proposing the project to the CEO. Everyone is on the same page from the start.

But no process is foolproof. When Jeff Bezos dreamed up the idea of a 3D phone display that would allow control by gestures in the air (the hand-waving again!), he fell in love with the concept. Later, he effectively co-authored the PR/FAQ that would launch the Amazon Fire Phone project. Bill Carr, an ex–vice president of digital media at Amazon, recalled wondering when he first heard about the Fire Phone in 2012 why anyone would want a battery-draining 3D display on a phone.[14] But work pressed on, occupying more than a thousand employees. When the Fire Phone was released in June 2014 at a price of $200, it didn't sell. The price was cut in half. Then the phone was free. Amazon couldn't give it away. A year later, it was discontinued and hundreds of millions of dollars were written off. "It failed for all the reasons we said it was going to fail—that's the crazy thing about it," said a software engineer. Asking "Why?" can work only where people feel free to speak their minds and the decision makers really listen. "Many employees who worked on the Fire Phone had serious doubts about it," concluded the journalist and author Brad Stone, who has written definitive histories of Amazon, "but no one, it seemed, had been brave or clever enough to take a stand and win an argument with their obstinate leader."[15]

Thinking from right to left is demanding because it's not natural. What's natural is WYSIATI—What You See Is All There Is—and focusing exclusively on what is in front of you. And when you are obsessed with a cool idea or you are deep into designing the project or buried in a thousand and one details, the box on the right is nowhere to be seen. That's when trouble starts.

Robert Caro can help with that.

Caro is the greatest living American biographer, famous for long, deeply researched, massively complex books about President Lyndon B. Johnson and Robert Moses, the man who built New York, which take as much as a decade or more to write. He starts all his mammoth projects the same way: He fills in the box on the right.

"What is this book about?," he asks himself. "What is its point?" He forces himself to "boil the book down to three paragraphs, or two, or one."[16] These paragraphs express the narrative theme with perfect simplicity.

But don't mistake simple for easy. Caro writes a draft and throws it out. Then another. And another, in seemingly endless iterations. This can go on for weeks as he compares his summary with his voluminous research. "The whole time, I'm saying to myself, 'no, that's not exactly what you're trying to do in this book.'" He gets into foul moods. "I come home and [my wife] doesn't even want to see me for the first several hours." But the struggle is worth it. When he finally has his precious paragraphs, he pins them to the wall behind his desk, where it is literally impossible for him to lose sight of his goal.

In the long years ahead, as he writes his book, pushing ever deeper into the jungle of his research, in growing danger of getting lost in its complexity, Caro constantly looks at his summary and compares it with what he is currently writing. "Is this fitting in with those three paragraphs?," he asks himself. "How is it fitting in? What you wrote is good, but it's not fitting in. So you have to throw it away or find a way to make it fit in."

With the goal always in view, there is no getting lost. That's thinking from right to left.

BACK TO COBBLE HILL

Let's imagine that it's 2011. David and Deborah are sitting in their little kitchen, drinking coffee and talking about the kitchen renovation. How should that conversation go in order to give the project a sound foundation? It should start with Frank Gehry's question: Why are you doing this project?

They would probably start with the obvious, something like "It would be nice to spend more time cooking in the kitchen." But that's the surface. They need to go deeper. For whom will they cook? If it's guests, are they close family? Friends? Business acquaintances? Why do they want to do more of that?

So what should go into the box on the right? That can't be decided without getting into lots more detail about David and Deborah's lives, aspirations, and priorities. But one possibility is "more entertaining at home." That should be elaborated upon. Why are they entertaining? The project needs a clear, explicit goal. That cannot be settled casually; it's what the whole project is about, and it must be treated accordingly.

If the goal is entertaining at home more, how would David and Deborah best achieve it? They can't do that without a kitchen renovation. But will that get them to their goal? Guests will use not only the kitchen but also the living room, with its ugly DIY fireplace, and that awful powder room. If that thought makes them cringe, they have discovered that the scruffiness of the kitchen is not the only barrier to their goal. They also need to move the powder room and redo the fireplace.

By carefully working through what must be done to get to their goal, the logic that surfaced midconstruction and convinced David and Deborah to make piecemeal expansions of the project will instead surface up front in a conversation about what other renovations they might consider. And if major work is under way and they would have to move out anyway, would it not make sense to also consider other work they might want to do in the future? To get it all over with at once. Plus it's cheaper to have workers come on-site once and do many jobs rather than come back multiple times.

If the scope of the project expands this way—in conversation, remember, not in reality—it will surely raise the question of money. Can they afford this? That depends not only on their present finances but also on their future plans. Property values are way up since they moved in, so they could get back some of the money when they sell the apartment. But *will* they sell the apartment? Do they intend to stay there until the ends of their careers? Where will they live when they retire? These decisions may be too far off to be of concern, or they may be important considerations. They can know only by bringing them up and discussing them.

Maybe the conversation would lead David and Deborah to expand the project a little. Or a lot. Maybe they would decide that the project should have a more ambitious goal—something like "making time at home more enjoyable in all aspects and raising the value of the apartment to its full market potential"—and conclude that they should do a top-to-bottom renovation.

Or maybe they would look at the cost, their finances, and their retirement plans, and scale it back. Maybe they would decide it would be too expensive to do fully and not worth doing partially, so they'd call the whole thing off.

Maybe they'll decide that the farmhouse where they spend their summers is where they should put their money. Or that instead of making capital improvements, they should invest the money.

But there are two things we can be certain of: Had they asked these questions, David and Deborah would never have decided to do the renovation the way they did. And every one of the possible approaches would have produced an outcome superior to what they got. Planning would have been done once. Plans would have been filed once. The work would have been done in the most efficient order, faster. And only once. The project would have cost David and Deborah far less money, time, and pain.

More fundamentally, the project would not have gotten out of control and would have remained the product of their informed choices. Instead of something that happened to them, it would have been something they made happen.

POSTSCRIPT

In writing this chapter, I omitted a substantial piece of the David-and-Deborah story. Recall that the town house is four stories plus a basement. David and Deborah own only the bottom two floors and the basement. Their neighbors own the top two floors. David and Deborah were legally obligated to get their neighbors to sign off on their proposed kitchen renovation, and they did, but they and their neighbors did not seriously discuss their plan, much less what they might do jointly within what is, after all, a single small building.

That was unfortunate, because after David and Deborah had gone through eighteen months of hell, their neighbors saw the finished apartment, liked the look of it, and decided to do the same thing, the same way. Like David and Deborah, they didn't carefully decide what goal should go into the box on the right. Like David and Deborah, they didn't carefully think about the best means of achieving that end. They even hired David and Deborah's contractor.

The result was the same, except that it was spread out over two more agonizing years. The work upstairs showered the downstairs apartment with dust and occasionally caused damage. Deborah couldn't take it. She moved out for the duration. At one point, David spent three months in the dark because sheets of plywood covered his windows. He finally got fed up and stayed with a friend for a year. Work that had been done in the first renovation had to be torn out and redone in the second. The bleakest moment was when the neighbors discovered that the building's brick facade was in danger of crumbling, which required that all the bricks be removed and relaid. David and Deborah's portion of that bill came to $180,000.

By David's rough estimate, he and Deborah and their neighbors spent a total approaching $1 million *each* renovating the little town house. If someone had suggested doing that at the start, he says, they would have called it "crazy." But that's where they got to, paradoxically, because they started the project "locked into a limited vision of what we wanted to achieve," in David's words. That lock-in wouldn't have happened if David and Deborah had started their project with Gehry-style questions and some hard right-to-left thinking—and included their neighbors in the discussion. But they didn't.

It was only a small kitchen renovation, after all. What could go wrong?

4

PIXAR PLANNING

People are terrible at getting things right the first time. But we're great at tinkering. Wise planners make the most of this basic insight into human nature. They try, learn, and do it again. They plan like Pixar and Frank Gehry do.

This is a tale of two masterpieces.

The first stands on a rocky outcrop of Sydney Harbor on the Australian coast. The Sydney Opera House is a collage of graceful white curves that call to mind billowing sails, clouds, or bird wings. Defying mass and scale, the building elevates you. It feels light and joyous, as if it may just lift off in the wind. When it was completed half a century ago, it astonished. Nothing like it had been seen before. The opera house became a proud national symbol and an international treasure. "It stands by itself as one of the indisputable masterpieces of human creativity," declared an expert evaluation report commissioned by UNESCO. In 2007, it was designated a UNESCO World Heritage site, alongside the Taj Mahal and the Great Wall of China, a first for a building whose architect was still alive.[1]

We have already encountered the second masterpiece. It is the Guggenheim Museum Bilbao. The renowned American sculptor Richard Serra called it "one of the greatest achievements of architecture in the twentieth century."[2] When a 2010 survey asked the world's leading architects and architecture experts to name the most important works since 1980, the Guggenheim Bilbao was by far the top choice.[3]

Many people consider the Sydney Opera House and the Guggenheim Museum Bilbao the greatest buildings of the past century. I agree.

The design of the Sydney Opera House sprang from genius. The architect was Jørn Utzon, a relative unknown when he won the global competition to conceive it.

The Guggenheim Bilbao was also the product of genius. Designed by Frank Gehry, it is arguably the greatest work of an architect so original that the only category he can be placed in is his own.

But there is one difference between these two buildings. And it is a big one.

The construction of the Sydney Opera House was an outright fiasco. Setbacks piled up. Costs exploded. Scheduled to take five years to build, it took fourteen. The final bill was 1,400 percent over the estimate, one of the largest cost overruns for a building in history. Worse, the Sydney Opera House destroyed Jørn Utzon's career.

The Guggenheim Bilbao was delivered on time and on budget. To be precise, it cost 3 percent *less* than expected.[4] And as we saw in the previous chapter, it produced the expected benefits and more, giving the project very select company in the only 0.5 percent of big projects that deliver on all promises. That success vaulted Frank Gehry to the top tier of the world's architects, leading to many more commissions and a vast and distinguished body of work all over the world.

There is much to learn from that contrast.

EXPERIRI

"Planning" is a concept with baggage. For many, it calls to mind a passive activity: sitting, thinking, staring into space, abstracting what you're going to do. In its more institutional form, planning is a bureaucratic exercise in which the planner writes reports, colors maps and charts, programs activities, and fills in boxes on flowcharts. Such plans often look like train schedules, but they're even less interesting.

Much planning does fit that bill. And that's a problem because it's a serious mistake to treat planning as an exercise in abstract, bureaucratic thought and calculation. What sets good planning apart from the rest is something completely different. It is captured by a Latin verb, *experiri*. *Experiri* means "to try," "to test," or "to prove." It is the origin of two wonderful words in English: *experiment* and *experience*.

Think of how people typically learn: We tinker. We try this. We try that. We see what works and what doesn't. We iterate. We learn. This is experimentation creating experience. Or, to use the phrase of theorists, it is "experiential learning." We're good at learning by tinkering—which is fortunate, because we're terrible at getting things right the first time.

Tinkering sometimes requires tenacity, and it always requires a willingness to learn from failure. "I have not failed ten thousand times," Thomas Edison said. "I've successfully found ten thousand ways that will not work." That wasn't hyperbole. Merely to figure out how to make a low-cost, long-lasting filament for a lightbulb, Edison had to churn through hundreds of experiments with different substances before he found the one—carbonized bamboo—that worked.[5]

Experimentation in planning requires a simulation of the project to come. With that, you can make changes in the simulation and see what happens. Changes that work—changes that will get you to the box on the right—are kept. Those that don't are chucked. With many iterations and serious testing, the simulation evolves into a plan that is creative, rigorous, and detailed, which is to say, a *reliable* plan.

The genius of our species, however, is that we can learn not only from our own experience but that of others. Edison himself started his experiments on lightbulb filaments by studying the results of the many other scientists and inventors who had tried to create an efficient lightbulb before him. And once he had cracked the problem, anyone could skip the experiments, study what he had done, and make a working lightbulb.

Still, even if I know Edison's solution to the lightbulb problem, my first attempt to make a working lightbulb will almost surely be a struggle. It will be slow, and my lightbulb may not work well. So I do it again. And I get a little better. And I do it again and again and again. And I get a lot better. That's called a "positive learning curve": Things get easier, cheaper, and more effective with each iteration.[6] This, too, is experience, and it is invaluable. As the old Latin saying goes, *"Repetitio est mater studiorum"*—"Repetition is the mother of learning."

A good plan is one that meticulously applies experimentation or experience. A great plan is one that rigorously applies both. In this chapter, I'll look at how to use experimentation in planning; in the next chapter, experience.

"A MAGNIFICENT DOODLE"

A bad plan is one that applies neither experimentation nor experience. The plan for the Sydney Opera House was *very* bad.

The Australian art critic Robert Hughes described Jørn Utzon's entry in the design competition as "nothing more than a magnificent doodle."[7] That's a little exaggerated, but not much. Utzon's entry was so sparse that it didn't even satisfy all the technical requirements set by the organizers, but his simple sketches were indisputably brilliant—perhaps too brilliant. They mesmerized the jury and swept objections aside, leaving a host of unanswered questions.

The principal mystery lay in the curved shells at the heart of Utzon's vision. They were beautiful on two-dimensional paper, but what three-dimensional constructs would enable them to stand? What materials would they be made of? How would they be built? None of that had been figured out. Utzon hadn't even consulted engineers.

At that point, the organizers of the competition should have congratulated Utzon on his vision and asked him to take whatever time was necessary to experiment with his ideas and draw on the experience of others to develop a serious plan. With that in hand, cost and time estimates could have been made, budgets authorized, and construction begun. That would have been a "Think slow, act fast" approach. But that's not what happened; the opposite did. The Sydney Opera House is an exemplary case of "Think fast, act slow."

The key force behind the opera house project was Joe Cahill, the premier of the state of New South Wales. Cahill had held office for many years and was ill with cancer. Like so many politicians before and since, his thoughts turned to his legacy. And like other politicians before and since, he decided that the public policies he had ushered in were not enough, that his legacy must take the tangible form of a grand building. But Cahill's Australian Labor Party colleagues did not share his dream. New South Wales faced a severe shortage of housing and schools, and pouring public money into an expensive opera house struck them as folly.

Facing a classic political dilemma, Cahill chose a classic political strategy: He lowballed the cost, helped in part by an estimate prepared for the contest judges that simply filled the large blanks in the plan with optimistic assumptions and concluded that Utzon's design was the cheapest of the leading contenders.

And Cahill rushed the process. He decreed that construction would start in February 1959, whatever the state of planning. Not coincidentally, an election was due in March 1959. He even instructed his officials to start building and "make such progress that no one who succeeds me can stop this."[8] It was the "start digging a hole" strategy discussed in chapter 2. And it worked for Cahill. By October 1959, he was dead, but the opera house was alive and under construction—although no one knew precisely what they were building because the final design had not been decided and drawn.

As Jørn Utzon worked, he saw that the challenges ahead were many and daunting, which would have been fine if the project had existed solely on his drafting table. But with construction ongoing, it was only a matter of time until unresolved problems and nasty surprises would surface and plunge the project deeper and deeper into delays and red ink. Utzon labored mightily, and he ultimately did crack the puzzle of how to build the curved shells, substituting an ingenious but substantially more upright design than the one he had first sketched.[9] But by then, it was much too late to avoid disaster.

Thanks mostly to the rushed start of construction, all that went up rapidly was the cost. Completed work even had to be dynamited and cleared away to start again. Inevitably, the project became a political scandal. The new minister in charge, who despised Utzon, bullied and harassed him and even deprived him of his fees. In 1966, Utzon was effectively pushed out and replaced in the middle of construction, with the shells barely erected and no interior work done.[10] He and his family left Australia in secret, slipping aboard a plane just minutes before the doors closed to avoid the press.

When the opera house was finally opened by Queen Elizabeth II in October 1973, it was acoustically unsuited for opera and internally flawed in many other ways thanks to the shambolic process of its creation and the dismissal of its creator. The man whose vision had created the soaring structure was not even present at the ceremonies, and his name was not mentioned.[11]

Utzon never returned to Australia. He died in 2008, never having beheld his completed masterpiece with his own eyes. It's a tragedy fit for opera.

THE BUMP THAT REDEFINED ARCHITECTURE

The story of how the Guggenheim Museum Bilbao came into existence is much less dramatic—and much happier. Although it was

Gehry who convinced officials in Bilbao to build a new museum on the riverfront site, he still had to win the competition to design it. To develop his entry, he went through an intensive period of what he calls "play"—trying out ideas. In its simplest form, Gehry sketches ideas on paper with scrawls that would be mystifying to anyone who didn't know what he was working on. But mostly he works with models, starting with wooden building blocks of various sizes that he stacks first one way, then another, looking for something that seems functional and visually pleasing. Working with Edwin Chan, an architect at Gehry's firm, Gehry started with a preliminary block model, then added scraps of white paper twisted into various shapes. He studied each change intently and discussed whether it should be kept or removed. Assistants built a new model of wood and cardboard, and the process was repeated. "There were often multiple models in a single day, as Frank would test and reject various ideas in quick succession," wrote Paul Goldberger, Gehry's biographer.[12] Two weeks of such iterations created Gehry's winning entry—after which the process continued: try, learn, again.

Gehry has worked with models his whole career. His studio is filled with them. In fact, he has a whole warehouse containing decades of models. He starts at one scale. Then, to see the project from a different perspective, he typically tries another and then another and so on. He zeroes in on some aspect of the project in a model and pulls back to see the whole in another, zooming in and out until he is satisfied that he understands how the building will look and work from every viewpoint. And always he is trying new ideas, discussing the results with his team and with clients, deciding what works and what doesn't. And this is just the beginning of his process.

After landing the contract to design the Guggenheim Bilbao, Gehry and Chan spent the better part of two years working through iteration after iteration, with the work moving from the decidedly analog world of building blocks and cardboard to sophisticated digital simulation using software called CATIA.¹³ Originally developed in 1977 by the French aerospace giant Dassault to design jets, it was modified for Gehry to design buildings in all their three-dimensional complexity. The level of detail and precision that CATIA enables is astonishing. It has empowered Gehry's work and imagination as has no other tool.

Earlier in his career, Gehry worked mostly with straight lines and box-like shapes, but when his thoughts increasingly turned to curves, he found that what he envisioned, once built, made him cringe. He showed me a photo of one of his first buildings with curves, the Vitra Design Museum in Weil am Rhein, Germany, completed in 1989. It's a beautiful building, but the roof on the spiral staircase at the back of the structure has a bump that doesn't seem intentional.¹⁴ That's because it wasn't. Gehry could not make his two-dimensional drawings work so that the builders could actually build what was in his head. So they didn't—due to no fault of theirs. Gehry's vision was simply not translating into the real world. But CATIA had been created to work with curves as subtle as the lines of a jet's fuselage and physics as unforgiving as aerodynamics beyond the speed of sound. For the first time, Gehry and his team could experiment with the full palette of shapes, confident about which could be built.

Three years after making that unwieldy roof in Germany, Gehry built the Olympic Fish in Barcelona for the 1992 Summer Games. That was his first design entirely done by CATIA and was made possible only by CATIA. The curves now flowed. Only five years later, in 1997, the Guggenheim Museum Bilbao opened. The transformation from the bump in Germany to the elegant curves of Bilbao only eight years later is nothing less than exceptional both technologically and aesthetically. It's as radical—and happy—a transformation of architectural style as any in architectural history.

CATIA's possibilities proved to be inexhaustible. Gehry and his team could alter a curve here or change a shape there, and the computer would quickly calculate the implications for every other aspect of the building, from the structural integrity (Will it stand?) to the functionality of the electrical and plumbing systems (Will it work?) and the budget (Can we afford it?). Iteration was now supercharged. Gehry took full advantage of the software's capabilities, trying yet more ideas. In a real sense, the Guggenheim building was first fully and successfully constructed on a computer. Only after the completion of its "digital twin"—a term that would be coined years after Gehry first created one—did construction begin in the real world.

That approach enabled not only artistic daring but astonishing efficiency, as Gehry and his team demonstrated when they later tackled 8 Spruce Street in New York City, a seventy-six-story apartment building. Gehry had the brilliant idea of making the stainless steel facade bulge and recede to resemble cloth rippling in the wind. But to do that, each piece of the facade would be different, manufactured in a factory, then assembled on-site. It all had to fit together seamlessly and do all the practical work a facade must do, while creating the gorgeous illusion of billowing cloth. And it couldn't cost much more than an ordinary facade. To do that required relentless testing. "If you were to do this by hand, you might get two or three tries within the allowable design period," noted Tensho Takemori, an architect at Gehry's firm.[15] But thanks to the digital simulation, "We had thousands of iterations. And because of that, we were actually able to hone the thing down to such great efficiency that we could essentially reduce the cost to almost the same as a flat curtain wall. The proof in this is there were no change orders, and that's a pretty unheard-of result for a 76-story tower."

Years after the Guggenheim Bilbao made Gehry one of the world's most celebrated architects, he made a guest appearance on an episode of *The Simpsons:* Marge sends a letter to the renowned architect asking him to design a concert hall for Springfield. Gehry crumples the letter and throws it onto the ground, but then gasps when he sees its shape. "Frank Gehry, you're a genius!" he shouts. Cut to Gehry presenting a model of Springfield's new concert hall, which looks remarkably like the Guggenheim Bilbao.[16] Gehry came to regret the episode. He did it as a joke, but people took it seriously. "It has haunted me," he explained to a TV interviewer. "People who've seen *The Simpsons* believe it."[17] Frank Gehry is indeed a genius, but everything else about that image of how he works is wrong. In fact, it's the opposite of the truth.

The degree of care and precision that Gehry brought to the planning of the Guggenheim Bilbao was, and is, highly unusual in the world of architecture—and elsewhere. I've spoken with Gehry several times over the years, in his studio, at Oxford where I invited him to lecture, and on the road, and he is adamant that precise planning is essential. "In our practice, we don't allow the client to start construction until we are sure we are doing a building that's within their budget and meets their requirements. We use all the technology available to us to quantify in the most precise way the elements of the build so there's not a lot of guessing," he told me.[18] Another time he stated, "I want to guarantee that we can build that vision. And I want to guarantee that we can build it at a price that the owner can afford."[19]

It's hard to overstate the contrast between the planning of the Guggenheim Bilbao and that of the Sydney Opera House. The former is the perfect illustration of "Think slow, act fast"; that is, of how to do projects. The latter is a painful example of "Think fast, act slow"; that is, how *not* to do projects. In that sense, this tale of two masterpieces is about much more than architecture.

THE PIXAR WAY

Today, Pete Docter is the three-time Oscar-winning director of the animated movies *Up, Inside Out,* and *Soul.* He is also the creative director of Pixar, the renowned studio behind a long string of era-defining movies, starting with the world's first computer-animated feature, *Toy Story*, in 1995. But when Docter joined Pixar in 1990, the studio was tiny. Digital animation was in its infancy. And Docter was young and naive.

"I figured that people like Walt Disney would be like, lying in bed, and suddenly shout 'Dumbo!'" he said and laughed. "The whole thing would be in their head, and they could tell you the story from beginning to end."[20] With experience, he discovered that the stories filmmakers tell do not come so easily. "It starts as a gray blob," he said.

In a long conversation, Docter detailed the process Pixar uses to go from "gray blob" to an Oscar-winning movie in theaters. I was prepared for it to be quite different from what Gehry did to plan the Guggenheim Bilbao. After all, an animated movie is as different from an art museum as an opera house is from a wind farm. Yet in its fundamentals, the process that Docter described bears a close resemblance to Gehry's process.

It starts with time. Pixar gives its directors months to explore ideas and develop a concept for a movie. At that point, it is a minimal idea, no more than what a seed is to the tree it will become. "A French rat loves to cook," for example. "A grouchy old man." Or "Inside the head of a girl." Nothing more than that. "All I want is some catchy, intriguing idea," Docter said.[21]

The first, small step is an outline of roughly twelve pages explaining how the idea can be the basis of a story. "It's mostly a description of what happens. Where are we? What's going on? What happens in the story?," said Docter. That is given to a group of Pixar employees—directors, writers, artists, and executives. "People read it and come back with criticisms, questions, concerns. And then typically the person [the director] will go back and redo the outline again." After which there may be another round of comments and redrafting.

Once "we can see where this is going," said Docter, the writing of the script starts. The first draft will be around 120 pages, and it will go through the same process, likely with "a couple of iterations." Docter emphasized that it is never mandatory for the director to respond to feedback from anyone, at this stage or later. "It's all just, hey, this is a free idea for you to use or not. The only thing that is required is that it gets better."

That part of the process will be at least broadly familiar to anyone who has written a script. But once there is a decent script in hand, Pixar does something unusual: The director and a team of five to eight artists turn the entire script into detailed storyboards that are photographed and strung together into a video that roughly simulates the movie to come. With each storyboard covering about two seconds of film time, a ninety-minute movie requires approximately 2,700 drawings. Dialogue read by employees is added, along with simple sound effects.

Now the whole movie exists in crude form. The process to that point takes about three or four months. "So it's a fairly big investment," Docter told me. But it is still small compared with the cost of actual production.

Next, Pixar employees, including many who have no other involvement in the project, watch the video. "You can really feel when you have the audience and when you don't. Without anybody saying anything," noted Docter. "A lot of times, I already know the stuff I want to change." The director also meets with a small group of other Pixar filmmakers, called the "brain trust," who critique the film. "They'll say, 'I didn't understand something, I wasn't on board with your main character, you had me but then you confused me.' Whatever. It's a wide range of different things that get picked on."

Invariably, after that first screening, "a significant percentage of the film gets chucked," said Docter. The script is substantially rewritten. New storyboards are drawn and photographed and edited together, new voices are recorded, and sound effects are added. This second iteration of the movie is shown to an audience, including the brain trust, and the director gets new feedback.

Repeat.

Then do it again. And again. And again.

A Pixar movie usually goes through the cycle from script to audience feedback *eight times*. The amount of change between versions one and two "is usually huge," said Docter. "Two to three is pretty big. And then, hopefully, as time goes on, there are enough elements that work that the changes become smaller and smaller."

In the version of Docter's Oscar-winning *Inside Out* released to theaters, the story is set mostly inside the mind of a girl, with characters named Joy, Sadness, Anger, and others representing the emotions the girl experiences. But in the early versions of the movie, the cast was much larger, with characters representing the full array of emotions that Docter had learned about in discussions with psychologists and neuroscientists. Even Schadenfreude and Ennui were part of the cast. And the characters were given normal, human names. The audience was expected to know which emotion the character represented by the character's behavior. It didn't work. "That proved to be very confusing for people," Docter said with a laugh. So he threw out several characters and simplified the names of the rest. That was major surgery. But it worked.

In a later round, when Docter was working at a much more granular level, the script had Joy lost in the deeper regions of the brain, far from its control room, where decisions are made, and she says something like "I have to get back to the control room!" several times. The lines were important. They told the audience what the goal was and underscored its urgency. But the feedback told Docter that they made Joy sound self-important and therefore unlikable. Docter's solution? Give those lines to other characters. "So Sadness will say, 'Joy, you've got to get up there!'" That's a tiny tweak, "but it ends up having a fairly significant effect on how you feel about that character."

After eight rounds or so of this exhaustive and exhausting process, the director has an extremely detailed and rigorously tested proof of concept. The movie has been simulated much as Gehry simulates his buildings with physical models and on CATIA. Then real animation begins, using Pixar's state-of-the-art computers. Scenes are created one frame at a time. Famous actors do voice-overs. A professional score is recorded. Sound effects are created. All the elements are pulled together, and the actual movie that will fill theaters and be seen on televisions the world over is finally created. "By the time you see the film," Docter said, "it's about the ninth version of the movie that we've put up."

WHY ITERATION WORKS

This process involves "an insane amount of work," Docter acknowledged. But a highly iterative process such as Pixar's is worth the extraordinary work it entails, for four reasons.

First, iteration frees people to experiment, as Edison did with such success. "I need the freedom to just try a bunch of crap out. And a lot of times it doesn't work," Docter told me. With this process, that's fine. He can try again. And again. Until he gets something that burns bright and clear, like Edison's lightbulb. "If I knew I have to do this only once and get it right, I'd probably hew to the things that I know work." And for a studio built on creativity, that would be a slow death.

Second, the process ensures that literally every part of the plan, from the broad strokes to the fine details, is scrutinized and tested. Nothing is left to be figured out when the project goes into delivery. This is a basic difference between good and bad planning. In bad planning, it is routine to leave problems, challenges, and unknowns to be figured out later. That's how the Sydney Opera House got into trouble. In that case, Jørn Utzon did eventually solve the problem, but it was too late. The budget had exploded, construction was years behind schedule, and Utzon was ousted with his reputation in tatters. In many projects, the problem is *never* solved.

Such failure is so common in Silicon Valley that there is even a name for it. "Vaporware" is software that is publicly touted but never released because developers can't figure out how to make the hype real. Vaporware typically isn't fraud, or at least it doesn't start that way, as there is often honest optimism at work and every intention of delivering. But past a certain point, it can become fraud. *The Wall Street Journal* reporter and author John Carreyrou believes that exactly this dynamic lay behind one of the worst scandals in Silicon Valley history. Theranos, a company founded by its charismatic nineteen-year-old CEO, Elizabeth Holmes—with former secretaries of state George Shultz and Henry Kissinger as board members—raised $1.3 billion from investors after it claimed to have developed a spectacular new blood-testing technology.[22] It was a mirage, and Theranos collapsed amid a hailstorm of fraud charges and lawsuits.[23]

Third, an iterative process such as Pixar's corrects for a basic cognitive bias that psychologists call the "illusion of explanatory depth."

Do you know how a bicycle works? Most people are sure they do, yet they are unable to complete a simple line drawing that shows how a bicycle works. Even when much of the bicycle is already drawn for them, they can't do it. "People feel they understand complex phenomena with far greater precision, coherence, and depth than they really do," researchers concluded. For planners, the illusion of explanatory depth is obviously dangerous. But researchers also discovered that, unlike many other biases, there is a relatively easy fix: When people try and fail to explain what they mistakenly think they understand, the illusion dissolves. By requiring Pixar film directors to walk through every step from the big to the small and show exactly what they will do, Pixar's process forces them to explain. Illusions evaporate long before production begins, which is when they would become dangerous and expensive.[24]

That brings us to the fourth reason why iterative processes work, which I touched on in chapter 1: Planning is cheap. Not in absolute terms, perhaps. The rough videos Pixar produces require a director leading a small team of writers and artists. Keeping them all working for years is a significant cost. But compared to the cost of producing digital animation ready for theaters, which requires hundreds of highly skilled people using the most advanced technology in the world, movie stars doing voices, and leading composers creating the score, it is so minor that even making experimental videos over and over again is relatively inexpensive.

That cost difference is important for the simple reason that in a big project problems are inevitable. The only question is, When will they arise? An iterative process greatly increases the probability that the answer to that question is "in planning." That can make all the difference. If a serious problem is discovered in version five of a Pixar movie and whole scenes need to be thrown out and redone, the amount of time and money lost is relatively modest. If the same problem is discovered when the movie is in production and whole scenes need to be thrown out and redone, it could be horrendously expensive, create dangerous delays, and possibly sink the whole project.

This simple distinction applies in most fields: Whatever can be done in planning should be, and planning should be slow and rigorously iterative, based on *experiri*. Of course, there's more to Pixar's record of success than its remarkable development process, but there is no question that that process is a major contributor to a success record unlike any other in Hollywood history. Pixar hasn't only delivered movies that won critical praise, reaped box-office fortunes, and became cultural touchstones, it has done so with unprecedented consistency. When Pixar released *Toy Story*, its first feature film, in 1995, it was a little-known upstart. A decade later, Disney, the behemoth of entertainment, paid $9.7 billion in 2021 dollars to buy the company. More tellingly, Disney asked Ed Catmull, then the CEO of Pixar, to take control of both Pixar and Disney Animation, the legendary studio that had long been struggling.

It was a smart move. Catmull turned Disney Animation around while continuing Pixar's string of successes. Catmull is now retired from Pixar and Disney; under his leadership, Pixar successfully delivered twenty-one out of twenty-two projects he started, while Disney delivered ten out of eleven. No other studio in Hollywood's more than one-hundred-year history has had a similar success rate.

That is a process that works.

TESTING, TESTING

Anyone familiar with how Silicon Valley operates has probably been nursing an objection from the first chapter of this book. The United States' capital of information technology is arguably the most successful and influential business hub in history, and its entrepreneurs and venture capitalists quite explicitly do not slowly and meticulously plan their projects. In fact, they often scorn the words *plan* and *planning*.

In Silicon Valley, the standard approach for startups is to release a product quickly, even if it is far from perfect, then continue developing the product in response to consumer feedback. This is the "lean startup" model made famous by the entrepreneur Eric Ries in his 2011 book of the same name.[25] It sounds an awful lot like the rush to get projects under way before they have been slowly and carefully planned—the very thing I have condemned as a key cause of project failure from the first page of this book. The success of Silicon Valley would seem to be a rebuke to my whole approach.

In fact, the lean startup model squares well with my advice. The contradiction arises only if you take a narrow view of the nature of planning.

Planning, as I see it, is not merely sitting and thinking, much less a rule-based bureaucratic exercise of programming. It is an *active* process. Planning is *doing:* Try something, see if it works, and try something else in light of what you've learned. Planning is iteration and learning before you deliver at full scale, with careful, demanding, extensive testing producing a plan that increases the odds of the delivery going smoothly and swiftly.

It's what Frank Gehry did for the Guggenheim Bilbao and has done for all his projects since. It's what Pixar does to make each of its landmark movies. It's what fast-growing wind and solar farms do in a global attempt to outcompete fossil fuels, as we will see later. And it's the core of the lean startup model.

Ries wrote that startups operate in an environment of "extreme uncertainty" in which it is impossible to know whether the product they have developed is one that consumers will value. "We must learn what customers really want," he advised, "not what they say they want or what we think they should want." The only way to do that is to "experiment." Create a "minimum viable product," put it in front of consumers, and see what happens. With lessons learned, change the product, ship again, and repeat the cycle.

Ries called this the building phase, as multiple iterations gradually build the final product. I would call it the planning phase, as the design of the product evolves following the dictum "Try, learn, again." Semantics aside, the only real difference is the method of testing.

If there were no other considerations involved, such as money, safety, and time, the ideal testing method would be to simply do whatever it is you are thinking of doing in the real world with real people, and see what happens. That's what NASA effectively did with Project Apollo, as it conducted individual missions to test each of the steps that would be required to get to the moon and back: getting into orbit, maneuvering to another spacecraft, docking. Only when NASA had mastered a step did it go on to the next one. And only when it had mastered as many of the steps as it could test did it send Apollo 11 to the moon. But this sort of testing is almost never possible for big projects because it is too expensive. Project Apollo cost roughly $180 billion in 2021 dollars.[26] Worse, it can be dangerous. The astronauts in Project Apollo all knowingly risked their lives. Three died.

The "minimum viable product" model comes close to the impossible ideal by doing enough testing to bring the product up to the "minimum viable" standard before releasing it into the real world to get that valuable feedback. But it can be done with only a limited range of projects. You can't build a skyscraper, see how people like it, then knock it down and build another. Nor can you put a passenger jet into service to see if it crashes.

As John Carreyrou observed, one reason Theranos got into trouble was that it used a Silicon Valley model commonly applied to software, which can afford to have initial glitches and failures, for medical testing, which cannot. Even for software-based companies, the lean startup model can easily be taken too far, as when glitches cause reputation-damaging product failures, security risks, breaches of privacy, and scandals such as Cambridge Analytica's use of personal data. Or when Instagram is harmful to teenage girls' self-image. Or when Facebook and Twitter arguably contributed to the 2021 attack on the US Capitol. Here a motto like Facebook's "Move fast and break things" seems downright irresponsible. Users and policy makers understandably push back and insist that Silicon Valley figure out what's wrong with its products and fix them before releasing them into the real world.

MAXIMUM VIRTUAL PRODUCT

When a minimum viable product approach isn't possible, try a "maximum virtual product"—a hyperrealistic, exquisitely detailed model like those that Frank Gehry made for the Guggenheim Bilbao and all his buildings since and those that Pixar makes for each of its feature films before shooting.

However, the creation of a maximum virtual product requires access to the necessary technology. If that's not available, look to less sophisticated tools, even technology at the opposite end of the spectrum of sophistication. Remember that Gehry developed the basic design of the Guggenheim Bilbao, and so many other renowned buildings, using sketches, wooden blocks, and cardboard models—technologies available in the average kindergarten classroom. Pixar's mock-up videos may use more advanced tech than that, but photographing drawings, recording voices, and combining them into a crude video is something a twelve-year-old can—and does—do with an iPhone.

The fact is that a wide array of projects—events, products, books, home renovations, you name it—can be simulated, tested, and iterated even by amateurs at home. Lack of technology isn't the real barrier to adopting this approach; the barrier is thinking of planning as a static, abstract, bureaucratic exercise. Once you make the conceptual shift to planning as an active, iterative process of trying, learning, and trying again, all sorts of ways to "play" with ideas, as Gehry and Pixar do, will suggest themselves.

This is why Pete Docter is clear-eyed and humble about Pixar planning. Pixar puts more than $100 million on the line with each project. It has world-class employees and dazzling technology. But at its core, Docter said, Pixar's planning process is no different than if you were designing a carrot peeler in your basement. "You have an idea, you make something with it, you give it to a friend to try. The friend cuts himself. 'Okay, give it back. I'm going to change it. Here, try again.' And it's better!"[27]

Try, learn, again. Whatever the project or the technology, it's the most effective path to a plan that delivers.

5

ARE YOU EXPERIENCED?

Experience is invaluable. But too often it is overlooked or dismissed for other considerations. Or it is simply misunderstood and marginalized. Here's how to avoid that.

There is one small fact I didn't mention when contrasting the planning and construction of the Sydney Opera House and the Guggenheim Museum Bilbao: Jørn Utzon (born 1918) was thirty-eight years old when he won the competition to construct his visionary building while Frank Gehry (born 1929) was sixty-two when he won his.

In another context, that age discrepancy would be trivial. In this case, it's paramount. Age reflects time, and time enables experience. The gap in age of the two visionary architects when they undertook the works that would shape their lives and legacies tells us that there was a big gap in their experience.

And the age gap actually understates the experience gap. Utzon was Danish and graduated from architecture school during the Second World War, when Denmark was occupied by Nazi Germany. There was little work to be had during and after the war, so Utzon had done nothing notable before he started designing the Sydney Opera House. Gehry, in contrast, had spent his early career in booming postwar Los Angeles, where he took on a long list of small but increasingly ambitious projects. By the time he tackled the Guggenheim Bilbao, he had more experience than most architects do the day they retire. The experience gap—or rather, the experience canyon—

between the two architects is another major reason why the creation of the Sydney Opera House was a fiasco while that of the Guggenheim Bilbao remains a model to follow.

We all know that experience is valuable. All else being equal, an experienced carpenter is a better carpenter than an inexperienced one. It should also be obvious that in the planning and delivery of big projects experience should be maximized whenever possible—by hiring the experienced carpenter, for example. It shouldn't be necessary to say that.

But it *is* necessary to say it—loudly and insistently—because, as we shall see, big projects routinely do *not* make maximum use of experience. In fact, experience is often aggressively marginalized. This happens when priority is given to other considerations. One big one is politics. The ambition to be the first, the biggest, the tallest, or some other superlative is another.

More fundamentally, we do not make the most of experience because we do not appreciate how deeply experience can enrich judgment and improve project planning and leadership. Aristotle said that experience is "the fruit of years" and argued that it is the source of what he called "*phronesis*"—the "practical wisdom" that allows us to see what is good for people and to make it happen, which Aristotle saw as the highest "intellectual virtue."[1] Modern science suggests that he was quite right.

We should make more use of this ancient insight.

MARGINALIZING EXPERIENCE

Back in chapter 1, I mentioned the story of my father grumbling—presciently, as it turned out—about the Danish government awarding a contract to an inexperienced contractor to drill an undersea tunnel. Not coincidentally, the company was led by Danes. Politicians everywhere know that awarding contracts to domestic companies is a good way to make influential friends and win public support with promises of jobs, even if the domestic company will not perform as well as its foreign competitor because it is less experienced. When this happens—and it happens routinely—those responsible put other interests ahead of achieving the project's goal. At a minimum, such an approach is economically dubious, and sometimes it is ethically dodgy, too, or downright dangerous. And elected officials are far from alone in doing this. Big projects involve big money and big self-interest. And since "who gets what" is the core of politics, there is politics in every big project, whether public or private.

This fact helps explain why the California High-Speed Rail project became such a mess. There is no real high-speed rail in the United States, which suggests how much experience US companies have building it. When California started to seriously consider this type of rail, foreign companies with lots of experience—notably SNCF, the French National Railway Company—set up offices in California in the hope of landing a sole-source contract or at least being a major partner in the project's development. But the state decided not to go that way. Instead, it hired a large number of mostly inexperienced, mostly US contractors and oversaw them with managers who also had little or no experience with high-speed rail.[2] That's a terrible way to run a project. But it's common—because it's good politics.

A Canadian example is arguably even more egregious. When the Canadian government decided it wanted to buy two icebreakers, it didn't buy them from manufacturers in other countries that were more experienced with building icebreakers, deciding instead to give the contracts to Canadian companies. That's national politics. But rather than give the contracts to one company so that it could build one ship, learn from the experience, and deliver the second ship more efficiently, it gave one contract to one company and the other to another company. Splitting the contract "will not lead to these natural learning improvements," noted a report by the parliamentary budget officer, Yves Giroux—a report that found that the estimated cost of the icebreakers had soared from $2.6 billion (Canadian) to $7.25 billion. So why do it? One company is in a politically important region in Quebec, the other in a politically important region in British Columbia. Splitting the contracts meant twice the political payoff—at the cost of experience and billions of dollars.[3]

BEING FIRST

The ambition to be the first with something is another way experience gets sidelined. I personally saw how misplaced this ambition can be two decades ago. The Danish Court Administration, the body that governs city courts, regional courts, and the supreme court in Denmark, was considering the creation of two big new IT systems, one of which would digitize all real estate records in the country and another that would make the administration of the courts entirely digital, including all legal documents. I was a member of the board of directors of the courts making the decision.[4] At the time, I had been studying big projects for about a decade, and although I hadn't yet studied IT, the plan made me nervous. We didn't know of anyone who had done something like what we were planning. And if my studies had shown anything, it was that going first is dangerous. So I suggested that a team from the Court Administration visit other countries to investigate. If we found that others had done such a thing already, we could learn from them. If we didn't, we could wait.

Except that wasn't what happened. The team duly traveled to various countries and reported back in a board meeting. Had anyone else done this? "No!" was the excited reply. "We will be the first in the world!" I had mistakenly thought that my fellow board members would see being first as a strong argument *against* going ahead. In fact, they took it as a reason to charge onward. The desire to do what has never been done before can be admirable, for sure. But it can also be deeply problematic.

These two very expensive IT projects were authorized, and they quickly turned into epic fiascos. Deadlines were repeatedly pushed back and budgets badly overrun. When completed, the new systems were buggy and worked badly. They became a political scandal that made the front pages of newspapers over and over for years. Several staff had nervous breakdowns and went on sick leave.

The only upside to the misery was that those who went second, third, and fourth could study our experience and do better. But did they? Probably not. Similar large-scale IT projects continue to be deeply troubled. Planners don't value experience to the extent they should because they commonly suffer yet another behavioral bias, "uniqueness bias," which means they tend to see their projects as unique, one-off ventures that have little or nothing to learn from earlier projects.[5] And so they commonly don't.

These examples are from the public sector. Those in the private sector may object that, yes, experience is good and there is no upside to being the first court system to digitize its records. But a company that develops the first-ever widget and is first to bring it to market does have an upside, the famous "first-mover advantage."[6] Surely this advantage more than compensates for the downside of not being able to learn from the experience of others.

But the first-mover advantage is greatly overstated. In a watershed study, researchers compared the fates of "pioneer" companies that had been the first to exploit a market and "settlers" that had followed the pioneers into the market. Drawing on data from five hundred brands in fifty product categories, they found that almost half of pioneers failed, compared to 8 percent of settlers. The surviving pioneers took 10 percent of their market, on average, compared to 28 percent for settlers. Getting into the market early was indeed important—"early market leaders have much greater long-term success," the researchers noted—but those "early" market leaders "enter an average of 13 years after pioneers."⁷ The consensus of researchers today is that, yes, being first to market can confer advantages in certain specific circumstances, but it comes at the terrible cost of an inability to learn from the experience of others. Better to be—like Apple following Blackberry into smartphones—a "fast follower" and learn from the first mover.⁸

BIGGEST, TALLEST, LONGEST, FASTEST

Ambition not only urges us to be first, it can also drive us to deliver the biggest. The tallest. The longest. The fastest. This quest for other superlatives can be as dangerous as the desire to be first, and for the same reason.

Consider Seattle's State Route 99 tunnel. A decade ago, when Seattle announced that it would bore a tunnel under its waterfront to replace a highway on the surface, it was far from a first, so there was plenty of relevant experience to draw on. But Seattle decided that its tunnel would be the biggest of its kind in the world, with enough room for two decks, each with two lanes of traffic. Politicians boasted. "Biggest" is at least as exciting as "first." It gets you into the news, something most politicians find useful.

But to bore the world's biggest tunnel, you need the world's biggest boring machine. Such a machine, by definition, hasn't been built and used before. It would be the first. Seattle placed a custom order and the machine was duly designed, built, and delivered. That cost $80 million, which is more than double the price of a standard boring machine. After boring a thousand feet of a tunnel that would be nine thousand feet long, the borer broke down and became the world's biggest cork in a bottle. Extracting it from the tunnel, repairing it, and getting it back to work took two years and cost another $143 million. Seattle's new underground highway, needless to say, was completed late and over budget, with pending litigation making further overruns likely. If the city had instead chosen to drill two standard-sized tunnels, it could have used off-the-shelf drilling equipment that had already been widely used and was therefore more reliable, and they could have hired teams experienced at running these machines. But politicians wouldn't have been able to brag about the size of the tunnel.

Along with the usual political concerns, one reason why mistakes such as Seattle's happen is that we too often think that only people can be experienced, not things, and that therefore using new technology is not like hiring an inexperienced carpenter. That's a mistake—because it is.

Remember Pixar's Pete Docter explaining the design of a new carrot peeler at the end of the previous chapter? He makes one. A friend tries it and cuts himself. So he alters the design, and the friend tries again. In this way, the iterative process of trying and learning steadily improves the peeler's design. The carrot peeler embodies the experience that created it, and Docter wants a peeler that incorporates the best experience, just as his movies at Pixar do.

This doesn't end when the formal design process ends, either. If Docter's carrot peeler were to become a hit, sell millions, and be used by generations of cooks and the design was never changed because it worked so beautifully, all that subsequent experience could be said to be embodied in the object as its validation. That's reliable technology.

FROZEN EXPERIENCE

The German philosopher Friedrich von Schelling called architecture "frozen music."[9] It's a lovely and memorable phrase, so I'm going to adapt it: Technology is "frozen experience."

If we see technology this way, it is clear that, other things being equal, project planners should prefer highly experienced technology for the same reason house builders should prefer highly experienced carpenters. But we often don't see technology this way. Too often, we assume that newer is better. Or worse, we assume the same of something that is custom designed, which we praise as "unique," "bespoke," or "original." If decision makers valued experience properly, they would be wary of a technology that is new, because it is *inexperienced* technology. And anything that is truly "one of a kind" would set off alarm bells. But all too often, "new" or "unique" is treated as a selling point, not something to avoid. This is a big mistake. Planners and decision makers make it all the time. It's a main reason that projects underperform.

OLYMPIC BLOWOUTS

Combine all the wrongheadedness described in the preceding passages, and you get the Olympics.

Since 1960, the total cost of hosting the Games—six weeks of competitions, including the Paralympics, held once every four years—has grown spectacularly and is now in the tens of billions of dollars. Every Olympic Games since 1960 for which data are available, summer and winter, has gone over budget. The average overrun is 157 percent in real terms. Only nuclear waste storage has higher cost overruns of the twenty-plus project categories my team and I study. Scarier still, the overruns follow a power-law distribution, meaning that really extreme overruns are surprisingly common. The current holder of the one Olympic record no one wants—in cost overrun—is Montreal, which went 720 percent over budget in 1976. But thanks to the power law, it is likely only a matter of time before some unlucky city becomes the new Olympic champion.[10]

There are many reasons for the sorry record of the Olympics, but much of the explanation lies in the way the Games aggressively marginalize experience.

There is no permanent host for the Games. Instead, the International Olympic Committee (IOC) calls on cities to bid for each Games. The IOC prefers to move the Games from region to region, continent to continent, because that's an excellent way to promote the Olympic brand and therefore serves the interests of the IOC—which is to say, it is excellent politics. But it also means that when a city and a country win the right to host the Games, it is likely that neither the city nor the country has any experience in doing so. Or if it has hosted the Olympics before, it was so long in the past that the people who did the work are retired or dead. London, for example, has hosted the Olympics twice—with sixty-four years between events. Tokyo hosted twice, with fifty-seven years between events. Los Angeles will host twice, with forty-four years between events. One solution would be for Olympic host cities to hire the people and companies that did the work four and eight years earlier, and that happens to an extent. But politics would never allow that to prevail. The bill for hosting the Olympics is massive. Only by promising lucrative contracts and jobs to locals can governments win support for a bid. And whether locals or professional Olympic nomads do the job, the host will have no experience in leading such a workforce, for the reasons mentioned above.

As a result, even if the Games repeat every four years, hosting performance is not driven up a positive learning curve by experience. The Olympics are forever planned and delivered by beginners—a crippling deficiency I call "Eternal Beginner Syndrome."[11]

On top of this come pride and the quest for gold. The Olympic motto is "Faster, higher, stronger," and host cities aspire to their own superlatives in constructing facilities. Rather than using existing designs or repeating designs shown to work by experience elsewhere, they routinely seek to build the first, the biggest, the tallest, the most unusual, the most beautiful, the unique, experience be damned. These pathologies can be seen in the Olympic record holder for cost overrun, the Montreal Games of 1976. "All the structures were dramatic, modern, and complex," noted a 2013 case study written by engineers, "none more so than the main stadium."[12]

The architect of the stadium was Roger Taillibert, a personal favorite of Mayor Jean Drapeau, who envisioned a clamshell with a hole in the roof over which a tall, curved tower would lean dramatically. Tension cables would connect the tower to the stadium, allowing a retractable roof to be raised or lowered over the hole. Nothing like it had been done before, which was what seemed to most delight Drapeau and Taillibert, but which should have triggered alarm bells.

Taillibert's plans showed little regard for mere practicalities. "The stadium design did not consider constructability and did not leave room for interior scaffolding," the reviewing engineers wrote, leaving workers with no choice but to build the stadium by clustering scores of cranes so tightly together that they interfered with one another.[13]

With costs exploding and construction far behind schedule, the government of Quebec ousted Drapeau and Taillibert, sprayed a fire hose of money, and barely managed to start the Games on schedule. There was no roof on the stadium, and the tower that was supposed to be the dramatic centerpiece was still only an ugly stub.[14]

After the Games, costs kept escalating as engineers realized that the tower could not be built as Taillibert had planned. An alternative design was developed, and the roof was finally installed a decade later. A litany of mishaps, malfunctions, repairs, replacements, and more cost increases followed. When Roger Taillibert died in 2019, the obituary in the *Montreal Gazette* opened by noting that the Olympic stadium had cost so much that "it took 30 years" for Quebec to pay it off. "And more than four decades later, it is still plagued by a roof that does not work."[15]

In the years leading up to the Games, the stadium's shape had inspired the nickname "the Big O," but that quickly morphed into "the Big Owe." In that sense, Montreal's Olympic Stadium should be considered the unofficial mascot of the modern Olympic Games. But it's not alone. Search online for "abandoned Olympic venues," and you will find many more, and worse, monuments to Olympic folly.

MAXING OUT ON EXPERIENCE

The polar opposite of the Big Owe is the Empire State Building.

As I described at the beginning of this book, the legendary building was completed at astonishing speed, in large part due to architect William Lamb's focus on developing a carefully tested plan that would empower a smooth, swift delivery. But another factor was his insistence that the project use existing, proven technologies "in order to avoid the uncertainty of innovative methods."[16] That included avoiding "hand work" whenever possible and replacing it with parts designed "so that they could be duplicated in tremendous quantity with almost perfect accuracy," Lamb wrote, "and brought to the building and put together like an automobile on the assembly line."[17] Lamb minimized variety and complexity, including in floor designs, which were kept similar as much as possible. As a result, construction crews could learn by repeating. In other words, workers didn't build one 102-story building, they built 102 one-story buildings. The whole project shot up the learning curve, and the quick pace of construction only accelerated.[18]

Still, the plan might have failed to deliver if it had been handed to neophytes. But the general contractors who erected the giant were Starrett Brothers and Eken, "a company with a proven track record of efficiency and speed in skyscraper construction," noted the historian Carol Willis.[19]

It also helped that it wasn't the first time Lamb had designed the building. In Winston-Salem, North Carolina, the Reynolds Building, once the headquarters of the R. J. Reynolds Tobacco Company, is an elegant art deco structure that looks remarkably like a smaller, shorter Empire State Building. Lamb designed it in 1927, and it opened in

1929, the year before construction began on the Empire State Building, taking that year's National Architectural Association's Building of the Year Award.[20] In designing and erecting the Empire State Building, Lamb was informed by the best experience an architect can hope for: enhancing a prior success.

Is the Empire State Building diminished by the fact that core elements of its design were used in an earlier project? Or that the design is deliberately simple and repetitive? I don't see how one could make that case. The building is iconic. It even achieved one of those superlatives people so desire—"world's tallest"—without taking undue risks.

Anyone with a big project in mind should hope to have an equivalent success. Maximizing experience is an excellent way to boost the chances of that.

WE KNOW MORE THAN WE CAN TELL

But as important as "frozen experience" is to getting projects right, we also need to look at the "unfrozen" kind—the lived experience of people. That's because experience is what elevates the best project leaders—people like Frank Gehry and Pete Docter—above the rest. And in both planning and delivery, there is no better asset for a big project than an experienced leader with an experienced team.

How does experience make people better at their jobs? Ask someone that question, and you'll likely hear that with experience people know more. That's true as far as it goes. People who work with a tool learn how to use it, so they gain knowledge such as "The safety lock must be turned off before the tool can start."

You don't actually need experience to get that sort of knowledge. Someone can just tell you, or you can find it in a manual; it is "explicit knowledge." But as the scientist and philosopher Michael Polanyi showed, much of the most valuable knowledge we can possess and use isn't like that; it is "tacit knowledge." We *feel* tacit knowledge. And when we try to put it into words, the words never fully capture it. As Polanyi wrote, "We can know more than we can tell."[21]

When an adult gives a child what she thinks are complete instructions on how to ride a bike ("Put your foot on the pedal, push off, press down on the other pedal"), the child typically falls on her first tries, because the instructions are *not* complete. And they cannot be. Much of what the adult knows about how to ride a bike (for example, how exactly to maintain balance during a turn at a certain speed) is knowledge that she feels. It can't be put fully into words, no matter how many words she uses. So although the instructions are helpful, the only way for the child to learn how to ride a bike is to try, fail, and try again. That is, she needs to develop experience and get that tacit knowledge for herself.

This is obvious in the case of physical activities such as riding a bicycle or playing golf, but it applies to so much more. Polanyi actually developed the concept of tacit knowledge in an exploration of how scientists do science.

Highly experienced project leaders like Frank Gehry and Pete Docter overflow with tacit knowledge about the many facets of the big projects they oversee. It improves their judgment profoundly. Often, they will *feel* that something is wrong or that there is a better way without quite being able to say why. As a large research literature shows, the intuitions of such experts are, under the right conditions, highly reliable. They can even be astonishingly accurate, as in the famous story of the art experts who instantly felt, correctly, that a supposedly ancient Greek statue was a fraud, even though it had passed various scientific tests and even if they couldn't say why they felt the way they did.[22] This is "skilled intuition," not garden-variety gut feelings, which are unreliable. It is a powerful tool available only to genuine experts—that is, people with long experience working in their domain of expertise.[23]

When a highly experienced project leader uses a highly iterative planning process—what I earlier called "Pixar planning"—good things happen. When writing scripts or dreaming up images, Pete Docter said, "I just dive in and do stuff completely intuitively. I'm going to be more accurate. I'm funnier. More truthful." But Docter then puts his intuitive judgments to the test by turning his scripts and images into a video mock-up and seeing how an audience responds. He analyzes what's working and what isn't and adjusts accordingly. By shifting from one mode to the other, over and over again, he gets the most from both intuition and careful thought.

But the value of judgment enriched by experience is not limited to planning. When Jørn Utzon won the competition to design the Sydney Opera House, he entered a complex, difficult political environment, far from his home turf, where an array of powerful figures were pressing their own interests and agendas. Lacking relevant experience in navigating this environment, he was a babe in the woods. And the wolves got him.

Frank Gehry's climb up the ladder of experience, in contrast, gave him an escalating education in the politics of big projects. His toughest lessons came in his biggest commission before the Guggenheim Bilbao: the Walt Disney Concert Hall in Los Angeles. Like the Sydney Opera House, it was conceived in a difficult political environment with powerful people and clashing views that resulted in conflicts, a rushed start, and a project that dragged on and on, getting deeper and deeper into cost overruns.[24] Like Utzon's, Gehry's reputation suffered. He might ultimately have shared Utzon's fate if not for the intervention of supporters, notably the Disney family, whose original gift of $50 million had gotten the project started and who made it a condition of their continued support that Gehry remain the architect when his detractors tried to oust him from the project. When finally completed, the building was a wonder. But it was very late and badly over budget and gave Gehry a scare.

As brutal as the experience was, the process of building the Disney

Concert Hall taught Gehry a host of lessons that he used in building the Guggenheim Bilbao and has used in projects ever since. Who has power, and who doesn't? What are the interests and agendas at work? How can you bring on board those you need and keep them there? How do you maintain control of your design? These questions are as important as aesthetics and engineering to the success of a project. And the answers can't be learned in a classroom or read in a textbook because they are not simple facts that can be put fully into words. They need to be learned as you learn to ride a bike: try, fail, try again. That was what Gehry did and Utzon didn't. One had built experience, the other had not.

When Aristotle discussed the nature of wisdom more than 2,300 years ago, he didn't scorn the knowledge we get from classrooms and textbooks. It is essential, he said. But practical wisdom, the wisdom that enables a person to see what's right to do and get it done, requires more than explicit knowledge; it requires knowledge that can be gained only through long experience—a view supported by Michael Polanyi and a great deal of psychological research 2,300 years later. As previously mentioned, that practical wisdom is what Aristotle called "*phronesis*." He held it in higher regard than any other virtue, "for the possession of the single virtue of phronesis will carry with it the possession of them all [i.e., all the relevant virtues]," as he emphasized.[25]

In short, if you have *phronesis*, you've got it all. Therefore, a project leader with abundant *phronesis* is the single greatest asset a project can have. If you have a project, hire a leader like that.

BACK TO *EXPERIRI*

To go back to where I started in the previous chapter: When planning, remember the Latin word *experiri*, the origin of the English words *experiment* and *experience*. Whenever possible, planning should maximize experience, both frozen and unfrozen.

Most big projects are not the first, tallest, biggest, or anything else too remarkable. They are relatively ordinary highways and rail lines, office buildings, software, hardware, change programs, infrastructure, houses, products, movies, events, books, or home renovations. People don't expect them to be grand cultural landmarks and legacies. Nor do they demand that they be wildly creative and unusual. But they do want them to be excellent. They want them to finish on budget and on time, do what they're supposed to, do it well and reliably, and do it for a long time. For such projects, experience can help enormously. If there is a design—or a system, process, or technique—that has delivered many times before, use it, or tweak it, or mix-and-match it with similarly proven designs. Use off-the-shelf technologies. Hire experienced people. Rely on the reliable. Don't gamble if you can avoid it. Don't be the first. Remove the words *custom* and *bespoke* from your vocabulary. They're a desirable option for Italian tailoring if you can afford it, not for big projects.

Similarly, whenever possible, maximize experimentation using a highly iterative "Pixar planning" process. Whatever the relevant mechanisms of testing, from simple trial and error to sketches, wood-and-cardboard models, crude videos, simulations, minimum viable products, and maximum virtual products, test everything from the big ideas down to the small details. With good testing mechanisms that make failure relatively safe, take calculated risks and try new ideas. But recognize that the less proven something is, the more it must be tested.

When something works, keep it. When it doesn't, get rid of it. Try, learn, again. And again. And again. Let the plan evolve.

Testing is all the more critical for those very rare big projects—such as finding solutions to the climate crisis, getting people to Mars, or permanently storing nuclear waste—that must do what has never been done before because that is the heart of the project. They start with a deep deficit of experience. To deliver their vision, on time and budget, that deficit must be turned into a surplus with the relentless application of *experiri*.

A good plan, as I said, is one that maximizes experience or experimentation; a great plan is one that does both. And the best plan? That's one that maximizes experience and experimentation—and is drafted and delivered by a project leader and team with *phronesis*.

But even with all that in hand, you still have to answer some of the toughest questions in any project: How much will it cost? How long will it take? Even superb plans delivered by excellent leaders and teams can be undone if those forecasts are off. And thanks to a ubiquitous bias, they routinely are.

Let's look at that bias—and how to overcome it.

6

SO YOU THINK YOUR PROJECT IS UNIQUE?

Think again. Understanding that your project is "one of those" is key to getting your forecasts right and managing your risks.

In 2010, as China was launching one giant infrastructure project after another, Hong Kong's Legislative Council approved a megaproject that was ambitious even by Chinese standards: the world's first fully underground high-speed rail system, to be known as "XRL," including the world's largest underground high-speed rail station, four stories deep, dynamited into bedrock, smack in the center of Hong Kong. The twenty-six-kilometer (sixteen-mile) line would halve the travel time between Hong Kong and the mainland city of Guangzhou, further integrating one of the world's most important ports and financial centers with the largest urban agglomeration on Earth, including the Pearl River Delta Economic Zone.

XRL would be built by Mass Transit Railway (MTR), the corporation that operates Hong Kong's giant rail network. MTR has an excellent track record, both in its daily operations and in delivering big projects. Yet it soon got into trouble with XRL. When construction began in 2011, it was scheduled to be finished in 2015. But when that date arrived, less than half the work had been done, with more than half the budget spent. A tunnel under construction, with an expensive tunnel-boring machine inside, had flooded. It was a mess.

MTR's CEO and project director resigned over the delay. The project was now in full meltdown. That was when I got a call from MTR, asking me to come to Hong Kong and help.

With my team, I sat down with the MTR board of directors in their thirty-third-floor boardroom, spectacularly overlooking Hong Kong's skyscrapers and harbor.[1] The atmosphere was tense. Was it even possible to clean up the mess?

I assured the board that it was. I'd seen worse. But there was no margin for error. The board had already gone back to the government to warn that more money and time would be needed. Now the board would have to go back again and explain exactly how much, which was excruciating in a culture that emphasizes not losing face. We had to make sure that there wouldn't be a third time, which meant getting the schedule and budget right for the remaining part of the project—and delivering on both. Everyone agreed.

Doing so required that we first understand how the mess had been created. So we did a postmortem, as always. It is seldom pretty.

When we asked MTR what had gone wrong, we were handed the usual dirty laundry list: Community protests had delayed the start. There had been problems with the giant tunnel-boring machines. There had been labor shortages. Tunneling had revealed unexpected underground conditions. The construction site had flooded. Mitigation measures had been ineffective. Management had felt underinformed. On it went. Combined, those factors had created a chain of delays followed by failed efforts to catch up, followed by more delays and more failed efforts. Staff had become demoralized, further dragging down performance. The situation had steadily worsened.

The specifics mattered, but the general litany was grimly familiar to me. What was the cause? Bad planning? Bad delivery? Should we blame managers, workers, or both? Why had a previously successful organization failed so spectacularly on this particular project?

When delivery fails, efforts to figure out why tend to focus exclusively on delivery. That's understandable, but it's a mistake, because the root cause of why delivery fails often lies outside delivery, in forecasting, years before delivery was even begun.

How did MTR know that its delivery was failing? By the schedule and budget slipping. But slippage was measured against MTR's forecasts of how long and how costly the various stages of the project would be. If those forecasts were fundamentally unrealistic, a team expected to meet them would fail no matter what they did. The delivery would be doomed before it started. That should be obvious. But when things go wrong and people get desperate, the obvious is often overlooked, and it's assumed that if delivery fails, the problem must lie with delivery, when in fact it lies with forecasting.

How long will it take? How much will it cost? Forecasting is critical to any project. In this chapter, I'll explain how to get estimates right by using a surprisingly simple and highly adaptable forecasting technique. However, even excellent forecasts cannot cope with the rare but disastrous turn of events such as the flooding in Hong Kong, also known as "black swans." Those call for risk mitigation, not forecasting. I'll show how. Then we'll get XRL back on track. That work started with a simple question: "How did you make your forecasts?"

IT'S THE ESTIMATE, STUPID!

We met Robert Caro, the acclaimed biographer, in chapter 3, where he diligently filled the box on the right before starting a new book. But before Caro began writing his Pulitzer Prize–winning biographies, he had spent six years as an investigative reporter with the Long Island newspaper *Newsday*. After writing a series of stories about a bridge proposal backed by Robert Moses, a long-serving state bureaucrat, Caro realized how powerful Moses was and decided to write his biography. He knew it was an ambitious project. Moses had been shaping New York City for more than forty years and had built more megaprojects than any other person in history. He was also secretive, preferring to stay far from public view. Still, Caro was fairly confident that he could complete his book in nine months and certain that he would finish within a year.[2]

That forecast was critically important. Caro and his wife, Ina, had a young son and modest savings. His advance on the book was only $2,500 ($22,000 in 2021 dollars). He could not afford for the project to drag on.

But it did drag on. One year went by. Two. Three. "As year followed year, and I was still not nearly done, I became convinced that I had gone terribly astray," Caro recalled decades later. In conversations, people would inevitably ask how long he had been working on the book. "When I said three years, or four, or five, they would quickly disguise their look of incredulity, but not quickly enough to keep me from seeing it. I came to dread that question."[3]

Caro and his wife "watched our savings run out, and we sold our house to keep going, and the money from the sale ran out."[4] They struggled on somehow. It took Caro *seven* years to finish his book. But a story that seemed destined to be a tragedy ended in triumph. When *The Power Broker: Robert Moses and the Fall of New York* was finally published in 1974, it won the Pulitzer Prize and became an improbable bestseller. Not only is the book still in print, it is considered one of the greatest dissections of political power ever written.

For our purposes, what matters is *why* there was such a vast and dangerous gap between Caro's expectation and how long the work actually took. There are two possible explanations.

One puts the blame on Caro's work. In this explanation, the forecast was reasonable. The book would have taken a year or less to complete if someone more experienced had written it, but Caro so badly bungled the research and writing that he took seven times as long as necessary. For years, he suspected that that was the case, but he couldn't figure out what he was doing wrong. It tormented him.

The other is that the forecast was a laughable underestimate and no one could possibly have written the biography Caro had in mind in one year. Five years into the project, when it seemed as if the book would never be finished, Caro discovered that that was in fact the correct explanation.

The discovery was accidental. After learning that the New York Public Library had a room with dedicated office space for chosen writers working on books, Caro applied and was granted a spot. For the first time, he found himself among other book authors. Two happened to be the authors of major historical biographies that Caro loved and considered to be models for his own book. Caro introduced himself, and they talked. Inevitably, Caro was asked the question he had learned to dread: "How long have you been working on your book?" Reluctantly, he answered, "Five years." But the other authors weren't shocked; far from it. "Oh, that's not so long," one said. "I've been working on my Washington for nine years." The other said that his book about Eleanor and Franklin Roosevelt had taken seven years. Caro was ecstatic. "In a couple of sentences, these two men—idols of mine—had wiped away five years of doubt."[5] Caro's work was not to blame; his forecast was.

So how had Caro convinced himself that a book that would take seven years to write could certainly be done in one? As an investigative reporter, he had been used to taking a week or two to research and write an article, a generous amount of time by newsroom standards. He might spend three weeks writing a particularly long article or series of articles, the word count of which would be roughly equivalent to that of a book chapter. A book may have twelve chapters. So the estimate was easy: $12 \times 3 = 36$ weeks, or nine months. It was not clear at the start how many chapters the book would have, but even if it went as high as seventeen, the book could still be finished in less than a year. For a newspaper reporter, a year is an almost incomprehensibly long period of time to devote to one piece of writing. It's small wonder then that Caro was confident.

In psychology, the process Caro used to create his forecast is known as "anchoring and adjustment."⁶ Your estimate starts with some fixed point, twelve chapters of three weeks each in Caro's case. That's the "anchor." Then you slide the figure up or down as seems reasonable, to one year for Caro. That's "adjustment." Caro was exactly right to call his thinking "naïve but perhaps not unnatural" because, as abundant research shows, anchoring and adjustment, particularly when immediate experience is used as the anchor, is a natural way of thinking. It's likely that most people in Caro's position, with his specific experience, would have made a forecast the same way and come up with a similar result.

But basing forecasting on anchoring and adjustment is tricky. As psychologists have shown in countless experiments, final estimates made this way are biased toward the anchor, so a low anchor produces a lower estimate than a high anchor does. That means the quality of the anchor is critical. Use a good anchor, and you greatly improve your chance of making a good forecast; use a bad anchor, get a bad forecast.

Unfortunately, it is easy to settle on a bad anchor. Daniel Kahneman and Amos Tversky pioneered research on this in a famous 1974 paper that included one of the stranger experiments in the history of psychology. They created a "wheel of fortune," the dial of which displayed numbers from 1 to 100. Standing in front of test subjects, they gave the wheel a spin, and it stopped on a number. They then asked subjects to estimate the percentage of UN members that are African. Even though the number the wheel had selected was blatantly irrelevant, it made a big difference to the final estimate: When the wheel of fortune stopped on, for instance, 10, the median guess was 25 percent; when it landed on 65, the median guess was 45 percent.⁷ (The correct answer at the time of the experiment was 29 percent.) Much subsequent research revealed that people will anchor in almost any number they happen to be exposed to prior to making their forecast.

Marketers often make use of this phenomenon. When you encounter a "limit six per customer" sign at the grocery store, there's a good chance that the sign is there to expose you to the number six, making it the anchor when you decide how many items to buy.

In this light, Robert Caro's thought process doesn't seem so unusual. It used a bad anchor—his experience as a newspaper journalist—and produced a terrible forecast that nearly ruined him and his family. But at least it made some superficial sense.

As I discovered, it was just such a "sensible" forecast that had gotten MTR into trouble. When MTR was planning XRL, it had lots of experience planning and delivering big transportation infrastructure projects. But it had no experience with high-speed rail, which is exceptionally complex and demanding even when it doesn't involve, as it did in that case, a cross-border and underground system. In that sense, MTR was in a position similar to that of the young Robert Caro when he set out to write his first book. And MTR had made its forecasts much the same way that Caro did, using its prior experience as an anchor. The result was similar, too; MTR's forecast for XRL— the basis of its delivery schedule and budget—was a clear underestimate of how long a project like this takes.

I happened to know a number of Hong Kong government insiders from previous work in the region, whom I saw while there working for MTR on XRL. I learned through the civil service grapevine that senior officials had, in fact, quietly and internally questioned the XRL anchor and suggested an upward adjustment. In big organizations there's almost always somebody with a sense of realism. But they were lone voices. Others were optimistic and had an interest in keeping estimates low, so realism was seen as pessimism and ignored. Such behavior is as common as bad anchoring and reinforces it.

The truth is that the managers and workers on XRL could not meet the schedule they were given, no matter how hard they worked. It's unlikely that anyone could have. From the beginning, they were sure to fall behind. When that happened, MTR reacted just as Robert Caro did—blaming the work, not the forecast—and demanded improvements and mitigations the managers and workers could also not deliver. More demands were made, but to no avail. The project fell further and further behind. Then came the meltdown.

The mistake the planners made is as basic as it is common: When we experience delays and cost overruns, we naturally go looking for things that are slowing the project down and driving up costs. But those delays and overruns are measured against benchmarks. Are the benchmarks reasonable? Logically, that should be the first question that is asked, but it rarely comes up at all. Once we frame the problem as one of time and money overruns, it may never occur to us to consider that the real source of the problem is not overruns at all; it is *underestimation*. This project was doomed by a large underestimate. And the underestimate was caused by a bad anchor.

To create a successful project estimate, you must get the anchor right.

"ONE OF THOSE"

In 2003, I got a call from the UK government. Gordon Brown, who was then finance minister and in charge of the national budget and would later become prime minister, had a problem with major projects. They were so routinely blowing past their expected time and cost that the government had lost confidence in its own forecasts. And because major projects made up a big chunk of the British budget, the government had lost confidence in its own bottom line. By that time, making a diagnosis—cognitive biases plus strategic misrepresentation equals trouble—was relatively easy. Finding a cure was more work.

I started with an obscure phrase found within a paper that Daniel Kahneman and Amos Tversky published in 1979—not the famous

1979 paper on "prospect theory" that won Kahneman the Nobel Prize in Economic Sciences in 2002 but another paper the prolific duo published the same year. The phrase is "reference class."[8]

To understand what a reference class is, bear in mind that there are two fundamentally different ways to look at a project. The first is to see it as its own special undertaking. All projects are special to some degree. Even if the project isn't something as wildly creative as making a Pixar film, going to Mars, or fighting a pandemic, even if it's as mundane as remodeling a suburban house or as common as building a small bridge, developing a software program, or hosting a conference, at least some aspects of the project will be unique. Maybe it's the people who will do the work or how they will do it. Or the location. Or current economic circumstances. Or a unique combination of these factors. There will always be *something* that makes this project different from all others.

People have no trouble grasping that. In fact, in my experience and in line with the results of behavioral science, people not only tend to naturally look at their projects this way, they tend to exaggerate just how unusual their specific project really is. This is the "uniqueness bias" we encountered in the previous chapter.[9] We all have it. It makes us love our kids. But it's unfortunate in some circumstances because it blinds us from seeing our project in the second way.

The cultural anthropologist Margaret Mead supposedly told her students, "You're absolutely unique, just like everyone else." Projects are like that. Whatever sets a project apart, it shares other characteristics with projects in its class. An opera house may be one of a kind because of its design and location, but it still has plenty in common with other opera houses, and we can learn a lot about how to construct a particular opera house by looking at opera houses in general and considering our opera house to be "one of those." The category of opera houses is the reference class.

Kahneman and Tversky dubbed these two perspectives the "inside view" (looking at the individual project in its singularity) and the "outside view" (looking at a project as part of a class of projects, as "one of those"). Both are valuable. But they're very different. Although there's little danger that a forecaster will ignore the inside view, overlooking the outside view is routine. That's a fatal error.

To produce a reliable forecast, you need the outside view.

THE OUTSIDE VIEW

Consider a scenario that is as common as it is simple: You are thinking about renovating your kitchen, even after reading about David and Deborah's nightmare in chapter 3, and you want to estimate the cost. This is a DIY job, so you don't have to include labor costs. How will you make a forecast?

If you're like almost everyone else, including many contractors, you start by taking careful measurements. How big will the floor space be? The walls? The ceilings? What size of cupboards and countertops do you want? Then you decide on the type of flooring, walls, ceiling, cupboards, drawers, countertops, sinks, faucets, fridge, oven, lights, and so on. You find out how much those things sell for, then use the measurements and unit costs to calculate what you must spend for each item. Add it all up, and you have your cost estimate, simple and easy. And thanks to the care you took in measuring and counting everything down to the smallest detail and getting the right prices, it must be reliable, too. Or so you assume.

You start the project by tearing out the existing flooring. And you discover mold in the floorboards.

Then you tear out drywall. And you discover old wiring that violates the current building code.

Later, your prized granite countertops are delivered. You slip while carrying a slab, breaking it in two.

Just like that, your estimate goes up in flames. You are on your way to a major cost overrun.

Maybe you think I'm being unreasonable with this illustration. After all, each of the nasty surprises I imagined is unlikely. That is true. But even with a project as simple as a kitchen renovation, the number of possible surprises, each unlikely, is long. Many small probabilities added together equal a large probability that at least some of those nasty surprises will actually come to pass. Your forecast did not account for that. That means your forecast, which seemed perfectly reasonable and reliable, was actually a highly unrealistic things-will-go-according-to-plan best-case scenario, like the best-case scenarios I described in chapter 2. And things almost *never* go according to plan. On big projects, they don't even come close.

You may think, as most people do, that the solution is to look more closely at your kitchen renovation, identify all the things that could possibly go wrong, and work them into your forecast. It's not. Spotting ways that things can go wrong is important because it enables you to reduce or eliminate risks or mitigate them, as I'll discuss below. But it won't get you the foolproof forecast you want, for the simple reason that no matter how many risks you can identify, there are always many more that you can't. They are the "unknown unknowns," to use the term Donald Rumsfeld, then the US secretary of defense, made famous.[10]

But there's a way around them. You just need to start over with a different perspective: See your project as one in a class of similar projects already done, as "one of those." Use data from that class—about cost, time, benefits, or whatever else you want to forecast—as your anchor. Then adjust up or down, if necessary, to reflect how your specific project differs from the mean in the class. That's it. It couldn't be simpler.

That kitchen renovation? The class it belongs to is "kitchen renovations." Get the mean actual cost of a kitchen renovation. That's your anchor. If there are good reasons to think your specific project will be above or below the mean—if, for example, you will use high-end countertops and fixtures that cost three times what standard items cost—adjust up or down accordingly. With that, you have your forecast.

I know from experience that people sometimes struggle with this, not because it's complicated but because it's simple. It's *too* simple. Their project is special, after all, or so they think, and this process doesn't emphasize that, so they complicate the process. They think that if they're doing a kitchen renovation, they shouldn't say that "one of those" is "the class of kitchen renovations." That's too easy. Instead, they try to create a tightly drawn, complicated definition of the class that seems to neatly fit their particular project. Instead of seeing the class as "kitchen renovations," they call it "kitchen renovations with granite countertops and German appliances in high-rise condominium units located in my neighborhood." That's a mistake. It ignores a lot of useful information. And it makes it much harder to gather the necessary data, a challenge I'll discuss below.

The same can happen with adjustments. These should be made only if there are clear, compelling reasons to think that your project will be well above or below the mean. But the more you adjust, the more your project is *different* from the average project. And your project is special! So it feels right to adjust, adjust, and adjust some more, even if the adjustments are based on little more than vague feelings. That, too, is a mistake.

This is all uniqueness bias talking, wanting to be reintroduced into your decisions when you're trying to eliminate it. Don't listen to it. Keep the process simple: Define the class broadly. Err on the side of inclusion. And adjust the average only when there are compelling reasons to do so, which means that data exist that support the adjustment. When in doubt, skip adjustment altogether. The class mean is the anchor, and the anchor is your forecast. That's very simple, yes. But simple is good; it keeps out bias.

I came to call this process "reference-class forecasting" (RCF).[11] After I developed it for Gordon Brown, the British government used it to forecast the time and cost of major projects and was so satisfied with the results that it made the process mandatory.[12] Denmark did the same.[13] RCF has also been used in the public and private sectors in the United States, China, Australia, South Africa, Ireland, Switzerland, and the Netherlands.[14] All that experience has enabled rigorous testing, and a slew of independent studies has confirmed that "RCF indeed performs the best," in the words of one.[15]

It performs the best by a large margin. The gap between a conventional forecast and one that uses RCF varies by project type, but for over half the projects for which we have data, RCF is better by 30 percentage points or more. That's on average. A 50 percent increase in accuracy is common. Improvements of more than 100 percent are not uncommon. Most gratifyingly, given the method's intellectual roots, Daniel Kahneman wrote in *Thinking, Fast and Slow* that using reference-class forecasting is "the single most important piece of advice regarding how to increase accuracy in forecasting through improved methods."[16]

WHY DOES IT WORK?

The core of reference-class forecasting is an anchor-and-adjustment process similar to what Robert Caro and MTR did—but using the *right* anchor.

What makes the reference class the right anchor is what I emphasized in the previous chapter: relevant real-world experience. One person did a kitchen renovation using basic fixtures and appliances; with no surprises and a smooth delivery, it cost $20,000 and took two weeks. Another went with granite countertops and lots of stainless steel, then discovered that the house's wiring wasn't up to code; the project wound up costing $40,000, and thanks to an electrician who was overbooked, it took two months to finish. Collect lots of these numbers, and you may find that the average kitchen renovation cost $30,000 and took four weeks to complete. These are experience-based, real-world outcomes, not estimates, so they're not distorted by psychology and strategic misrepresentation. Use them to anchor your forecast, and you will create an estimate that is rooted in reality, undistorted by behavioral biases, making it a better estimate.

This also explains why adjustment should be used cautiously and sparingly, if at all. It is an opportunity for biases to creep back in. Overdo it, and the value of your unbiased anchor may be lost.

RCF also lets you come to grips with the seemingly intractable problem of Donald Rumsfeld's unknown unknowns. Most people think that unknown unknowns cannot be forecasted, and that sounds reasonable. But the data for the projects in the reference class reflect *everything* that happened to those projects, including any unknown unknown surprises. We may not know precisely what those events were. And we may not know how big or how damaging they were. But we don't need to know any of that. All we need to know is that the numbers for the reference class do reflect how common and how big the unknown unknowns really were for those projects, which means that your forecast will reflect those facts, too.[17]

Remember David and Deborah's renovation in the Cobble Hill neighborhood of Brooklyn? It started going downhill when the contractor tore out the kitchen floor and discovered shoddy work done when the building had gone up in the 1840s. The whole floor had to be torn out and supports in the basement installed. That was an unknown unknown that would have been difficult to spot before work began. But if the project's time and cost had been forecast using renovations of old New York homes as the reference class, the frequency and severity of such nasty surprises would have been encoded into the data. As a result, the estimated cost and time would have accounted for unknown unknowns that can't be predicted.

So reference-class forecasting is better on biases. It's better on unknown unknowns. It's simple and easily done. And it has a proven track record of delivering more accurate forecasts. I'm happy that it has been taken up to the extent that it has by different organizations around the world—much more than I thought would ever happen when I first developed the method for Gordon Brown—but I wouldn't blame anyone for wondering why, given all its strengths, it isn't used even more than it is, across the board.

There are three reasons for this. The first is that for a lot of people and organizations, the fact that RCF eliminates biases is a bug, not a feature. As I discussed in chapter 2, shoddy forecasting is the bread and butter of countless corporations. They do not want the people who authorize projects and pay the bills to have a more accurate picture of what projects will cost and how long they will take. They're going to stick with the status quo, at least until they're forced to change—for instance, by assigning legal liability for blatantly biased forecasts, which is increasingly happening.[18]

A second challenge to overcome is the strength of uniqueness bias. Kahneman writes about a time when he and some colleagues set out to compose a textbook together. They all agreed that it would take roughly two years. But when Kahneman asked the only member of the group with considerable experience in producing textbooks how long it usually takes, that expert said he couldn't recall any project taking less than seven years. Worse, about 40 percent of such projects are never finished, he said. Kahneman and his colleagues were briefly alarmed—but then they moved on just as if they had never heard those unwelcome facts because, well, their project felt different. It always does. "This time is different" is the motto of uniqueness bias. The textbook was ultimately finished *eight* years later.[19] If the greatest living student of cognitive bias can be suckered by uniqueness bias, it's small wonder that the rest of us are vulnerable, too, or that avoiding the trap requires awareness and sustained mental effort.

The third reason RCF is still not as widely used as it should be is the simplest. It's the data. Calculating an average is easy, but only once you have the numbers in hand. *That* is the hard part.

FIND THE DATA

In the aforementioned kitchen renovation example, I took for granted that you have data on kitchen renovations that will allow you to calculate the average cost. But you probably don't. And you'll struggle to find them. I know from experience, because I've looked for reliable kitchen renovation data, couldn't find them, and was told by an economist who studies the home renovation economy that, as far as he knows, they haven't been collected. True, if you search "average cost of kitchen renovation," you'll find companies suggesting various figures, usually wide ranges. But where did those numbers come from? Are they based on many actual results, or are they just a sales pitch? You can't know. And you *must* know, if you want a reliable forecast.

This is a common problem. Old project data are seldom considered a valuable resource and collected. In part, that's because project planners and managers have a mindset that is focused on the future, not the past. As soon as a project is over, their focus is on the next new thing, and no one thinks about looking back to collect data on the old project. But it's also because those who do see value in data often have an interest in keeping theirs under wraps. For instance, how many big construction companies want homeowners to have good data on home renovation costs? This helps explain why my database of big projects, spanning many different project types, has taken decades to develop and is the only one of its kind in the world.

But these are not insurmountable barriers. Governments and corporations can review their old projects and create their own databases.

In fact, I've helped several do so. So can small businesses—and trade associations, if they can convince their members to participate. Highly experienced professionals naturally learn from past projects—a contractor who has done dozens of kitchen renovations will have a strong sense of what an average kitchen renovation costs—but they can refine and improve their understanding simply by gathering numbers from their old projects and adding to those numbers every time a project is finished.

As for those who do not have access to a database like mine or cannot create their own, reference-class forecasting is still useful; you just have to take a rough-and-ready approach to it.

Think about the young Robert Caro, contemplating writing his first book. He could easily have used RCF to forecast how long his project would take: Make a list of books he considers broadly similar to what he plans to write, call their authors, and ask how long it took them to write those books. If he gets twenty responses, he adds them up, divides by twenty, and has his anchor. Even drawing upon a sample of only twenty, he would find a ton of real-world experience packed into the number. Then he would ask himself if there were strong reasons why he should expect to be much faster or slower than the average. If yes, he could adjust accordingly. If no, he has his estimate. It wouldn't be perfect, but it would be miles better than Caro's actual estimate, because it would be anchored in past projects like the one he was actually doing—writing a book—instead of what he used to do, writing a set of long newspaper articles.

In fact, Caro did something like this later, by accident, when he met his fellow authors in the New York Public Library writing room and was relieved to hear that they had each spent seven years or more writing their books. But that happened long after he had started his project—and after he had taken his family to the brink of financial ruin and spent years tormenting himself for not finishing in one year, as planned.

The same goes for your kitchen renovation. Look around for others who have done a kitchen renovation in, say, the past five to ten years. Ask friends, family, co-workers. Kitchen renovations are common, so let's say you come up with fifteen such projects. Get the total cost of each, add them, divide by fifteen. That's your anchor.

Even simpler and even more accurate, you could get the percentage cost overrun for each renovation and calculate their mean. Percentages are easier to remember, and they compare better than totals do. You could then take the estimate made the usual way—by carefully measuring your specific project—and increase it by that percentage. In that way, you would combine the value of the inside view (detail) with the value of the outside view (accuracy), which is the whole game.

Of course, when it comes to the outside view, more is better, so data from thirty projects beat data from fifteen, and data from a hundred beat data from thirty. But it's essential to recognize that RCF can deliver a lot of value even when there are many fewer data than we want. With a little logic and imagination and an understanding of why RCF works, it's possible to wring at least some value out of it even when you have small numbers.

Even the data from just one completed project are valuable. Obviously, it would be wrong to call that a "reference *class*." But it *is* real-world experience. Call it a "reference *point*." Then compare it to your planned project and ask, "Is our project likely to perform better or worse than this reference point?" I know from experience that that discussion can be surprisingly useful.

A TRULY UNIQUE PROJECT?

The smallest natural number is zero. In the truly rare cases in which a project can accurately be described as unique—the one and only of its kind—that's how many projects there are in the reference class. Yet even in that case, RCF may be useful.

In 2004, I got a call from Anders Bergendahl, the Swedish official in charge of decommissioning nuclear power plants. He needed a reliable estimate of how much it would cost to decommission Sweden's fleet of nuclear power plants, which would take decades, and safely store nuclear waste, which would last for centuries. Sweden's nuclear industry would be asked to pay into a fund to cover those costs, so the government needed to know how much the industry should pay. "Can you help?" he asked.

I was stumped. At the time, I did not have data on nuclear decommissioning projects (I do today). And I didn't think I could get any. Very few nuclear plants had been decommissioned worldwide, and those few had been done under very special circumstances; think Chernobyl and Three-Mile Island. Sweden would be the first country to carry out a planned decommissioning of a fleet of reactors. "I can't help," I said. "Sorry."

But Bergendahl saw something I didn't. He said that consultants had given him a report estimating the cost and the "cost risk," meaning the risk of the cost being higher than expected. But he had noticed a strange thing when he had compared the consultants' report with an academic book in which my team and I had documented the cost risk for transportation infrastructure such as roads, bridges, and rail lines.[20] According to our book, the cost risk was higher for that very ordinary sort of infrastructure. "That makes no sense," Bergendahl said. It takes from five to ten years to complete transportation projects, and people have been building them for centuries. How can it be less risky to decommission nuclear power when it takes much longer and we have almost no experience doing it? I agreed. That made no sense. The consultants and their report would have to go.

But Bergendahl had an idea for a replacement. Why not use our data on transportation infrastructure costs as a "floor"—a minimum—and assume that the real cost of nuclear decommissioning and storage would be somewhere above that? That would be far from a perfect estimate. But it made a lot more sense than the one the consultants had put together. And decommissioning wasn't starting soon. If the Swedish government put that estimate into place now and got the nuclear industry to start paying into the fund, the government could adjust the estimate later as more was learned about decommissioning in Sweden and elsewhere. I was impressed. It was such a common-sense approach—*phronesis*, again. We worked to develop it, and it became Swedish policy.[21]

The uncomfortable truth is that I myself had fallen for "uniqueness bias" by assuming that a project as unprecedented as nuclear power plant decommissioning had nothing to learn from the experience of other projects. Not true; as Bergendahl showed, it just took a little logic and imagination to see it.

REGRESSION TO THE TAIL

There is, however, a big, fat-tailed caveat on all this. Imagine you have a graph with the costs of one thousand kitchen renovations that takes the shape of a classic bell curve—with most projects clustered around the mean in the middle, very few projects on the far right or far left, and even the most extreme data points not far removed from the mean. As I discussed in chapter 1, that's what statisticians call a "normal distribution."

In a normal distribution, there is regression to the mean, meaning that the observations in a sample tend to move back toward the mean of the population as more observations are included. So if a contractor completes an unusually expensive kitchen renovation, it is likely that the next one, other things being equal, will be closer to the mean and therefore cheaper.

When you're dealing with a normal distribution, it's fine to use the mean cost in a reference-class forecast, as I described above, and call it a day. But as noted in chapter 1, my analysis revealed that only a minority of the many project types in my database are "normally" distributed. The rest—from the Olympic Games to IT projects to nuclear power plants and big dams—have more extreme outcomes in the tails of their distributions. With these fat-tailed distributions, the mean is not representative of the distribution and therefore is not a good estimator for forecasts. For the most fat-tailed distributions, there isn't even a stable mean that you can expect outcomes to cluster around because an even more extreme outcome can (and will) come along and push the mean further out, into the tail toward infinity. So instead of good old regression to the mean, you get what I call "regression to the tail."[22] In that situation, relying on the mean and assuming that your result will be close to it is a dangerous mistake.[23]

So much for the theory. What does this mean in practice?

Ideally, you'd always want to know whether you're facing a fat-tailed distribution or not. But if you're a private individual doing a kitchen renovation or a small business doing a minor project, you might not know. Even if you're a top civil servant in control of a national program with the firepower of your national statistical agency at your disposal, like Anders Bergendahl, you may not know. In that case you're better off using the average—or using your imagination, as Bergendahl, who didn't even know his average, did—than using nothing.

But following the precautionary principle, you should also err on the side of caution and assume that your project is part of a fat-tailed distribution, because this is more likely to be the case than not. That means you should assume that your project has at least some risk of not merely finishing a little late or a little over budget; it may go haywire and end very badly. To protect yourself against that, you need to mitigate risk, as I describe below.

If you're a professional at a large organization, you should do better than this rough-and-ready approach. You need to get serious about gathering enough data to allow you to statistically analyze the distribution and determine if it's normal or fat-tailed. If it's normal or near normal, do a reference-class forecast using the mean. This would still give you an approximately 50 percent risk of a small cost overrun. If you want to reduce this risk further, add a 10 to 15 percent contingency (reserve), and you're done.[24]

If you face a fat-tailed distribution, shift your mindset from forecasting a single outcome ("The project will cost X") to forecasting risk ("The project is X percent likely to cost more than Y"), using the full range of the distribution. In a typical fat-tailed distribution in project management, about 80 percent of the outcomes will make up the body of the distribution. That's pretty normal; nothing really scary there. For that portion of the distribution, you can protect yourself the usual way with affordable contingencies that will fit into a budget. But the tail outcomes—the "black swans"—cover about 20 percent of the distribution. That means a 20 percent chance of ending up in the tail, which is too much risk for most organizations. Contingencies might have to be 300, 400, or 500 percent over the average cost—or 700 percent, as we saw for the Montreal Olympics in chapter 2. That's prohibitive. Providing such contingencies would not be budgeting; it would be blowing up the budget. So what can you do about the tail? Cut it off.

You can do that with risk mitigation. I call it "black swan management."

BLACK SWAN MANAGEMENT

Some tails are simple to cut. Tsunamis are fat-tailed, but if you build well inland or erect a high enough seawall, you eliminate the threat. Earthquakes are also fat-tailed, but build to an earthquake-proof standard, as we did with the schools in Nepal, and you are covered. Other tails require a combination of measures; for a pandemic, for instance, a blend of masks, tests, vaccines, quarantines, and lockdowns to prevent infections from running wild.[25] That's black swan management.

For big projects, black swan management typically requires a combination of measures. I started this book with one: "Think slow, act fast." We saw that delivery is when things can go horribly and expensively wrong. Exhaustive planning that enables swift delivery, narrowing the time window that black swans can crash through, is an effective means of mitigating this risk. Finishing is the ultimate form of black swan prevention; after a project is done, it can't blow up, at least not as regards delivery.

The critical next step is to stop thinking of black swans the way most people do. They are not bolt-from-the-blue freak accidents that are impossible to understand or prevent. They can be studied. And mitigated.

My team and I were asked to do just that for High Speed 2, or HS2, a $100 billion–plus high-speed rail line that will run from London to northern England, if and when it is completed.[26] Using our database, we first explored the cost distribution of comparable high-speed rail projects around the world. Sure enough, the distribution had a fat tail. High-speed rail is risky business, as we saw in Hong Kong. So we zeroed in on the projects in the tail and investigated what exactly had made each project blow up. The answers were surprisingly simple. The causes had not been "catastrophic" risks such as terrorism, strike actions, or other surprises; they had been standard risks that every project already has on its risk register. We identified roughly a dozen of those and found that projects were undone by the compound effects of these on a project already under stress. We found that projects seldom nosedive for a single reason.

One of the most common sources of trouble for high-speed rail was archaeology. In many parts of the world, and certainly in England, construction projects are built on layers of history. The moment a project starts digging, there's a good chance it will uncover relics of the past. When it does, the law requires that work stop until a qualified archaeologist can survey the site, document it, remove artifacts, and ensure that nothing significant is lost. Experienced managers know this and keep an archaeologist on speed dial.

Normally, that's enough. But sometimes big projects cut through cities and landscapes, so when artifacts are discovered at one site and the archaeologists get to work, artifacts are found at another site soon after. And another. And another. There just aren't that many archaeologists, and, unlike plumbers or electricians, responding to emergency calls isn't a normal part of their work. So when multiple discoveries overlap, the delays can become severe. And those delays can in turn delay other work. The result is a chain reaction of setbacks, like a line of cars sliding into one another on an icy street. In this way, what starts as one minor fender bender becomes gridlock capable of derailing the whole project.

Given the amount of digging HS2 would require, that was a major risk. The solution? Put every qualified archaeologist in the country on a retainer. That's not cheap. But it's a lot cheaper than keeping a multibillion-dollar project on hold. So it makes sense. And after construction started, it had the additional effect of archaeology becoming the one area where news perceived as positive by the general public originated directly with the project, promoted by HS2 as the largest archaeology program ever undertaken in the United Kingdom.[27]

We also found that early delays in procurement and political decisions correlated with black swan blowouts in the HS2 reference class. Interestingly, early delays are not seen as a big deal by most project leaders. They figure they have time to catch up, precisely because the delays happen early. That sounds reasonable. But it's dead wrong. Early delays cause chain reactions throughout the delivery process.

The later a delay comes, the less remaining work there is and the less the risk and impact of a chain reaction. President Franklin Roosevelt got it right when he said, "Lost ground can always be regained—lost time never."[28] Knowing this, we advised measures that would cut the probability of early delays and chain reactions.

After dealing with archaeology and early delays, we had ten more items on the list of causes of high-speed rail black swans, including late design changes, geological risks, contractor bankruptcy, fraud, and budget cuts. We went through one after another, looking for ways to reduce the risk. By the end, we had a bundle of measures that reduced black swan risk arising from each cause *and* from their interaction.

That's how you cut the tail of a big, complex project. The procedure will be somewhat different from project to project, but the principles are the same. And the answers are right under your nose in the tail of the reference class; you just need to dig them out.

As with reference-class forecasting, the big hurdle to black swan management is overcoming uniqueness bias. If you imagine that your project is so different from other projects that you have nothing to learn from them, you will overlook risks that you would catch and mitigate if you instead switched to the outside view. A startling illustration—a cautionary tale, in fact—is provided by the Great Chicago Fire Festival.

THE GREAT CHICAGO FIRE FESTIVAL

The story of the fire that destroyed most of Chicago in 1871 runs deep in local culture, so Jim Lasko, the creative director of a Chicago theater company, pitched the idea of a one-day festival that would culminate in the spectacular burning of replica Victorian houses. The mayor's office loved it and signed off on it.

The very name Great Chicago Fire Festival highlighted the potential for disaster, so the fire department carefully examined Lasko's plans and demanded a litany of safety measures, including building the houses on a barge in the river and installing a sophisticated sprinkler system. For Lasko, it was aggravating and exhausting, but the months of this relentless focus on risk were also a comfort. If live events go wrong, they go wrong in front of an audience.

In October 2014, before a crowd of thirty thousand people, including the mayor and the governor, Lasko held up a walkie-talkie and gave the order to light the fire. Nothing happened. He waited. Still nothing. The ignition system had failed. There was no backup and no contingency plan. All the effort had gone into mitigating the risk of the fire spreading, not the risk of the fire not igniting in the first place.

A politician later called the festival "the fiasco on the river," and the name stuck. The event became a punch line. The theater company ultimately folded, and Lasko lost his job.[29]

What went wrong? Lasko and his team spent ages thinking about risk, but they never shifted their perspective from thinking of the Great Chicago Fire Festival as a unique project to seeing it as "one of those"; that is, part of a wider class of projects. If they had, they would have spent time thinking about live events. How do they fail? One common way is equipment failure. Mics don't work. Computers crash. How is that risk mitigated? Simple: Identify essential equipment, get backups, and make contingency plans. That kind of analysis is dead easy—but only *after* you have shifted to the outside view.

Notice that risk mitigation does not require predicting the *exact* circumstances that lead to disaster. Jim Lasko didn't need to identify when and how the ignition system would fail, only recognize that it could. And have a Plan B if it did.

Recall what Benjamin Franklin wrote in 1758: "A little neglect may breed great mischief." This is why high safety standards are an excellent form of risk mitigation and a must on all projects. They're not just good for workers; they prevent little things from combining in unpredictable ways into project-smashing black swans.

Black swans are not fate. We are not at their mercy. That said, it is important to acknowledge that risk mitigation—like most things in life—is a matter of probability, not certainty. I started this book with the story of the Empire State Building, which was so skillfully planned and swiftly delivered that it came in substantially under budget and a little ahead of schedule. That was superb risk mitigation. What I didn't mention is that, despite doing everything right, the project, which was launched in the Roaring Twenties, was unfortunately finished during the Great Depression, a turn of events no one had seen coming. In the devastated economy, the Empire State Building struggled to attract paying tenants and was nicknamed the "Empty State Building" during the 1930s. Not until the economy revived after the Second World War did it become profitable.

In this complex world, we can and must move the probabilities in our favor, but we can never achieve certainty. Good risk managers know this in their bones and are prepared for it.

BACK TO HONG KONG

Now let's go back to that underground high-speed rail project in Hong Kong.

MTR got into trouble with the XRL project when it used the wrong anchor—its own experience with urban and conventional rail. Toss in some optimism bias, add ambition, and MTR created a delivery schedule that was doomed from the outset. When work inevitably fell behind schedule, managers and workers were blamed. A downward spiral of failure and recrimination followed.

To get MTR out of that spiral, we started by going back to the beginning and making our own forecast of the project, but this time it was a reference-class forecast using the right anchor. Of course, we couldn't use a large reference class of underground high-speed rail projects because XRL was the world's first. Instead, we used worldwide data for 189 high-speed rail, tunneling, and urban rail projects that statistical tests had shown were comparable to XRL. This is RCF in its most sophisticated form, possible only when you have a rich database.[30] The forecast showed that what MTR had tried to do in four years should take six. No wonder it had gotten into trouble.

We also went back and did risk mitigation. We found, for example, that if a boring machine broke down, engineers and parts were ordered from the manufacturer. And people waited until they arrived. That made no sense. In Formula 1 racing, where every second counts, the pit stop has engineers and a wide array of spare parts on hand to keep delays to an absolute minimum. I told MTR that time was as important to them as it was to an F1 team, and MTR was spending a lot more money, so they should do the same. We also noted that procurement and delivery were often accompanied by delays as lower-level employees at MTR contacted lower-level employees at the supplier. We advised that such decisions be pushed up the ladder, so that the CEO of MTR would contact the CEO of the supplier— a remarkably effective way to accelerate response time, we found.

The next step was getting MTR back on track. To do that, we made another reference-class forecast for the remaining work, roughly half of the total. The estimate had to be high confidence because MTR had only one more shot at getting approval from the Hong Kong government for more time and money. Having data from almost two hundred relevant projects to draw on enabled us to statistically model the uncertainties, risks, and likely outcomes of various strategies. Then MTR could decide how much risk it was willing to take. I told the MTR board that it was like buying insurance. "How insured do you want to be against further time and budget overruns? Fifty percent?

Seventy? Ninety?" The more insured you want to be, the more money you have to set aside.[31]

A settlement was eventually reached between MTR and the government in November 2015. But even before then, we got to work on improving delivery.

If the data are detailed enough, as ours were, it's possible to forecast not only a whole project but sections of a project, using the same reference-class forecasting technique. Doing this, we set milestones, the well-known management tool that places markers for the project to pass by specified dates.

But if a project is falling behind, managers don't want to wait until the next milestone arrives before they are alerted to the delay. They need to know and act as quickly as possible. Our data were so detailed that we could make a further set of subforecasts, so we invented "inchstones." And we specified in detail beforehand who would be responsible for what. If MTR started falling behind under the new schedule, managers would know immediately, and they would know who must act, so no time would be wasted. With the Hong Kong government, we developed the inchstone approach into a general methodology based on artificial intelligence, which today is used on other Hong Kong projects and can be used on any project anywhere.[32]

The final step in turning XRL around was owning the mistake. MTR did that, starting with a public apology by a top official. New leaders were hired and policies changed to reflect the problems we identified. Perhaps most important, management started celebrating progress against inchstones and milestones. The spiral of negativity was replaced by an updraft of accomplishment that everyone could feel. The whole turnaround process took ninety very intense days and nights.

Four years later, early on the morning of September 22, 2018, Hong Kong's spectacular new underground railway station with its dramatically curved rooftop green spaces welcomed the first travelers. At precisely 7:00 A.M., the first bullet train slipped quietly into a tunnel and raced to mainland China. The project had been concluded on budget and three months ahead of schedule—the budget and schedule created by using the right anchor.

So now we can put reference-class forecasting and risk management into the toolbox, along with experience, Pixar planning, and thinking from right to left. These are the essential tools for thinking slow in planning before acting fast in delivery.

That said, I have to admit something: Some people think my approach is not only wrong but the opposite of how we should tackle big projects. In the next chapter, I'll examine their argument and put it—and mine—to the test.

7

CAN IGNORANCE BE YOUR FRIEND?

Planning ruins projects, some say. Just get going! Trust your ingenuity! It's a wonderful sentiment backed by superb stories. But is it true?

As the 1960s were coming to a close, Jimi Hendrix was a twenty-five-year-old psychedelic rock star who spent his nights soaking up the bohemian atmosphere of Manhattan's Greenwich Village. One of his favorite nightclubs was a little place called the Generation. In early 1969, Hendrix took over the lease.

Hendrix luxuriated in the club's laid-back vibe, relaxing for hours with friends and jamming with other musicians. He wanted more of that—plus a space where musicians could record jam sessions on a simple eight-track tape machine. To redesign the club, he hired John Storyk, a twenty-two-year-old who had recently graduated from Princeton University's architecture school and whose only building experience was designing the decor of an experimental nightclub that Hendrix had wandered into and loved. That was enough. Storyk started drawing.

Hendrix also asked Eddie Kramer, his twenty-six-year-old sound engineer, to take a look. Kramer had worked with Hendrix for two years. He knew him as an artist and a person, and he knew his business affairs. Kramer had a strong reaction when he first visited the club, accompanied by the man Hendrix had hired to manage it. "I walked down the stairs at what was the Generation nightclub," he recalled half a century later, "and I said, 'You guys are out of your f***ing minds.'"[1]

It would cost Hendrix a fortune to remodel the club, Kramer reasoned. And what would he get in exchange? A nightclub where he could relax and jam, sure. But the recordings produced during those jam sessions would be suboptimal. Meanwhile, Hendrix would continue to spend as much as $200,000 a year (roughly $1.5 million in 2021 dollars) for studio sessions to record his albums. Why not build a private recording studio instead? It could be a place designed from top to bottom as an expression of Hendrix's personal aesthetic and artistic spirit, a place as inspiring and comfortable for him as any nightclub could be. But it would also be a top-quality recording studio where he could record top-quality albums—and keep the fortune he spent every year on studio time.

In 1969, that was a daringly innovative idea. Not even the biggest stars owned their own studios. And commercial studios tended to be sterile boxes where technicians wore white lab coats. Hendrix was convinced; the nightclub project was now a studio project.

ELECTRIC LADY

John Storyk had almost finished redesigning the Generation when he was told about the change of plans. He was crushed. He thought he was fired. But Kramer and Hendrix's studio manager said no. "They said, 'You can stay, and you can become the designer for the studio.'"

"I said, 'Guys, I don't know anything about studios. I've never even been in a studio.'

"They said, 'That's okay.'"[2]

That freewheeling spirit permeated the project. Hendrix gave Kramer and Storyk a remarkably free hand to create a studio unlike any other—a studio designed exclusively to cater to one artist's "needs, tastes, whims, and fancies," as Eddie Kramer described it. But Hendrix did have one, very specific request. Recalling it, Kramer dropped his voice and did an excellent impression of the 1960s icon. "Hey, man," he said. "I want some round windows."

Storyk made six drawings on tracing paper of what he thought a recording studio fit for Jimi Hendrix should look like. Those drawings became the plan. The whole plan. There was no schedule. There was no budget. "The entire studio was built from six drawings and a lot of pointing," Storyk said with a laugh.

When construction began, problems sprouted like magic mushrooms. A major one was the discovery of an underground river flowing beneath the building. It required the installation of sump pumps that would have to operate around the clock. But the pumps created background noise that was unacceptable for a recording studio, so they had to be muffled somehow. "That set the project back weeks and weeks," Storyk said with a sigh.

They invented on the fly. In most rooms, ceilings are afterthoughts, nothing more than a place to hang light fixtures. But in a recording studio, the ceiling has to absorb ambient sound. Storyk and Kramer learned from acousticians that they inject air into plaster to make it more sound absorbent, so they dreamed up a way to get extra air into the plaster by whipping it with commercial eggbeaters.

Financing was a bigger problem. Hendrix made a lot of money from concerts and records, but his cash flow was irregular. "We would do construction for a month, a month and a half, two months, and the money would run out," Kramer recalled. The tradesmen would be laid off, "the site would be shut down, and Jimi would go on the road." When Hendrix did a concert, he was paid in cash. Bags were stuffed with tens of thousands of dollars. Someone in the Hendrix entourage flew the bags back to Manhattan and handed them to Hendrix's managers. "And we could get the project started again."

As construction dragged on and bills piled up, Hendrix couldn't sustain the airdrops, but his manager convinced Warner Bros., Hendrix's record label, to put in hundreds of thousands of dollars. That barely got the project over the finish line. It had taken a year and cost more than $1 million—adjusted for fifty years of inflation, that's roughly $7.5 million—but it was done. Inspired by his most recent album, *Electric Ladyland*, Hendrix called the studio Electric Lady, later renamed Electric Lady Studios.

An opening party was held on August 26, 1970. Patti Smith, Eric Clapton, Steve Winwood, Ron Wood, and other fellow stars were there.[3] The studio had the perfect Hendrix vibe, with ambient lighting, curved walls, and, of course, round windows. "It was a womblike place to be in," Kramer recalled. "Jimi felt incredibly happy, comfortable, and creative in it." And the sound blew people away. Musicians call it "tight." Only decades later did Storyk have the technology to take measurements that confirmed why: The plaster on the ceiling absorbed midrange sound, as expected, but also, to his surprise, low-frequency sound. The eggbeaters turned out to be a stroke of genius.

Tragically, Jimi Hendrix died less than a month after his studio opened, and the world lost the lifetime of brilliant music he surely would have produced. But his studio lived on. Stevie Wonder recorded there. Then came Led Zeppelin, Lou Reed, the Rolling Stones, John Lennon, David Bowie, AC/DC, the Clash, and a long list of others. And it's *still* going. U2, Daft Punk, Adele, Lana Del Rey, and Jay-Z have all recorded in what is now the oldest working recording studio in New York City and one of the most famous studios in the world.

"I still have the six drawings," Storyk said of the original design. A famous tech mogul once offered to buy them for $50,000. "Not for sale. Still in the tube. The Museum of Modern Art has said they'll take them."

The project was a leap in the dark: An ethereal artist impulsively authorized two kids with little experience and no plan to design and deliver an unprecedented project that he paid for with literal bags of cash. By all rights, it should have ended badly. At some points, such as when Hendrix ran out of cash, it seemed it would. It took ages to complete. It cost a fortune. But in the end, the project paid off beyond anyone's wildest dream.

JUST DO IT

I love Jimi Hendrix, and I love this story. Who wouldn't? There's something deeply appealing about people daring to skip planning and just throw themselves into a big project—then dreaming, scheming, and hustling their way through challenges to deliver a grand success. It's romantic—which is not a word people often use to describe planning.

The story of Electric Lady also squares with a widespread view of creativity as something that is mysterious and spontaneous. It can't be scheduled and planned. The most you can do is put yourself into a position where creativity is needed and trust that it will appear. "Necessity is the mother of invention," after all.

From this, it's easy to conclude that the sort of careful planning I advise in this book is unnecessary—or worse, that careful planning reveals problems. With problems revealed and no solutions in hand, you may decide that the project is too difficult and give up—and never discover the solutions you would have invented if you had blindly plunged ahead.

According to this perspective, "Just do it" is much better advice. "I think things are better done spontaneously," said a woman whose major house renovation was featured in a BBC series. She bought the house at auction without first doing a proper inspection or any serious planning of the renovation. That was deliberate, she said. "Too much planning, and you tend not to do it."[4]

This thinking has some powerful intellectual backing. Half a century ago, Albert O. Hirschman was a renowned economist at Columbia University when he wrote an essay that has been influential ever since.[5] In recent years, the journalist Malcolm Gladwell wrote glowingly about it in *The New Yorker*, as did Harvard professor and former White House official Cass R. Sunstein in *The New York Review of Books*.[6] In 2015, the Brookings Institution, a prominent Washington, DC, think tank, reissued the book in which Hirschman's text first appeared as a Brookings Classic, with a new foreword and afterword, to celebrate Hirschman's thinking and the upcoming fiftieth anniversary of the book's publication.[7]

Hirschman argued that planning is a bad idea. "Creativity always comes as a surprise to us," he wrote. "Therefore, we can never count on it and we dare not believe in it until it has happened." But if we know that big projects pose big challenges that can be overcome only by creativity and we don't trust creativity to deliver its magic when we need it, why would anyone ever launch a big project? They shouldn't. Yet they do. For that, Hirschman argued, we must thank ignorance; it's our friend in getting projects started. He called it "providential ignorance."[8]

When we ponder a big project, Hirschman observed, we routinely fail to see the number and severity of the challenges the project will pose. This ignorance makes us too optimistic. And that's a good thing, according to Hirschman. "Since we necessarily underestimate our creativity," he wrote, "it is desirable that we underestimate to a roughly similar extent the difficulties of the tasks we face, so as to be tricked by these two offsetting underestimates into undertaking tasks which we can, but otherwise would not dare, tackle."

In Hirschman's view, people "typically" underestimate the costs and difficulties of big projects, leading to budget overruns and blown schedules.[9] But these negatives are dwarfed by the projects' larger-than-expected benefits. He suggested a name for this principle: "Since we are apparently on the trail here of some sort of Invisible or Hidden

Hand that beneficially hides difficulties from us, I propose 'the Hiding Hand.'"

Hirschman illustrated his idea with a story about a paper mill built in what is now Bangladesh. The mill was designed to exploit nearby bamboo forests. But shortly after the mill started operating, all the bamboo flowered and died, a natural cycle that happens every half century. With the mill's raw material gone, the operators had no choice but to find alternatives. They came up with three: They created new supply chains to bring bamboo from other regions; they developed and planted a faster-growth species to replace the bamboo that was lost; and they invented new methods to substitute other kinds of lumber.

In the end, according to Hirschman's telling of the story, a burst of creativity born of desperation made the mill better off than if the original bamboo had lived. But what if the planners had done a better job and had become aware of the fact that the bamboo in the region would soon die off? The mill might never have been built. As strange as it sounds, in this case bad planning saved the day, or so Hirschman argued.[10]

Hirschman provided a handful of other examples from the economic development projects that were his specialty, but it's not hard to find others in radically different fields. One of my favorites is *Jaws*, the movie that made director Steven Spielberg a household name. By common agreement, the production was a mess. The script was terrible. The weather was uncooperative. The mechanical sharks malfunctioned—one sank—and they looked goofy, not scary. According to Peter Biskind's classic film history, *Easy Riders, Raging Bulls: How the Sex-Drugs-and-Rock 'n' Roll Generation Saved Hollywood*, filming took three times longer than expected, costs went three times over budget, and Spielberg was driven to the edge of a nervous breakdown, fearing his career would be destroyed.

So how did *Jaws* become one of the most successful movies of all time? The terrible script compelled the actors and director to invent scenes and dialogue together, including moments that gave the characters real depth. And the deficiencies of the mechanical sharks forced Spielberg to shift the focus to the people and only hint at the terror in the water for most of the movie, which turned out to be a lot scarier than any image of a shark. Those two innovations elevated a schlocky B-movie into a box-office smash hit and a masterpiece of suspense.[11]

We saw another epic story that fits Hirschman's argument a couple of chapters back: The difficulty of turning Jørn Utzon's "magnificent doodle" into the Sydney Opera House was badly underestimated, but construction went ahead, Utzon eventually cracked the puzzle, and although the project went vastly over budget, took far too long, and was internally flawed, the opera house ultimately became one of the world's great buildings.

And we have to put Electric Lady onto the list. The project those two kids took on in 1969 was insanely difficult, but they plunged ahead, worked hard, and invented solutions as they moved along. When I spoke with Storyk and Kramer recently, it was obvious how much pride they have in what they accomplished. And rightly so.

These are compelling stories. And that's a problem for me because I can't overstate how contrary Hirschman's argument is to mine. If he's right, I'm wrong and vice versa. It's that simple.

STORIES VERSUS DATA

So how can we figure out who's right? Typically, people don't have sufficient data to determine that, so they try to settle the debate—creative chaos versus planning—with stories. I get this all the time, even from scholars. It's how Hirschman made his argument in the first place. And it's how Cass Sunstein, Malcolm Gladwell, and many others were enticed by it.

On one side are stories such as *Jaws*, the Sydney Opera House, Electric Lady, and more.

And on the other? I could respond by noting, for example, that the woman I quoted above—who said, "Too much planning, and you tend not to do it"—is one-half of the London couple I mentioned in chapter 1 whose house renovation soared from an initial estimate of $260,000 to more than $1.3 million and counting. It might not have been a bad thing if "too much planning" had stopped them from buying that house.

That would be a good story. But let's be honest, it wouldn't be nearly as good as the one about *Jaws*.

It's not just the drama of my story that would come up short. So would the number of stories I could collect, for a simple reason: Projects that run into trouble and end in miserable failure are soon forgotten because most people aren't interested in miserable failures; projects that run into trouble but persevere and become smash successes are remembered and celebrated.

Consider *Jaws*: When it was finished and about to be released, Steven Spielberg was sure that it would bomb and destroy his career. If it had, only Spielberg and a few film historians would even remember *Jaws* today. The same is true of the Sydney Opera House and all the rest. If the Electric Lady project had been abandoned before it was completed or if the finished studio had possessed terrible acoustics, it would have been sold off—to be turned into a shoe store, perhaps—and the only lingering traces of the story would be found in the endnotes of Jimi Hendrix biographies. And maybe the round windows.

We can see this reality in the first and second movies directed by the young Dennis Hopper. In the late 1960s, Hopper was a volatile, drug-taking hippie who didn't believe in scripts, plans, and budgets. The first movie he directed was *Easy Rider*. I vividly remember watching it several times, transfixed, as a teenager in Denmark. And I was far from alone. *Easy Rider* was a global commercial and critical success and is generally considered a landmark of the era. And the second one? I don't know if I ever saw it. At first, I couldn't even recall its title. Hopper brought the same manic, improvisational approach to that movie, but it was a disaster that only serious film buffs can name today. (I looked it up. It's called *The Last Movie*.)

In the social sciences, "survivorship bias" is the common mistake of noting only those things that made it through some selection process while overlooking those that didn't. Someone could note, for example, that Steve Jobs, Bill Gates, and Mark Zuckerberg all dropped out of university and conclude that a key to success in information technology is to leave school. What's missing, and what makes that odd conclusion possible, are the dropouts who went nowhere in information technology and are ignored. That's survivorship bias.

If we consider only stories, survivorship bias will always favor Hirschman's account because projects that overcome adversity with a burst of creativity and deliver great triumphs are like dropouts who become billionaires; they're great stories, so they get noticed. To get at who's right, we need to know about the other dropouts, too, even though they are not great stories and no one has ever heard of them. We need more than stories. We need data.

WHAT THE DATA SAY

Hirschman never produced data, only eleven case studies, which are far too few to establish that the pattern he claimed was, in his words, "typical" and a "general principle" was in fact real, let alone typical or general.[12] But as I discussed in chapter 1, I've got lots of numbers thanks to spending decades building a big database of big projects. So

I did some analysis using a sample of 2,062 projects comparable to those studied by Hirschman—everything from dams to rail lines, tunnels, bridges, and buildings. In 2016, I published the resulting paper in the academic journal *World Development*.

If Hirschman is right, a typical project should see parallel mistakes: A failure to foresee the difficulty in the project should produce an underestimate of the final cost, while a failure to foresee how creative the project leaders would be in response to difficulties should produce an underestimate of the project's benefits. That's the pattern with *Jaws*, the Sydney Opera House, and Electric Lady: They fit Hirschman's theory.

We should also see that the overrun on benefits—the extent to which the good stuff generated by the project exceeded what was expected—is bigger than the overrun on costs. Again, that's what we see in all these cases: The 300 percent cost overrun on *Jaws* was big, but the movie crushed expectations at the box office to more than compensate. Much more.

So what did the data show? Not that. The benefit overrun of the average project does not exceed the cost overrun. In fact, there is no benefit overrun.[13]

Put simply, the typical project is one in which costs are *underestimated* and benefits are *overestimated*. Picture a big project that costs *more* than it was supposed to and delivered *less* than expected: That description fit four out of five projects. Only one in five squared with what Hirschman's theory says should be the norm. To be blunt, the typical leap in the dark ends with a broken nose. Jimi got lucky. So did Spielberg and Sydney.

However, for people such as CEOs and venture capitalists—and even governments—what matters isn't the performance of any one project but how a whole portfolio of projects performs. For them, it may be fine to take big losses on 80 percent of projects as long as the gains from the 20 percent of projects that deliver Hirschman's happy ending are so big that they more than compensate for the losses. So I checked the data and found that the results were equally clear: Losses far exceeded gains. Whether it's the average project or a portfolio of projects, Hirschman's argument just doesn't hold up.

These conclusions are overwhelmingly supported by logic and evidence, including the main findings of Daniel Kahneman and behavioral science. Simply put, if Kahneman is right, Hirschman is wrong. Kahneman identified optimism bias as "the most significant of the cognitive biases."[14] An optimistic benefit estimate is clearly an overestimate, which is the prediction of Kahneman and behavioral science for project planning. But Hirschman and the Hiding Hand predict the exact opposite, as we saw earlier: underestimated benefits. So it's a clear-cut case of which of the two opposite predictions is supported by the data. And the verdict comes down overwhelmingly in favor of Kahneman and behavioral science and against Hirschman and the Hiding Hand.

I know this conclusion is not emotionally satisfying. How could it be? The rare exceptions Hirschman incorrectly thought are typical are, almost by definition, fantastic projects that make irresistible stories. They follow the perfect Hero's Journey, with a narrative arc from great promise to near ruin to an even greater accomplishment and celebration.[15] We seem hardwired to love such stories. We crave them in all cultures and times. So there will always be authors telling those stories. Like Hirschman. Or Malcolm Gladwell.

In the presence of such glory, who gives a damn about statistics?

THE REAL HERO'S JOURNEY

Some years ago, I gave a lecture about big projects in Sydney's beautiful Aurora Place skyscraper, designed by one of my favorite architects, Renzo Piano, to correspond spatially with the elegant curves of the opera house, which it overlooks. After I spoke, someone in the audience made exactly that point. "No one cares about the costs," he said, waving to the opera house shells below. "Just build." I nodded. I'd heard this sentiment many times.

"The genius who designed the opera house was a fellow Dane," I answered. "His name was Jørn Utzon. He was young when he won the commission, in his thirties. He died at the age of ninety. Can you name any other building he designed during his long lifetime?"

Silence.

"There's a reason for that. The government here mismanaged the planning and construction of the Sydney Opera House so badly that the costs and schedule exploded. Little of that was Utzon's fault. But he was the architect, so he was blamed and fired midconstruction. He left Australia in secret and in disgrace. His reputation was ruined. Instead of being showered with commissions to build more masterpieces, Utzon was marginalized and forgotten. He became what no masterbuilder wants to be or deserves to be. He became a *one-building architect*.[16]

"What you call the costs are not the full costs," I continued. "Yes, the Sydney Opera House cost a large amount of money, far more than it should have. But the full cost of that building includes all the other architectural treasures that Jørn Utzon never built. Sydney got its masterpiece, but cities around the world were robbed of theirs."

More silence.

There are always other costs—costs that never appear on any spreadsheet—when a project spirals out of control. The simplest are what economists call "opportunity costs": the money unnecessarily burned by bad planning that could have been used to fund something else, including other projects. How many triumphs and wonders has bad planning stolen from us? We'll never know. But we do know that bad planning stole the buildings Jørn Utzon would have designed just as surely as we know that Jimi Hendrix's untimely death stole the music he would have composed.

My disagreement with Hirschman—and with my interlocuter in Sydney—isn't just about dollars and cents and statistics. There is so much else at stake, including people's lives and life's work. This is part of the equation we need to get right to get projects right. And we should be grateful when things work out, needless to say, as we are for the Sydney Opera House and Electric Lady.

So yes, it *is* possible to take a leap in the dark and land gracefully. If it happens, it will make for a wonderful story. But that happy ending is highly unlikely, and sometimes it requires turning a blind eye to major negative consequences, such as the tragic destruction of Utzon's career. My data put the odds of having a benefit overrun that exceeds the cost overrun, even if by only a little, at 20 percent. Contrast that with the 80 percent probability of failure. It's a dangerous bet—and an unnecessary one.

Good planning that sweeps away ignorance will indeed reveal difficulties ahead, but that is no reason to quit and walk away. Hirschman was right in saying that people are ingenious, but he was wrong to think we have to be deep into the delivery of a project, with our backs against the wall, to summon up that creativity.

Just look at Frank Gehry. He is a wildly creative architect, but contrary to the ridiculous popular image of how he works—perfectly captured by that episode of *The Simpsons*—his creative process is slow, painstaking, and relentlessly iterative. This is true of his planning, not when the project is under construction and problems arise. In fact, Gehry plans meticulously precisely to avoid getting himself into desperate situations that he has to invent his way out of. For him, careful planning doesn't obstruct creativity; it enables it.

The same is true of the torrent of creativity that has poured out of Pixar Animation Studios over the decades, as we saw in chapter 4. It overwhelmingly emerges during planning. Pixar would have been out of business long ago if it had relied on Hirschman's model.

We do not have to be desperate to be creative. Indeed, there's reason to think that desperation may actually *hinder* the imaginative moments that elevate a project to glory. Psychologists have studied the effects of stress on creativity for decades, and there is now a substantial literature showing that it has a largely—though not entirely—negative effect. A 2010 meta-analysis of seventy-six studies found that stress is particularly corrosive in two circumstances: when we feel that the situation is mostly beyond our control and when we feel that others are judging our competence. Now imagine a project spiraling out of control. The very phrase "out of control" tells you that the first condition is probably present for those involved. And reputations are likely on the line, satisfying the second condition. So a project in trouble is exactly the sort of situation in which we can expect stress to hamper creativity.[17]

Imaginative leaps belong in planning, not delivery. When stakes and stress are low, we are freer to wonder, try, and experiment. Planning is creativity's natural habitat.

A STORY SUPPORTED BY DATA

John Storyk understands this as well as anybody. When Jimi Hendrix decided that a twenty-two-year-old who had never seen the inside of a recording studio should design Electric Lady, he instantly made Storyk famous in music circles. Storyk was given two more commissions to design studios before he had even finished Electric Lady, and a career was accidentally born. Whereas Eddie Kramer went on to become a legendary rock producer, John Storyk became one of the world's premier designers of studios and acoustics. His firm, the Walters-Storyk Design Group, has worked everywhere from Lincoln Center in New York to the Swiss Parliament Building to the National Museum of Qatar.

Storyk was seventy-four and still hard at work when we spoke and he recalled the unforgettable start of his career. Not surprisingly, given how his big break came about, he's a believer in serendipity and often uses the word. It's an open, smiling philosophy of life. But today he doesn't rely on happy accidents to make his projects successful. He plans carefully. And that means slowly. Everybody wants things done yesterday, but "what I'm constantly trying to do is slow things down," he says. Take time to develop ideas. Take time to spot and correct problems. Do it on the drafting table, not the construction site. "If you slow things down sometimes and you take a second and a third look, you end up making less mistakes," he says. "And that means [the project gets done] faster."

Storyk's career may have started with a leap in the dark that fit Albert Hirschman's story. But his half century of successful projects around the world is testament to the approach I advocated in the previous chapters: Think slow, act fast. And *that* is supported by data.

So yes, all that slow thinking and the thoroughly detailed and tested plan it produces is a good idea. But not even a superb plan delivers itself. To take the final, critical step, you need a team—a single, determined organism—to act fast and deliver on time.

In the next chapter, I'll show you how to forge one.

8

A SINGLE, DETERMINED ORGANISM

As important as it is to do the slow thinking that produces excellent planning and forecasting, acting fast in delivery takes more than a strong plan; you need an equally strong team. How are diverse people and organizations with different identities and interests turned into a single "us"—a team—with everyone rowing in the same direction: toward delivery?

After the goal of the project has been decided and placed in the box on the right.

After the plan has been developed using experiments, simulations, and experience.

After accurate forecasts have been made, and risks mitigated, based on real-world performance of past projects.

After all that, you have done your slow thinking and you have a plan worthy of the name.

Now it's time to act fast and deliver.

A strong plan greatly increases the probability of a swift and successful delivery. But it's not enough. As any experienced project manager will tell you, you also need a capable, determined delivery team. The success of any project depends on getting the team right—"getting the right people on the bus," as one colleague metaphorically put it, "and placing them in the right seats," as another added.

I know a highly sought-after manager of multibillion-dollar IT projects. He's the sort of person who is brought in when everything is going wrong and executives know their careers are on the line, which happens all too often with IT projects. His condition for tackling any project? That he can bring his own team. That's how he gets the team right. They are a tried and tested delivery force, which makes them worth every penny of the many dollars spent to hire them.

Examine any successful project, and you're likely to find a team like that. Frank Gehry's many successes—on time, on budget, with the vision the client wants—have depended not only on Gehry but also on the superb people who have worked with him for years; in some cases, decades. The Empire State Building had excellent planning, as we have seen, but it also had a construction firm renowned for putting up skyscrapers fast.

Then there's the Hoover Dam. A soaring structure that awes tourists as much today as it did when it was finished in 1936, the Hoover Dam was a gigantic project built in what was a remote, dusty, dangerous location. Yet it came in under budget and ahead of schedule. In the annals of big projects, it is a legend. In large part, that triumph was owed to Frank Crowe, the engineer who managed the project. Before tackling the Hoover Dam, Crowe had spent a long career building dams across the western United States and over those many years had developed a large and loyal team that followed him from project to project. The experience contained within that team was profound. So were the mutual trust, respect, and understanding.[1]

The value of experienced teams cannot be overstated, yet it is routinely disregarded. A Canadian hydroelectric dam I consulted on is one of countless examples. It went ahead under the direction of executives who had zero experience with hydroelectric dams. Why? Because executives *with* experience were difficult to find. How hard can it be to deliver a big project?, the owners pondered. The oil and gas industry delivers big projects. A hydroelectric dam is a big project. Ergo, executives from oil and gas companies should be able to deliver a dam. Or so the owners reasoned—and hired oil and gas executives to build the dam. The reader will not be surprised to learn that in sharp contrast to the Hoover Dam, this project turned into a fiasco that threatened the economy of a whole province. That was when I was brought in to diagnose the problem—too late.[2]

So how do you get the team right? The simple solution, whenever possible, is to hire the equivalent of Frank Crowe and his team or Gehry and his. If they exist, get them. Even if they are expensive—which they are not if you consider how much they will save you in cost, time, and reputational damage. And don't wait until things have gone wrong; hire them up front.

Unfortunately, sometimes such teams don't exist. Or if they do, they're already engaged elsewhere. When a team cannot be hired, it must be created. That's a common situation, and it was the challenge facing the British Airports Authority (BAA) in 2001, when it announced that it would build a new multibillion-dollar terminal at London's Heathrow Airport.

A DEADLINE SET IN STONE

Heathrow was, and is, one of the world's busiest airports, and the new terminal—Terminal 5 (T5)—would be an immense addition. The main building would be the largest freestanding structure in the United Kingdom. Add two more buildings, and T5 would have fifty-three gates and a total footprint of 3.8 million square feet. When we think of airports, we imagine runways and large buildings like these. In reality, however, airports are complex agglomerations of infrastructure and services, like little cities. So T5 also required a long list of other systems—tunnels, roads, parking facilities, rail connections, stations, electronic systems, baggage handling, catering, safety systems, and a new air traffic control tower for the whole airport—that had to work together seamlessly.

All that would be built between two runways with the existing central terminal area at one end and a busy freeway at the other. And the airport could never shut down. The whole project had to be built without interrupting Heathrow's hectic operations for even a minute. Apparently that wasn't enough pressure for BAA, a private company that ran most of the major airports in the United Kingdom, so in 2001 it announced that, after many years of planning, construction of T5 would begin the following year and the project would be completed in six and a half years. T5 would open on March 30, 2008. At 4:00 A.M., to be precise. "That meant at four in the morning, the coffee had to be hot, the food available, and the gates ready," recalled Andrew Wolstenholme, the BAA executive and engineer who oversaw the construction of T5.[3]

To publicly declare the opening date of such an enormous project so early was ambitious, to say the least. Some would say foolhardy; certainly unusual. Heathrow was badly congested, with tens of millions of weary passengers dragging luggage through its crowded, run-down halls, and the need for a new terminal had been settled a decade and a half earlier. But it had taken ages to make progress, in part due to opposition in the communities around the airport and the longest round of public consultations in British history. Up to the point when BAA made its announcement, everything about T5 had been ponderous.

Further ratcheting up the pressure, BAA examined major UK construction projects and international airport projects, using something like the reference-class forecasting approach described in chapter 6, and concluded that if T5 merely delivered typical results, it would come in one year late and $1 billion over budget—a result that could sink the company.[4] The word *deadline* comes from the American Civil War, when prison camps set boundaries and any prisoner who crossed a line was shot.[5] For BAA, the metaphor fit uncomfortably well.

To succeed, the delivery of T5 had to far outperform the norm. BAA had three key strategies for making that happen.

The first was planning. In line with what I called "Pixar planning" in chapter 4, T5 was planned using highly detailed digital representations that were used to run rigorous simulations. T5's creation and operation worked on computers before they were attempted in reality.

Digital simulation enabled the second strategy: a radically different approach to construction. Instead of sending materials to a worksite to be measured, cut, shaped, and welded into buildings—the conventional way since the building of the pyramids—the materials were sent to factories, which used the detailed, precise digital specifications sent to them to manufacture components. Then the components were sent to the worksite to be assembled. To the untrained eye, T5 would have looked like a conventional construction site, but it wasn't; it was an *assembly* site.[6] The importance of this difference cannot be overstated, and every large construction site will need to follow suit if construction is going to make it into the twenty-first century. This process, called "design for manufacture and assembly," is how the hyperefficient car industry operates. Sir John Egan, the CEO of BAA and a former head of Jaguar, had argued in an influential report to the UK government that this approach would produce major efficiency gains in construction.[7] With T5, he put his thinking into practice.

The third strategy was all about people. We perform at our best when we feel united, empowered, and mutually committed to accomplishing something worthwhile. Much psychological and organizational research tells us so.[8] It's also common sense. There's a word to describe a group of people who feel that way: they are a team. That was what T5's workforce had to become, Wolstenholme and other BAA executives knew, if the project was to have any chance of succeeding. They also knew what a tall order that was. T5 would be built by thousands of people, from executives and lawyers to engineers, surveyors, accountants, designers, electricians, plumbers, carpenters, welders, glaziers, drywallers, drivers, pipefitters, landscapers, cooks, and many others. They would be white collar and blue collar, management and union. They would come from different organizations with different cultures and interests. Yet somehow this fractious bunch would have to become a coordinated, purposeful, creative whole.

From the outset, Wolstenholme led a deliberate campaign to make that happen. "Our approach wasn't for the faint-hearted," he says. "You have to have very strong leaders who don't just understand the what but the how."

HOW TO BUILD A TEAM

The first "how" was BAA's decision to do much more than hire firms and oversee their work. It would actively lead and share risks. That meant getting involved in disputes as early as possible.

Richard Harper is a construction supervisor who spent four and a half years at T5, directing the hundreds of workers erecting the steel frames of the main terminal and other buildings. In the early stages of the project, Harper's steel company had to work behind one of BAA's principal contractors, a major British engineering firm that was pouring concrete. Harper warned BAA that the principal contractor wouldn't be able to work fast enough to stay ahead of him, which would result in his crew being "stood"—workers and equipment standing around waiting, a costly sin in construction. If that happened, Harper's company would take the financial hit because its contract with BAA called for it to be paid a flat fee. Despite assurances from the principal contractor that it wouldn't fall behind, it did. The owner of Harper's company was furious, and the two companies argued about who was to blame.

"BAA could see there was trouble looming," Harper recalled in the

"Brummie" accent of his native Birmingham. His company could sue the principal contractor. Or worse. The owner of Harper's company "was very short fused. He could very easily have walked away from the project, which he'd done many times [on other projects]."[9]

BAA intervened. It changed its contract with Harper's company to a cost-reimbursable arrangement with a percentage profit on top when milestones were met. With that revised incentive structure BAA defused the conflict. No longer required to protect their separate self-interests, Harper's company and the principal contractor stopped pointing fingers at each other and instead discussed how best to tackle the problem. The principal contractor agreed to bring in hundreds more workers. Harper's company agreed to shuffle workers to other jobs while the principal contractor caught up. A conflict that could have turned into a meltdown quickly cooled, and the project rolled along.

Contracts such as that between BAA and Harper's company became a hallmark of the project, meaning that BAA assumed far more risk than it would have under ordinary contracts. But by giving companies only positive incentives to perform well—including bonuses for meeting and beating benchmarks—it ensured that the interests of the many different companies working on the project were not pitted against one another. Instead, everyone had the same interest: completing T5 on time.[10] With their interests aligned, cooperation between Harper's company and the principal contractor flourished. At one point, the principal contractor's work made it impossible for Harper to operate his cranes. Rather than fight about it or complain to BAA, the two companies' executives sat down, explored solutions, and agreed that building a temporary ramp would enable both companies to keep working simultaneously. The principal contractor quickly built the ramp—and paid for it. "It must have cost, at a minimum, £100,000," Harper said. The project kept rolling.

It helped that many of the managers of the various companies knew one another. "We'd all worked together on sites in London and around England and Wales," said Harper, who, like most of his colleagues, had already had decades of experience when he arrived at T5. "So there was a good rapport there in the first place." That was also by design. BAA understood, as so many others do not, that "lowest bid" does not necessarily mean "lowest cost," so rather than follow the common practice of hiring the lowest bidders, BAA stuck with companies it had worked with for years and that had proven their ability to deliver what BAA needed. And it encouraged those companies to do the same with specialized subcontractors—experience again.

"If you're going to win a football game, you need to play with the same squad every season," Andrew Wolstenholme said, using an impeccably British metaphor. "We'd built up trust. We understood each other."

But when you work on a joint project with people from many companies, which squad are you playing for? Who are your teammates? Teams are identities. To truly be on one, people must know it. So BAA gave everyone working on T5, including its own employees, a clear and emphatic answer: Forget how things are usually done on big projects. Your team is not your company. Here, your team is T5. We are *one* team.

Wolstenholme is an engineer with decades of experience in construction, but he started his career in the British military, where the squad you play for is literally on your forehead—in the form of your unit's "cap badge." When people came to T5, Wolstenholme says, they were told, "Take off your cap badge and throw it away, because you work for T5."

That message was explicit, blunt, and repeated. "We had posters on the walls of people with lightbulbs going on, and they were saying, you know, 'I get it. I work for T5.'"

MAKING HISTORY

Identity was the first step. Purpose was the second. It had to *matter* that you worked for T5. To that end, the worksite was plastered with posters and other promotions comparing T5 with great projects of the past: the partially completed Eiffel Tower in Paris; Grand Central Terminal under construction in New York; the massive Thames Barrier flood controls in London. Each appeared on posters with the caption "We're making history, too." When important stages of T5 were completed, such as the installation of the new air traffic control tower, they went up alongside the Eiffel Tower and all the rest. "One day," the posters promised, "you'll be proud to say, 'I built T5.'"

"The whole philosophy," Andrew Wolstenholme recalled, was to "share the culture right from the top to the person sweeping the dust off the runway or finishing off the concrete or putting the tiles on the floor. They had to feel equally part of what we're building, that we're making history here in delivering T5."

I grew up in construction and know from firsthand experience that construction workers are sharp as knives at understanding what's happening on their worksites. Moreover, they have a well-founded skepticism of management. They know corporate propaganda when they see it, and they distrust it. "Most guys turn up with cynicism on any site we go to," Richard Harper said. They are usually right to be cynical "because it's all bollocks what the people [management] are saying." Promises aren't kept. Work conditions are poor. Workers aren't listened to. When reality doesn't match the words, corporate PR about teamwork and making history is worse than useless on the shop floor.

The workers brought their usual cynicism to T5, Harper said. "But with that site, within, if not forty-eight hours, a week maximum, everybody had bought into the philosophy of T5. Because they could see T5 was implementing what they said they would do."

It started with the on-site facilities. "It was just something mind-boggling," Harper told me, sounding amazed even now. "The guys had never seen this. The toilets, the showers, the canteens were the best I've ever seen on any site I've worked on in the world. They were fantastic."

BAA ensured that whatever workers needed, they got, right away, particularly when it involved safety. "All the PPE [personal protective equipment] was provided," Harper said. "If guys had wet gloves, they only had to take them back to the store and they got a fresh pair of gloves. If they had a scratch on the glasses and couldn't see properly, they'd take the glasses back, and they were changed. Guys weren't used to this. This was totally new to them. On other jobs, they told you, 'If you're not happy with the glasses or whatever, buy your own.'" These may sound like small things to outsiders, but as Harper pointed out, for workers they are "massive, just massive. You set a man to work in the morning and you've put the things there that he wants, then you get a good day's work. You start them off in a bad way, and you know the next eight to ten hours, it's going to be very difficult." Multiply that by thousands of workers and thousands of days, and you do indeed get something massive.

T5's managers not only listened to workers, they consulted them, asking some to sit down with designers to explore how designs and workflows could be improved. Once the standards for finished work were agreed upon, skilled workers developed their own system of benchmarks to establish the quality of workmanship required for both themselves and everyone else to follow. Some 1,400 of these samples were photographed, cataloged, and put on display at the worksite. Because the benchmarks came from the workers, the workers took ownership of them, increasing the effectiveness of implementation.

With a shared sense of identity, purpose, and standards, open communication is easier, but BAA further cultivated the feeling that everyone on the project had both a right and a responsibility to speak up. Everyone knew "you had the backing of BAA" if you wanted to say something, Harper said. "If any of the guys had ideas, you know, 'I think we could do this or that,' you were free to say it. If anybody felt aggrieved about something, you were free to say that as well."

Harvard professor Amy Edmondson dubbed this sense of being free to speak your mind "psychological safety." It's hard to overstate its value. Psychological safety boosts morale, fosters improvements, and ensures that, in Andrew Wolstenholme's words, "bad news travels fast"—so problems can be tackled quickly.[11]

4:00 A.M.

It worked. "I'm sixty years old. I've been in construction since I was fifteen," said Harper, who has worked across the United Kingdom and in countries around the world. "I have never, ever seen that level of cooperation."

From the suits to the hard hats, the spirit was the same. "There wasn't one man came to me and said anything detrimental about T5. Everybody had nothing but praise. What a great job it was. How the management and workers on-site worked together. No shouting, no screaming. Everybody happy." The most telling evidence, Harper told me, was the shirts and jackets emblazoned with the project logo. All big construction projects hand them out to workers, but they're seldom worn anywhere but on the worksite. "The job I'm at now, the guys can't wait to get them off. They hate the contractor." To Harper's amazement, workers wore T5 gear the way passionate soccer fans wear their team's jersey. "The guys used to go straight to the pub from work and still have 'em on! They were proud to be part of a project like that."

T5 finished on budget and on time. And at precisely 4:00 A.M. on March 27, 2008—the date had been moved up three days—the new terminal opened. The coffee was indeed hot. The project wasn't perfect, to be sure. Problems with baggage distribution systems in the first several days forced British Airways to cancel flights, which was embarrassing and expensive, but the kinks were worked out and the terminal operated well within a few months—and has done so ever since. In an annual survey of global travelers, T5 routinely ranks among the world's favorite terminals. It took the top spot six times in its first eleven years of operation.[12]

Success didn't come cheaply. "We spent quite a lot of money on developing the team dynamics," Andrew Wolstenholme said. BAA also put a lot of time and effort into it. Plus, it shouldered more direct financial risk. But if the delivery had merely been average, the deadline would have been missed and the cost overrun could easily have run into billions of pounds. That made the money spent on getting the team right a stellar investment.

That lesson was driven home by another giant project that, coincidentally, was under way elsewhere in London. The original Wembley Stadium was the most famous soccer stadium in the world and something of a national shrine until it was demolished in 2002 to make way for a new stadium. If ever there was a project that could inspire teamwork, it would surely be the construction of the new home of Britain's national sport. Yet nothing remotely like the T5 spirit of shared purpose and "making history" emerged at Wembley; quite the opposite. It was a project rife with conflicts. Work stoppages were routine. "The guys there had no pride in constructing our national stadium," said Richard Harper. Inevitably, the project dragged on years past its deadline, forcing the Football Association (FA) Cup Final and other events to be moved. The cost, according to *The Guardian*, doubled from a forecast £445 million to £900 million (US $1.2 billion). Inevitably, it spawned a massive lawsuit.[13]

T5 is an unlikely object of affection. It's just an airport terminal, after all. Yet the workers who built T5 were so committed to the project that when it was done and they all put their cap badges back on and left, "people sort of found it quite difficult to go back," Wolstenholme observed.

Thirteen years had passed since T5's completion when I spoke with Richard Harper, but the wistfulness in his voice was unmistakable. "I loved it," he said.

THE SECRET TO SCALING UP

When your team has delivered your project on time, on budget, with the expected benefits, it's time to pop the champagne and celebrate. So you may think that this is the end of the book. But I can't stop yet because I still haven't told you the solution to the puzzle I mentioned in the first chapter.

You will recall that most project types are not only at risk of coming in late, going over budget, and generating fewer benefits than expected. They are at risk of going *disastrously* wrong. That means you may not wind up 10 percent over budget; you may go 100 percent over. Or 400 percent. Or worse. These are black swan outcomes, and the project types at risk of them are called "fat-tailed." They include nuclear power plants, hydroelectric dams, information technology, tunnels, major buildings, aerospace, and many more. In fact, almost all the project types in my database are fat-tailed. But not quite all.

There are five project types that are not fat-tailed. That means they may come in somewhat late or over budget but it's very unlikely that they will go *disastrously* wrong. The fortunate five? They are solar power, wind power, fossil thermal power (power plants that generate electricity by burning fossil fuels), electricity transmission, and roads. In fact, the best-performing project types in my entire database, by a comfortable margin, are wind and solar power.

So this is the puzzle: Why are these project types exceptional? What makes them a safer bet than all the rest? And why are wind and solar power the most reliable projects of all, more likely than any other project type to be delivered successfully?

I'll provide the illuminating answer in the next and final chapter. And I'll assemble the ideas from earlier chapters into a model that anyone can use to lower cost and improve quality for projects at all scales, from wedding cakes and kitchen renovations to subways and satellites.

But for projects that have to scale up—*way up*—this model is more than valuable; it is essential. With this model, truly huge projects can be carried out at far less cost and risk far more quickly and reliably. We can build at colossal scale with higher quality and accelerated speed, saving sums of money substantial enough to change the fortunes of companies, industries, and countries.

This model could even help save us from climate change.

9

WHAT'S YOUR LEGO?

Get a small thing, a basic building block. Combine it with another and another until you have what you need. That's how a single solar cell becomes a solar panel, which becomes a solar array, which becomes a massive megawatt-churning solar farm. Modularity delivers faster, cheaper, and better, making it valuable for all project types and sizes. But for building at a truly huge scale—the scale that transforms cities, countries, even the world—modularity is not just valuable, it's indispensable.

In 1983, the government of Japan launched a new project that was as promising as it was enormous. Its name was Monju, meaning "wisdom." When completed, Monju would be both a nuclear power plant churning out electricity for consumers and a fast-breeder reactor, a new type of nuclear plant that would produce fuel for the nuclear industry. For a nation long threatened by energy insecurity, Monju was designed to deliver a better future.[1]

Construction started in 1986. It finished almost a decade later, in 1995. But a fire immediately shut down the facility. An attempt to cover up the accident became a political scandal that kept the plant closed for years.[2]

In 2000, the Japan Atomic Energy Agency announced that the plant could restart. Japan's supreme court finally authorized the restart in 2005. Operations were scheduled to begin in 2008, but they were postponed until 2009. Test runs started in 2010, with full operations scheduled to commence, for the first time, in 2013. But in May 2013, maintenance flaws were discovered on some fourteen thousand components of the plant, including critical safety equipment. The restart was halted. Further violations of safety protocols were uncovered. Japan's Nuclear Regulation Authority declared Monju's operator to be unqualified.[3] At that point, the government had spent $12 billion and the estimated cost of finally restarting Monju and operating it for ten years was another $6 billion—at a time when the 2011 Fukushima disaster had turned popular opinion against nuclear power. The government finally threw in the towel. In 2016, it announced that Monju would be permanently closed.[4]

Decommissioning Monju is expected to take another thirty years and cost a further $3.4 billion. If that forecast proves more accurate than the rest, the project will have taken sixty years, cost more than $15 billion, and produced zero electricity.[5]

Monju is an extreme case, but it's not in a category by itself. Far from it. Nuclear power plants are one of the worst-performing project types in my database, with an average cost overrun of 120 percent in real terms and schedules running 65 percent longer than planned. Even worse, they are at risk of fat-tail extremes for both cost and schedule, meaning they may go 20 or 30 percent over budget. Or 200 or 300 percent. Or 500 percent. Or more. There is almost no limit to how bad things can get, as Monju demonstrated so spectacularly.[6]

The problem isn't nuclear power; many other project types have track records only somewhat less bad. The problem lies in the way huge projects like Monju are typically designed and delivered. When we understand that problem, we will find a solution to building big that is, paradoxically, small. In fact, it is tiny, like a single block of Lego. But it's remarkable what you can do with blocks of Lego, as we will see.

ONE HUGE THING

One way to design and deliver a project on an enormous scale is to build one thing. One *huge* thing.

Monju is one huge thing. Most nuclear power plants are. So are giant hydroelectric dams, high-speed rail lines such as that in California, and mammoth IT projects and skyscrapers.

If you build like this, you build only one thing. By definition, that thing is one of a kind. To put that in the language of tailors, it is bespoke: no standard parts, no commercial off-the-shelf products, no simple repetition of what was done last time. And that translates into slow and complex. Nuclear power plants, for one, are the products of a staggering number of bespoke parts and systems that must all work, and work together, for the plant as a whole to work.

Complex bespokeness alone makes huge projects hard to deliver if done in this manner. But that is compounded by several more factors.

First, you can't build a nuclear power plant quickly, run it for a while, see what works and what doesn't, then change the design to incorporate the lessons learned. It's too expensive and dangerous. That means that experimentation—one-half of the *experiri* I discussed in chapter 4—is out. You have no choice but to get it right the first time.

Second, there's a problem with experience—the other half of *experiri*. If you are building a nuclear power plant, chances are that you haven't done much of that before for the simple reason that few have been built and each takes many years to complete, so opportunities to develop experience are scarce. Yet with no experimentation and little experience, you still have to get it exactly right the first time. That's difficult, if not impossible.

Even if you do have some experience building nuclear power plants, you probably won't have experience building this *particular* nuclear plant because, with few exceptions, each plant is specifically designed for a specific site, with technology that changes over time. Like Monju, it is bespoke, one of a kind. Anything bespoke is expensive and slow to make, like a tailored suit. But imagine a tailor who has little experience with suits making a bespoke suit for you and having to get it right on the first try. It's not going to end well. And that's just a suit, not a multibillion-dollar, fantastically complex nuclear power plant.

Lacking experimentation and experience, what you learn as you proceed is that the project is more difficult and costly than you expected—and not just the single project you're doing but the project type as such. Obstacles that were unknown are encountered. Solutions thought to work don't. And you cannot make up for it by tinkering or starting over with revised plans. Operations experts call this "negative learning": The more you learn, the more difficult and costly it gets.

Third, there's the financial strain. A nuclear power plant must be completely finished before it can generate any electricity. Even nine-tenths done, it's useless. So all the money that is poured into the plant produces nothing for the entire time it takes you to get to the ribbon-cutting ceremony—which, given the bespokeness, the complexity, the lack of experimentation, your lack of experience, the negative learning, and the need to get everything right the first time, will probably be a very long time. All this is reflected in the dreadful performance data for nuclear power plants.

Finally, don't forget black swans. All projects are vulnerable to unpredictable shocks, with their vulnerability growing as time passes. So the fact that the delivery of your one huge thing will take a very long time means that it is at high risk of being walloped by something you cannot possibly anticipate. That's exactly what happened to Monju. More than a quarter century after the project was launched, when the plant was still not ready to go, an earthquake caused a tsunami that struck the nuclear plant at Fukushima, producing the disaster that turned public opinion against nuclear power and finally convinced the

Japanese government to pull the plug on Monju. It is a giant understatement to say that that turn of events could not have been predicted in 1983. But when delivery takes decades, the unpredictable becomes inevitable.

Add up all this, and it's not remarkable that nuclear power plants and other "one huge thing" projects are painfully slow and expensive to deliver. It's remarkable that they are delivered at all. Fortunately, there is another way to build huge things.

MANY SMALL THINGS

At the beginning of this book, I mentioned a project that successfully delivered twenty thousand schools and classrooms to Nepal, which I designed, planned, and programmed with the architect Hans Lauritz Jørgensen.

There are two ways of looking at that project. Viewed one way, it was huge. After all, we built a major part of an entire national school system. But another way of looking at it is to focus on the classroom. In some instances, a single classroom was the whole school. In others, putting a couple of classrooms together made a school. In still others, three or more classrooms made a school. Assemble enough classrooms into enough schools, and you have the schools for a district. Do that for all districts, and you have a national school system.

A classroom is small, however many there are. So you could say that our project was small.

Small is good. For one thing, small projects can be simple. That's what Jørgensen and I aimed for from the outset. We wanted the schools to be functional, high quality, and earthquake proof. But within those parameters, they would be as simple as possible. That's why we decided, for example, that there would be only three main school designs, with the slope at the construction site—Nepal is extremely mountainous—the main variable.

The Nepalese government had emphasized that the schools were desperately needed, so we accelerated the program in every way. It took us only a few weeks to develop the first draft of the basic designs and construction program. Raising funds and final decisions took a few months. Then construction of the first schools began.[7]

It's relatively easy to build something small and simple. One classroom went up quickly. And another. For the many village schools that had only one or two classrooms, that was a complete school. For those that required more classrooms, more were built. When a school was finished, kids went to class and teachers started teaching. Experts assessed what worked and what didn't. Changes were made. The next batch of classrooms and schools got going. And the next.

Repeat this process over and over and over, and you have the whole story of the project. A number of classrooms becomes a school. A number of schools completes a district. A number of districts becomes a major new addition to a national school system in which hundreds of thousands of students are learning. That's a huge thing made of many small things.

There is, however, a big difference between this huge thing and those built as "one huge thing": The schools in Nepal were delivered on budget and years ahead of schedule. And they worked well, according to independent evaluations.[8]

Modularity is a clunky word for the elegant idea of big things made from small things. A block of Lego is a small thing, but by assembling more than nine thousand of them, you can build one of the biggest sets Lego makes, a scale model of the Colosseum in Rome. That's modularity.

Look for it in the world, and you'll see it everywhere. A brick wall is made of hundreds of bricks. A flock of starlings, which moves as if it were a unitary organism, may be composed of hundreds or thousands of birds. Even our bodies are modular, composed of trillions of cells that are themselves modular. There's an evolutionary reason for this ubiquity: In survival of the fittest, the "fittest" is often a module that is particularly successful in reproducing itself.[9]

The core of modularity is repetition. Put down one Lego block. Snap on another. And another. And another. Repeat, repeat, repeat. Click, click, click.

Repetition is the genius of modularity; it enables experimentation. If something works, you keep it in the plan. If it doesn't, you "fail fast," to use the famous Silicon Valley term, and adjust the plan. You get smarter. Designs improve.

Repetition also generates experience, making your performance better. This is called "positive learning," as we saw earlier. Repetition rockets you up the learning curve, making each new iteration better, easier, cheaper, and faster.

As the old Latin saying goes, *"Repetitio est mater studiorum"*— "Repetition is the mother of learning." Yes, I wrote that in chapter 4. But repetition is the mother of learning.

Wedding cakes are a wonderful illustration. Even the grandest wedding cake is mostly composed of a series of identical, flat, ordinary cakes. Stack several of those, and you get one tier. Bake more, stack them, and you get another tier. Assemble many tiers, and you get a great tower of cake. That sounds easy enough, but as many a baking enthusiast has discovered, even if your individual cakes are baked correctly, your first attempts to stack cakes are likely to produce something that looks more like the Leaning Tower of Pisa than the magnificent monuments in magazines. Bakers develop the ability to deliver perfect cakes only after trying many times, learning a little lesson here, a little lesson there. But because wedding cakes are so inherently modular and repetitive, bakers who keep at it get that experience rapidly—and they soon become highly skilled.

It's important to note that modularity is a matter of degree. The Empire State Building wasn't modular to the extent that a Lego model of the Empire State Building is modular, but its floors were designed to be as similar as possible, with many being identical, which meant that workers often repeated work, which helped them learn and work faster. Similarly, the construction of the Pentagon was accelerated by keeping the five sides of the building identical. Following this line of reasoning, I advised a company building a large nuclear power plant to duplicate exactly what it had done in building a recent plant, not because the earlier plant had been a great success but because even that degree of repetition would boost them up the learning curve. Every little bit helps.

In Nepal, our Lego was the classroom, with schools and districts being larger modules. So the project was very modular. But it could have been even more so. Our schools were built the traditional way, with building materials brought to the site and workers cutting, framing, laying, mortaring, nailing, sanding, and finishing the materials to build schools classroom by classroom. In other countries—it wasn't advisable in Nepal for a variety of reasons—that work could instead be done in a factory. The Lego that ships from the factory could be a complete classroom if it is small enough to fit onto the back of a flatbed truck and transported on the roads—if there are roads, which was not the case for many mountain villages in Nepal. If the classroom is too big for that, it could be built in chunks—half a classroom, perhaps, or the components of a classroom—and shipped. When the modules are delivered to the site, the building isn't constructed; it's assembled, like Lego. In this way, the construction site morphs into an assembly site, which is exactly what you want, as mentioned previously.

This is happening in England. Factories build half classrooms. Those Lego are shipped to the site and assembled into a new school. "It enabled us to be better and faster and indeed deliver higher quality," said Mike Green, the government official in charge of the program. It's also a lot cheaper. "We have already knocked a third off the per square meter cost of building schools," he told me, and he is convinced that there are more savings to be had.[10] My data confirm he is right.

Manufacturing in a factory and assembling on-site is far more efficient than traditional construction because a factory is a controlled environment designed to be as efficient, linear, and predictable as possible. To take an obvious example, bad weather routinely wreaks havoc on outdoor construction, while production in a factory proceeds regardless of the elements. As I mentioned in the previous chapter, this process—properly known as "design for manufacture and assembly"—is a big part of the explanation of the success of Heathrow's Terminal 5.

When Lego shipped from factories is assembled, scaling up is mainly a matter of adding more of the same. The best illustration is a facility that few people have seen and fewer think about but that is indispensable in our digital world: the server farm. The Lego is the server. Stack a number of servers, and you get a rack. A number of racks forms a row. A number of rows forms a room. A number of rooms forms a building. A number of buildings, and you have a server farm. If you are Apple, Microsoft, or some other large corporation that needs even more server power, you build more farms. In principle, there's no limit to the server capacity you can build in this manner, fast and at ever-falling cost.

SCALE-FREE SCALABILITY

Notice that I'm not using precise numbers. That's because the numbers can be scaled up or down as much as you like—from one to infinity and back again—without changing the character of the whole, much the same way that a flock of starlings is a flock of starlings and behaves like a flock of starlings whether it is made of fifty birds, five hundred, or five thousand. The technical term for this property is "scale free," meaning that the thing is basically the same no matter what size it is. This gives you the magic of what I call "scale-free scalability," meaning you can scale up or down following the same principles independently of where you are scalewise, which is exactly what you want in order to build something huge with ease. The mathematician Benoit Mandelbrot, who first laid out the science of scale-free scalability, called this attribute "fractal"—like one of those popular Internet memes in which you see a pattern, then zoom into a detail within the pattern and discover that it looks the same as the pattern as a whole, and you keep zooming in and keep discovering the same pattern.[11]

Modularity can do astonishing things. When the Covid pandemic first emerged in China in January 2020, a company that makes modular housing modified an existing room design and cranked out units in a factory. Nine days later, a thousand-bed hospital with fourteen hundred staff opened in Wuhan, ground zero of the outbreak. Other, bigger hospitals went up almost as fast.[12] Hong Kong did something similar to build quarantine facilities, preparing a site and assembling a thousand units of comfortable, fully equipped modern housing in four months. When the government later decided that anyone coming into Hong Kong would have to spend twenty-one days in quarantine, the facility was quickly expanded to thirty-five hundred units with room for seven thousand people. All the units can be disconnected and set up elsewhere—or put into storage.[13]

The obvious objection is that modules may be fine for emergencies and utilities such as server farms, but they're cheap and ugly and aren't suitable for anything more permanent and public. There's something to that view. Much of what passed for modular housing in previous generations was indeed cheap and ugly. But that doesn't mean it had to be. Some modular housing was considerably better than that, notably Sears Modern Homes. For much of the first half of the twentieth century, Americans could open a Sears, Roebuck catalog, order a house, and have a complete factory-built kit delivered. All the parts were included, with instructions for assembly, like IKEA furniture on a grand scale. Sears sold around seventy thousand kits. Many of the buildings are still standing 90, 100, or 110 years later and are prized for their high-quality construction and classic design.[14] And that was a century ago. Modern information and manufacturing technology make so much more possible, and easier, today.

When I spoke with Mike Green, he was working on an app that would allow local officials and citizens in the United Kingdom to design their own schools by dragging and dropping standard-sized classrooms and hallways. "And when you press finish, it holds up a component list which can be filed with a manufacturer instantly," he said. The goal is to make it possible for a school to be ordered in much the same way a car is.[15] The comparison is apt. Cars are extremely modular—even very expensive and sophisticated cars are assembled Lego style—yet no one complains that there are no aesthetically pleasing, high-quality cars. It is fully possible for the words *modular, beautiful,* and *high quality* to appear in the same sentence.

When the architect Danny Forster designed an elegant twenty-six-story Marriott hotel for a swanky street in Manhattan, he made it entirely modular. Rooms were his Lego. Each was constructed in a factory in Poland, complete with everything, even furniture, then shipped to a warehouse in Brooklyn. The Covid pandemic interrupted the plan, but when tourism rebounds and the numbers work again, the plan is that the rooms will be taken out of storage and the world's largest and coolest modular hotel will be assembled. "We want to demonstrate that modular building can do more than just harness the efficiencies of the factory," Forster said. "It can produce a graceful and iconic tower."[16]

Even further removed from cheap and ugly is Apple's dazzling, ethereal headquarters in Cupertino, California, designed by Norman Foster, Steve Jobs, and Jony Ive, where modularity played a major role, too. As conceived by Jobs, "This would be a workplace where people were open to each other and open to nature, and the key to that would be modular sections, known as pods, for work or collaboration," the journalist Steven Levy summarized. "Jobs' idea was to repeat those pods over and over: pod for office work, pod for teamwork, pod for socializing, like a piano roll playing a Philip Glass composition."[17] That extended to how the building was put together. "We viewed the construction process as a manufacturing project and wanted to do as much outside of here as possible," Apple's CEO Tim Cook told *Wired* magazine. "Then you begin to put together Legos."

The difference between cheap-and-ugly modular and these projects is imagination and technology. To fully unlock modularity's potential, to see how astonishingly versatile it can be, we need to "think different," as the old Apple slogan put it.

PLAYING WITH LEGO

What is our basic building block, the thing we will repeatedly make, becoming smarter and better each time we do so? That's the question every project leader should ask. What is the small thing we can assemble in large numbers into a big thing? Or a huge thing? *What's our Lego?* Explore that question, and you may be surprised by what you discover.

Consider a giant hydroelectric dam, for example. It may seem obvious that there's no alternative. Either you dam the river, or you don't. There's no role for modularity.

Except there is. You could divert some of the river's flow, run it through small turbines to generate electricity, and return it to the river. This is called "small-scale hydroelectric." An installation like that is relatively tiny, and it produces only a fraction of the power of a major dam. But treat it like Lego—repeat, repeat, repeat—and you will get substantial electricity production with less environmental damage, less citizen protest, less cost, and less risk. One of the world's leaders in hydroelectricity, Norway, a country of just 5 million inhabitants, has an active policy to enhance small hydro development and has commissioned more than 350 small-scale hydroelectric projects since 2003, with more to come.[18]

A giant factory, too, may seem to be one huge thing or nothing. But when Elon Musk announced that Tesla would build Gigafactory 1 (today known as Giga Nevada), the world's largest factory by footprint, he envisioned it in modular terms. His Lego was a small factory. Build one, get it working. Build another beside it and integrate the two. Build a third, a fourth, and so on. By building Gigafactory 1 this way, Tesla started turning out batteries and earning revenue within a year of the announcement, even as work continued on the whole giant facility, which will consist of twenty-one "Lego blocks" when completed.[19]

The key elements of modularity appear to be central to Elon Musk's general approach to engineering, and he uses them in remarkably different ventures. Tesla would seem to have nothing to do with SpaceX, a Musk creation that is revolutionizing space transport and services. But the use of replicability to shoot up the learning curve, accelerate delivery, and improve performance is woven into the company's planning and delivery model.[20]

Space has long been dominated by big, complex one-off projects, and priced accordingly, with NASA's James Webb Space Telescope—$8.8 billion, 450 percent over budget—just the latest example. But there are promising signs that the lessons of modularity are taking hold. To make satellites, a company called Planet (formerly Planet Labs, Inc.) uses commercial, off-the-shelf electronics, like those mass produced for cell phones and drones, made into 10 × 10 × 10 cm (4 × 4 × 4 inch) modules as cheaply and easily as possible. These are their Lego. They're assembled into larger so-called CubeSat modules. Assemble three CubeSat modules and you have the electronics for one Planet Dove satellite. In sharp contrast to the large, complex, expensive satellites that have long been the norm, each Dove satellite takes only a few months to build, weighs eleven pounds, and costs less than $1 million—peanuts by the standards of satellites and cheap enough that failure will result in learning, not bankruptcy. Planet has put hundreds of these satellites into orbit, where they form "flocks" that monitor the climate, farm conditions, disaster response, and urban planning. Despite privacy concerns that need addressing by policy makers, Dove satellites are a powerful illustration of the adaptability and scalability of modular systems, especially when contrasted with NASA's bespoke approach.[21]

Subways would seem to be an even harder case for modularization, but when Madrid Metro carried out one of the world's largest subway expansions between 1995 and 2003, it leaned on modularity in two ways. First, the seventy-six stations required for the expansion were treated like Lego, with all sharing the same simple, clean, functional design. Costs plunged, and speed of delivery soared. To amplify those effects, Madrid Metro shunned new technologies. Only proven technologies—those with a high degree of "frozen experience"—were used.

Second, the Metro leadership made an important conceptual breakthrough by also treating lengths of tunnel as Lego. Initially, they calculated the optimal length of tunnel that one boring machine and its crew could deliver—typically three to six kilometers in two hundred to four hundred days. Then they divided the total length of tunnels they needed to bore by that amount and hired the number of teams and machines they needed to meet the schedule. At times, they had up to six machines working at once, which was unheard of at the time.[22] Treating lengths of tunnel like Lego pushed the project further up the positive learning curve, cut the total time required, and saved buckets of money.[23] In total, Madrid Metro produced 131 kilometers (81 miles) of rail and seventy-six stations in just two stages of four years each. That's twice the speed of the industry average. And it did so at half the cost. We need more behavior like this in megaproject management.

Then there is freight shipping. Since time immemorial, stevedores carefully loaded a ship by hand, one item at a time, so the cargo wouldn't shift at sea, and when the ship got to its destination, the process was reversed. It was hard, dangerous, slow work. But in the 1950s, an American shipper named Malcolm McLean thought that maybe cargo should be put into identical steel boxes that could be stacked into ships and transferred directly to trains and trucks at the destination. It was a modest idea; McLean thought it would reduce costs somewhat.

But by turning cargo into Lego, it made shipping extremely modular and cost effective. The stacks on ships got taller. The ships got bigger. The transfer from one mode of transportation to another got quicker. The speed and ease of transporting goods soared, while costs plunged so steeply that the economics of production and distribution worldwide were changed. In *The Box: How the Shipping Container Made the World Smaller and the World Economy Bigger*, the definitive history of containerization, the economist Marc Levinson argued compellingly that the humble shipping container was nothing less than a major cause of globalization.[24]

It's no small accomplishment to drastically reduce costs and boost speeds. But modularization does more than that; it radically reduces risk—to such an extent that modularization may be the most effective way to "cut the tail," as recommended in chapter 6.

THIN-TAILED PROJECTS

By now you know the solution to the puzzle I discussed at the end of the previous chapter: Only five project types—solar power, wind power, fossil thermal power, electricity transmission, and roads—are not fat-tailed, meaning that they, unlike all the rest, do not have a considerable risk of going disastrously wrong. So what sets the fortunate five apart? They are all modular to a considerable degree, some extremely so.

Solar power? It's born modular, with the solar cell as the basic building block. In a factory, put multiple solar cells together onto a panel. Ship and install the panel. Install another, and wire them together. Add another panel. And another until you have an array. Keep adding arrays until you are generating as much electricity as you like. Even giant solar farms consist of little more than that. Solar power is the king of modularity. It is also the lowest-risk project type of any I've tested in terms of cost and schedule. That's no coincidence.

Wind power? Also extremely modular. Modern windmills consist of four basic factory-built elements assembled on-site: a base, a tower, the "head" (nacelle) that houses the generator, and the blades that spin. Snap them together, and you have one windmill. Repeat this process again and again, and you have a wind farm.

Fossil thermal power? Look inside a coal-burning power plant, say, and you'll find that they're pretty simple, consisting of a few basic factory-built elements assembled to make a big pot of water boil and run a turbine. They're modular, much as a modern truck is modular. The same goes for oil- and gas-fired plants.

Electricity transmission? Parts made in a factory are assembled into a tower, and factory-made wires are strung along them. Repeat. Or manufactured cables are dug into the ground, section by section. Repeat again.

Roads? A multibillion-dollar freeway consists of several multimillion-dollar freeway sections strung together. Repeat, repeat, repeat. Learning from the delivery of one section can be applied to another, just as the workers who put up the Empire State Building learned from one floor to the next. Moreover, once learning is in place, freeway sections can be built simultaneously to reduce time.

Following is a chart with all the project types arranged by how "fat-tailed" they are in terms of cost—meaning how much they are in danger of the extreme cost overruns that destroy projects and careers, blow up corporations, and humiliate governments.

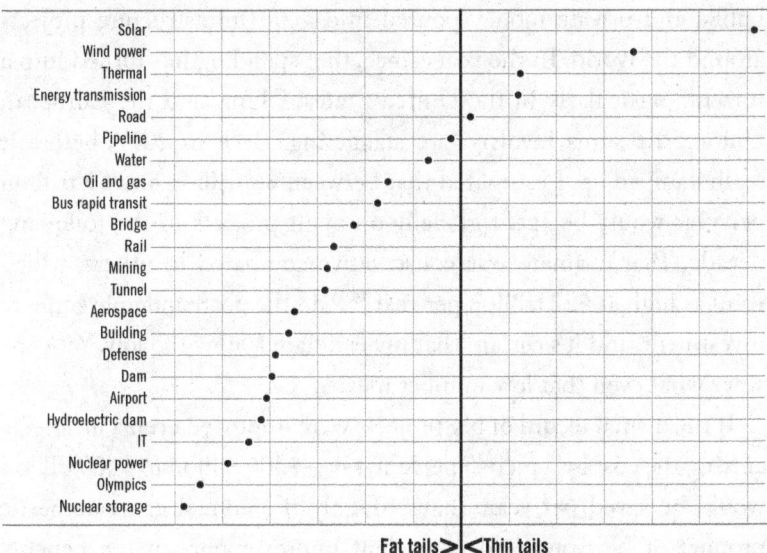

At one extreme—the terrifying place where no one wants to be—we find storage of nuclear waste, hosting the Olympic Games, construction of nuclear power plants, building information technology systems, and constructing hydroelectric dams. They are all classic "one huge thing" projects. At the other extreme, we find the five blessed project types that are not subject to fat-tailed risks. They're all modular. (So are pipelines, which fall a whisker below the cutoff line.) And look at solar and wind power: They're way out there, sitting pretty. And they are *extremely* modular. Which explains why they are fast outcompeting other energy sources—fossil, nuclear, hydro—on price.[25]

The pattern is clear: Modular projects are in much less danger of turning into fat-tailed disasters. So modular is faster, cheaper, *and* less risky. That is a fact of immense importance.

HOW TO SAVE *TRILLIONS* OF DOLLARS

In the years before the Covid pandemic, unprecedented amounts of public and private money poured into giant infrastructure projects around the world. In the years since, that spending has turned into a torrent, particularly in the United States, China, and the European Union. The sums involved are staggering. Back in 2017, before it really ramped up, I estimated that between $6 trillion and $9 trillion per year would be spent globally on giant projects in the following decade. That estimate was conservative compared to others, which went as high as $22 trillion per year.[26] Add the postpandemic surge of investment, and it's certain that my estimate is now too low. Yet consider what even that low number means.

If the dismal record of big projects were improved even a little—by cutting the cost by a mere 5 percent, say—$300 billion to $400 billion would be saved per year. That's roughly the annual gross domestic product of Norway. Add equivalent improvements in the benefits delivered by giant projects, and the gains would be in the range of the GDP of Sweden. Each year. But as Frank Gehry and the Madrid Metro leadership have demonstrated, a 5 percent improvement is nothing. Cutting cost by 30 percent—which is still modest and entirely possible—would create annual savings in the range of the GDP of the United Kingdom, Germany, or Japan.

Those are world-changing numbers. To put them in perspective, a 2020 study funded by the German government estimated that the total cost to end global hunger by 2030 would be $330 billion over ten years—a fraction of what could be gained by doing big projects a little better.[27]

THE CHINA EXPERIMENT

Some readers will object that I have been unfair to the "one huge thing" model. They will argue that "one huge thing" projects—for instance, nuclear power plants—are hamstrung by public opinion, hostile governments, and the burdens of excessive safety and environmental regulation. Break the chains, they say, and those projects could perform just as well as or better than their modular competitors, wind and solar power. It's an interesting hypothesis. Fortunately, a natural experiment put it to the test and we have the results.

The experiment was conducted in China over the past decade. Red tape and NIMBY opposition can and do indeed slow or stop projects in many countries, but not in China. In China, if the national government at the highest levels decides that a project is a priority, obstacles are eliminated and the project gets done.

For more than a decade, the Chinese government has deemed it nothing less than a national strategic imperative to massively grow China's capacity for nonfossil electricity generation. It wants more of everything: more wind power, more solar power, more nuclear power. And it wants it all as fast as possible.

So how quickly have those three project types been delivered in China? The chart on the next page, adapted from work done by the energy analyst Michael Barnard and updated with data from the International Renewable Energy Agency, shows the megawatts of new electricity-generating capacity added to China's national grid, by source, from 2001 to 2020.[28]

The results couldn't be clearer. The "one huge thing" model, exemplified by nuclear power, is the line crawling along the bottom of the diagram. It was crushed by "many small things"—wind and solar power—shooting up to the right. China is a critical case in the sense that it is the nation in the world with the most conducive conditions for nuclear power. So if nuclear power doesn't succeed in scaling up

NEW INSTALLED ELECTRICITY CAPACITY (MW), CHINA
by Technology and Year

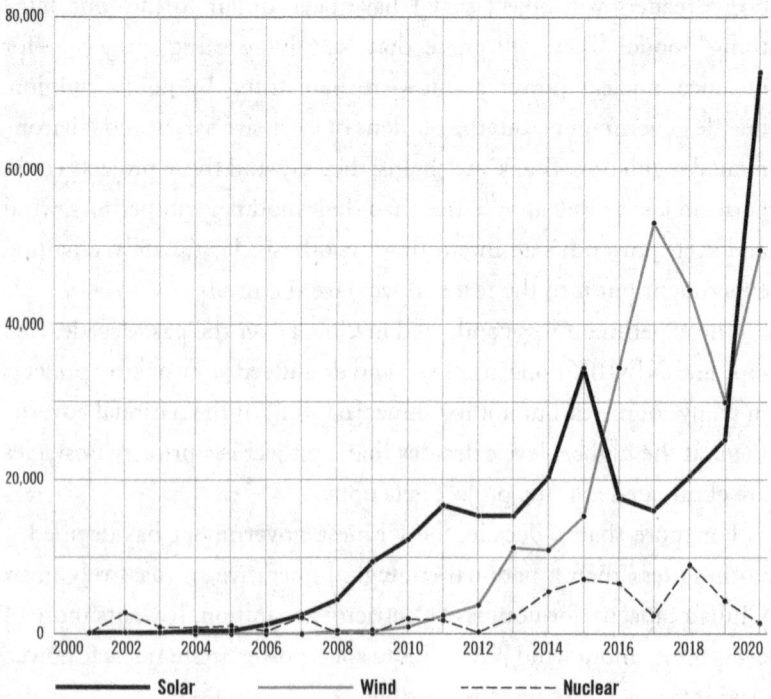

there, it is unlikely to succeed anywhere—unless, of course, the nuclear industry disrupts itself, which is exactly what its more enlightened proponents now suggest. They have come to accept the limitations of the "one huge thing" model and are trying to take nuclear power in a radically different direction. They call for scaled-down reactors to be built in factories, shipped to where they are needed, and assembled on-site, again transforming the construction site into an assembly site, which is rightly seen as the key to success. These reactors would each produce only 10 to 20 percent of the electricity generated by a conventional nuclear reactor. But if more electricity is needed, a second reactor could be added. Or a third. Or however many are required.[29] The name of this new model for nuclear power says it all: They are "small modular reactors," or SMRs.

At the time of writing, SMRs are an unproven technology. I won't guess if they will ultimately work as hoped or how long it will take for them to do so. But it is telling that after more than sixty years of civilian nuclear power development, much of the nuclear industry—supported by a roster of investors that includes Bill Gates and Warren Buffett—is finally shifting its thinking from "one huge thing" to "many small things."[30] Other "one huge thing" forms of global infrastructure should watch and learn.

CLIMATE CRISIS

I would have liked to end this book right there. But I can't because there is a far more urgent and frightening reason why we need to radically improve how we plan and deliver big projects. It is climate change.

In mid-July 2021, the skies opened and deluged western Germany, with some regions getting more rain in one day than they normally get in a month. Flash floods tore through the countryside. Towns were gutted. At least two hundred people died. While Germany was drowning, northwest America, from Oregon to British Columbia, baked in a heat wave that pushed temperatures to heights once thought impossible. Crops withered. Wildfires roared through forests, and a town in British Columbia was reduced to ash. One estimate of the number of Americans killed by the high temperatures put it at 600.[31] The number of Canadians killed by the heat wave in British Columbia is believed to be 595.[32] Globally, the World Health Organization estimates that between 2030 and 2050 "climate change is expected to cause approximately 250 000 additional deaths per year, from malnutrition, malaria, diarrhoea and heat stress."[33]

Extreme weather events have always happened, but climate change is making them more frequent and more extreme. And they will keep getting more frequent and more extreme. The only question is how much more.

Consider what the scientific panel that advises the United Nations said about a heat wave severe enough that, in the past, before humanity started changing the atmosphere, could be expected to happen once every fifty years. Today, the globe is 1.2 degrees Celsius warmer than it was then. As a result, that same heat wave can be expected to happen 4.8 times over fifty years, or once every ten years. If the temperature increase gets to 2 degrees, it will happen 8.6 times over fifty years, or once every six years. With a 5.3-degree increase, it will strike 39.2 times over fifty years—once every fifteen months—turning a rare and dangerous event into a new normal.[34]

The same holds true for hurricanes, floods, droughts, wildfires, ice melt, and more. With each, the fat tails—the extremes—are getting fatter and fatter. If that progression is soon slowed and eventually stopped, our world will continue to be one in which humanity can thrive. If not, we will be in deep trouble.[35]

To halt climate change before it becomes catastrophic, most of the nations of the world have committed to a target of "net zero by 2050," meaning that by midcentury they will emit no more greenhouse gases into the atmosphere than they take out. Scientists estimate that if the world collectively hits that target we will have a good shot at limiting the temperature rise to 1.5 degrees Celsius. That sounds simple enough. But it's hard to overstate how ambitious the goal is, and how central good project delivery is to achieving it.

In 2021, the International Energy Agency, an autonomous intergovernmental organization established within the framework of the Organisation for Economic Co-operation and Development (OECD), released a detailed report examining what would be required to get to net zero.[36] It found that fossil fuels, which today account for four-fifths of the world's energy production, could provide no more than one-fifth in 2050. Replacing them would require a vast increase in electrification—our grandchildren will encounter gas stations only in history books—and an explosion in the production of electricity by renewable energy sources. Wind power must grow elevenfold. Solar power must grow a mind-boggling twentyfold.[37] Investment in renewable energy must triple by 2030, mostly delivered as hundreds, if not thousands, of large-scale, multibillion-dollar wind and solar farms. New nuclear and new hydro may have a role to play for the 2050 deadline, but for 2030 they have already proven too slow.

Furthermore, technologies that are now only concepts and prototypes must soon be ready for massive rollouts. A major one, if it can be made to work at scale, is so-called carbon capture, utilization, and storage (carbon capture, for short), which takes carbon out of the air and either stores it underground or uses it as a raw material in industrial processes. Another is industrial-scale electrolyzer capacity that uses wind- or solar-powered electricity to generate hydrogen. Every month from 2030 onward, the International Energy Agency says, ten heavy industrial plants must be equipped with carbon capture, three new hydrogen-based industrial plants must be built, and two gigawatts of electrolyzer capacity must be added at industrial sites. *Every month.*

There's much more that must be done, but you get the idea: We're talking about projects at a scale and in numbers never seen before in human history, without which mitigating and adapting to climate change will be impossible. Fatih Birol, the executive director of the International Energy Agency, put it bluntly: "The scale and speed of the efforts demanded by this critical and formidable goal ... make this perhaps the greatest challenge humankind has ever faced."[38]

"Scale and speed"; those are the key words. To win the fight against climate change, we must build at a scale and speed that put to shame the long, sorry record of the giant projects of the past. We can no longer afford bloated budgets and deadlines that keep sliding into the future. And we absolutely cannot have projects that never deliver what they promise. There is no room for more Monjus or California High-Speed Rail. In our present situation, wasted resources and wasted time are a threat to civilization. We must build huge and fast. Fortunately, we have a strong precedent for how to do that. It's found back home, in Denmark.

BLOWIN' IN THE WIND

In the 1950s and 1960s, Denmark, like many other countries, became dependent on cheap oil from the Middle East. When OPEC embargoed the West in 1973, the Danish economy slumped, and its vulnerability became clear to all. A furious hunt for new sources of energy led Denmark to rapidly expand its use of coal, oil, and natural gas from nearby sources. But a few pioneers went in a different direction. Denmark is a small, flat country buffeted by ocean winds. We should harness that power, they said, and by 1978 the country had built the world's first multimegawatt wind turbine at Tvind in Jutland, which is still operating today.

People tinkered in garages and on farms, experimenting with designs, sizes, and locations. But even with tax breaks for investors, onshore wind power remained a modest, peripheral industry, in part because Denmark doesn't have lots of uninhabited land and people don't want to live in the shadow of wind turbines. In the late 1990s, a visionary Danish minister of the environment, Svend Auken, told companies seeking permission to build coal-powered generators that they could go ahead on the condition that they also build two of the world's first offshore wind farms. They did. One worked, the other was a mess. Both gave the owners *experiri*. It was a start.

When a group of Danish energy companies merged in 2006 and became DONG Energy, a company now known as Ørsted, the new company inherited the offshore wind farms, plus another in the Irish

Sea. They were minor assets for a company that worked almost exclusively with fossil fuels, but they were enough to ensure that "by coincidence we became the most experienced guys on offshore wind," recalled Anders Eldrup, the new company's first CEO.[39]

In 2009, the United Nations held a landmark conference in Copenhagen to discuss climate change, and Eldrup made a bold announcement there. Some 85 percent of his company's energy came from fossil fuels at the time and only 15 percent from renewables, mostly wind. Within a generation, he promised, his "85/15 plan" would reverse those numbers. That wasn't merely ambitious; lots of observers thought it was impossible. The technology of wind power was too immature and much too costly. Even with government contracts guaranteeing the purchase of electricity at generous rates for years to come, investors were wary. What they didn't appreciate was the extreme modularity of offshore wind farms. Assemble four Lego—foundation, tower, head, blades; click, click, click—and you have a turbine that can start generating electricity immediately. Assemble eight to ten turbines and wire them together, and you have a "string" that can be connected to a substation that feeds into the national electricity grid. It, too, can start delivering as soon as it is assembled. Put together a few strings, and you have a wind farm that is operational on day one. Repeat, repeat, repeat. It can scale up as much as you like, with each iteration pushing everyone up the learning curve.

"We knew that we had to reduce the cost of offshore wind dramatically to make it competitive, and we set a target to reduce it by thirty-five to forty percent over a seven-year period," recalled Henrik Poulsen, who took over from the retiring Anders Eldrup as CEO in 2012.[40] The company and its partners made improvements in every aspect of the business. The most dramatic was growth in the size of turbines. Whereas a turbine in 2000 might have been a little taller than the Statue of Liberty and able to power 1,500 homes, a turbine in 2017 was almost double that height and capable of powering 7,100 homes.

The size of wind farms grew even faster. An offshore wind farm the company completed in 2013 covered 88 square kilometers (34 square miles); the first phase of its Hornsea Project off the coast of England, completed in 2020, covered 407 square kilometers (157 square miles). When the second phase of the Hornsea Project is finished, the whole thing will cover 869 square kilometers (336 square miles), making it considerably bigger than the 784 square kilometers (303 square miles) of New York City's five boroughs.

The explosive growth drove down costs. "It turns out," said Poulsen, "that once we got going, once we started taking on offshore wind projects in the UK and later on in Germany, Denmark, and the Netherlands, once we started industrializing and standardizing the way we were building offshore wind farms, once we got the whole industry value chain focused on it, that within four years we had reduced the cost of offshore wind by 60 percent." That was more than expected and three years ahead of schedule. Wind power became cheaper than fossil fuels faster than anyone had dreamed of.[41] There was no optimism bias there; quite the opposite.

In 2017, with oil and gas vanishing from its business, Ørsted took its new name in honor of the Danish physicist Hans Christian Ørsted, who discovered electromagnetism. Two years later, Anders Eldrup's "impossible" 85/15 plan was achieved. It hadn't taken a generation; it had taken ten years.[42] Again that was better than expected and a full fifteen years ahead of schedule, unheard of for conventional Big Energy projects.

Over the same ten years, the percentage of Denmark's electricity generated by fossil fuels fell from 72 percent to 24 percent, while the share contributed by wind power soared from 18 percent to 56 percent.[43] Some days, Danish wind turbines produce more electricity than the country can consume. The surplus is exported to neighboring nations.

For Denmark, the benefits of this revolution are likely to be felt for decades. The global wind energy industry is booming, with ever-bigger developments popping up all over the world, and many of the leading companies are Danish thanks to Denmark's pioneering role. Ørsted has gone global. So has Vestas, one of the world's largest manufacturers of wind turbines, also Danish.[44] And many of the smaller, specialized firms in the industry not only come from Denmark, they come specifically from Jutland, the region where people first started experimenting with turbines in the 1970s. Henrik Poulsen, who now advises an investment company, described how his firm recently bought a Danish company that makes control systems for wind farms: "Now we want to expand this company and we're looking for companies that we could merge into this platform." Naturally, they're looking around the world. But the prospects they've found "are all located within a few hundred kilometers" of each other in Jutland. "Which is a bit crazy," said Poulsen. Economic geographers like myself call this "clustering" or "economies of agglomeration." It's what happened for film in Hollywood in the 1920s and for tech in Silicon Valley in the mid–twentieth century. Jutland is now the Silicon Valley of wind energy—which is striking for a country whose population is just over half that of Los Angeles County.

A FIGHTING CHANCE

But this isn't about Denmark. It's about the world and what we can learn from Denmark's wind power revolution. Part of the lesson is that government has a role in development. "Without the government-created framework, this never would have happened," noted Anders Eldrup. This approach may not be popular in the United States, but ironically, the United States is the model. The whole digital revolution, which the American giants of Silicon Valley dominate, could not have happened without US government support for the creation of digital technologies, including what became the Internet. If you want to start an avalanche big enough to change the world, government may have to help push the first boulder.

But the more fundamental lesson is the power of modularity. It was modularity that enabled learning so rapid and growth so explosive that Denmark was able to revolutionize both wind power technology and its own electricity supply faster than anyone expected, including the innovators themselves, and in less time than it takes many countries to deliver a single "one huge thing" project. That's huge and fast. That's the model we need: "many small things" manufactured at scale and assembled like Lego, click, click, click.

The implications for governments and corporations are clear: encourage, support, and practice a modular approach. But it is also empowering for individuals. When small can scale up and become huge fast, small experiments have huge potential. All it takes is imagination and tenacity. Remember that much of today's global wind industry can be traced back to a handful of Danes tinkering in garages and farms. Use your imagination. Get tinkering.

With new ideas and the relentless application of the modular model, we will have a fighting chance to deliver the transformation people and the planet need.

CODA

ELEVEN HEURISTICS FOR BETTER PROJECT LEADERSHIP

Heuristics are fast and frugal rules of thumb used to simplify complex decisions. The word has its origin in the ancient Greek word *Eureka!*, the cry of joy and satisfaction when one finds or discovers something.[1] "Think slow, act fast" is an example of a heuristic. Experts and laypeople alike use them when making decisions under uncertainty.[2] Heuristics are mental shortcuts used to reduce complexity, making decisions manageable. Heuristics are often tacit and need to be deliberately teased out before they can be shared verbally. Wise people, including successful project leaders—plus your grandmother and anyone else with *phronesis*—work to refine and improve their heuristics throughout life.[3]

The following are eleven of my favorite heuristics, developed during decades of studying and managing big projects.[4] But a word of warning: Heuristics should never be used like thoughtless paint-by-numbers rules. Check whether my heuristics resonate with your own experience before using them in practice. Even more important, use them as a source of inspiration for investigating, trying new things, and developing your own heuristics—which is what really matters. For how to do this and why, read the references, advance your experience, and watch your ability to turn bold visions into concrete reality radically improve.

HIRE A MASTERBUILDER

I sometimes say that this is my only heuristic because the masterbuilder—named after the skilled masons who built Europe's medieval cathedrals—possesses all the *phronesis* needed to make your project happen. You want someone with deep domain experience and a proven track record of success in whatever you're doing, whether it's a home renovation, a wedding, an IT system, or a skyscraper. But masterbuilders aren't always available or affordable, in which case you need to think further and consider some of the following.

GET YOUR TEAM RIGHT

This is the only heuristic cited by every project leader I've ever met. Ed Catmull explained why: "Give a good idea to a mediocre team, and they will screw it up. Give a mediocre idea to a great team, and they will either fix it or come up with something better. If you get the team right, chances are they will get the ideas right."[5] But who should pick the team? Ideally, that's the job of a masterbuilder. In fact, it's the masterbuilder's main job. This is why the role of masterbuilder is not as solitary as it sounds; projects are delivered by teams. So to amend my advice above: When possible, hire a masterbuilder. And the masterbuilder's team.

ASK "WHY?"

Asking why you're doing your project will focus you on what matters, your ultimate purpose, and your result. This goes into the box on the right of your project chart. As the project sails into a storm of events and details, good leaders never lose sight of the ultimate result. "No matter where I am and what I'm doing in the delivery process," noted

Andrew Wolstenholme, the leader who delivered Heathrow's Terminal 5 in chapter 8, "I check myself constantly by asking whether my present actions effectively contribute to the result on the right." (See chapter 3.)

BUILD WITH LEGO

Big is best built from small. Bake one small cake. Bake another. And another. Then stack them. Decoration aside, that's all there really is to even the most towering wedding cake. As with wedding cakes, so with solar and wind farms, server farms, batteries, container shipping, pipelines, roads. They're all profoundly modular, built with a basic building block. They can scale up like crazy, getting better, faster, bigger, and cheaper as they do. The small cake is the Lego brick—the basic building block—of the wedding cake. The solar panel is the Lego of the solar farm. The server is the Lego of the server farm. This potent little idea has been applied to software, subways, hardware, hotels, office buildings, schools, factories, hospitals, rockets, satellites, cars, and app stores. Its applicability is limited only by imagination. So what's your Lego? (See chapter 9.)

THINK SLOW, ACT FAST

What's the worst that can happen during planning? Maybe your whiteboard is accidentally erased. What's the worst that can happen during delivery? Your drill breaks through the ocean floor, flooding the tunnel. Just before you release your movie, a pandemic closes theaters. You ruin the most beautiful vista in Washington, DC. You have to dynamite months of work on the opera house, clear away the rubble, and start over. Your overpass collapses, killing dozens of people. And so much more. Almost any nightmare you can imagine can happen—and *has* happened—during delivery. You want to limit your exposure to this. You do it by taking all the time necessary to create a detailed, tested plan. Planning is relatively cheap and safe; delivering is expensive and dangerous. Good planning boosts the odds of a quick, effective delivery, keeping the window on risk small and closing it as soon as possible. (See chapter 1.)

TAKE THE OUTSIDE VIEW

Your project is special, but unless you are doing what has literally never been done before—building a time machine, engineering a black hole—it is not unique; it is part of a larger class of projects. Think of your project as "one of those," gather data, and learn from all the experience those numbers represent by making reference-class forecasts. Use the same focus to spot and mitigate risks. Switching the focus from your project to the class your project belongs to will lead, paradoxically, to a more accurate understanding of your project. (See chapter 6.)

WATCH YOUR DOWNSIDE

It's often said that opportunity is as important as risk. That's false. Risk can kill you or your project. No upside can compensate for that. For fat-tailed risk, which is present in most projects, forget about forecasting risk; go directly to mitigation by spotting and eliminating dangers. A rider in the grueling three-week Tour de France bicycle race explained that participating is not about winning but about not losing, each day for twenty-one days. Only after that can you consider winning. Successful project leaders think like that; they focus on not losing, every day, while keeping a keen eye on the prize, the goal they are trying to achieve.

SAY NO AND WALK AWAY

Staying focused is essential for getting projects done. Saying no is essential for staying focused. At the outset, will the project have the people and funds, including contingencies, needed to succeed? If not, walk away. Does an action contribute to achieving the goal in the box on the right? If not, skip it. Say no to monuments. No to untested technology. No to lawsuits. And so on. This can be difficult, particularly if your organization embraces a bias for action. But saying no is essential for the success of a project and an organization. "I'm actually as proud of the things we haven't done as the things we have done," Steve Jobs once observed. The things not done helped Apple stay focused on a few products that became wildly successful because of that focus, according to Jobs.[6]

MAKE FRIENDS AND KEEP THEM FRIENDLY

A leader of a multibillion-dollar public sector IT project told me he spent more than half his time acting like a diplomat, cultivating the understanding and support of stakeholders who could significantly influence his project. Why? It's risk management. If something goes wrong, the project's fate depends on the strength of those relationships. And when something goes wrong, it's too late to start developing and cultivating them. Build your bridges before you need them.

BUILD CLIMATE MITIGATION INTO YOUR PROJECT

No task is more urgent today than mitigating the climate crisis—not only for the common good but for your organization, yourself, and your family. Aristotle defined *phronesis* as the dual ability to see what things are good for people *and* to get those things done. We know what's good: climate mitigation, for instance, by electrifying everything—homes, cars, offices, factories, shops—and making sure that the electricity comes from abundant renewable sources. We have the ability to do this. In fact, it's already happening, as we saw in chapter 9. Now it's a matter of quickly accelerating and scaling up the effort with thousands more mitigation (and adaptation) projects, large and small, following the principles laid out in this book—which was a main motivation for writing it and for hammering out this list of heuristics.

KNOW THAT YOUR BIGGEST RISK IS YOU

It's tempting to think that projects fail because the world throws surprises at us: price and scope changes, accidents, weather, new management—the list goes on. But this is shallow thinking. The Great Chicago Fire Festival failed not because Jim Lasko couldn't predict the exact chain of circumstances that led to the malfunction of the ignition system (see chapter 6); it failed because he took the inside view on his project and didn't study how failure typically occurs for live events as a class. Why didn't he? Because focusing on the particular case and ignoring the class is what human psychology inclines us to do. The greatest threat Lasko faced wasn't out in the world; it was in his own head, in his behavioral biases. This is true for every one of us and every project. Which is why your biggest risk is you.

APPENDIX A

BASE RATES FOR COST RISK*

The table on the next page shows cost overruns for twenty-five project types covering sixteen thousand–plus projects. Overrun is measured as (a) mean cost overrun, (b) percentage of projects in the upper tail (defined as ≥ 50 percent), and (c) mean overrun in the tail. Overrun is measured in real terms.

The numbers in the table are base rates for cost risk in project management. For example, if you're planning to host the Olympic Games, your base rate (expected value) for cost overrun will be 157 percent, with a 76 percent risk of ending up in the tail with an expected overrun of 200 percent and substantial further risk of overrun above this. If you're the sponsor or project leader, your key question should be "Can we afford this risk?" and if not, "Should we walk away or can we reduce the risk?"

We see from the table that the base rates are very different for different project types for both mean risk and tail risk. The highest mean risk is found for nuclear storage, at 238 percent, while the lowest is found for solar power, at 1 percent. The highest risk for ending up in the tail is held by the Olympics, at 76 percent, while the highest mean overrun in the tail is found for IT projects, at 447 percent. Differences in base rates must be taken into account when planning and managing projects but often are not. Frequently, empirical base rates are not considered at all.

---

*Results for schedule risk and benefit risk are similar, albeit based on fewer data; see Bent Flyvbjerg and Dirk W. Bester, "The Cost-Benefit Fallacy: Why Cost-Benefit Analysis Is Broken and How to Fix It," *Journal of Benefit-Cost Analysis* 12, no. 3 (2021): 395–419.

APPENDIX A

PROJECT TYPE	(A) MEAN COST OVERRUN (%)*	(B) % OF PROJECTS IN TAIL (≥ 50% OVERRUN)	(C) MEAN OVERRUN OF PROJECTS IN TAIL (%)
Nuclear storage	238	48	427
Olympic Games	157	76	200
Nuclear power	120	55	204
Hydroelectric dams	75	37	186
IT	73	18	447
Nonhydroelectric dams	71	33	202
Buildings	62	39	206
Aerospace	60	42	119
Defense	53	21	253
Bus rapid transit	40	43	69
Rail	39	28	116
Airports	39	43	88
Tunnels	37	28	103
Oil and gas	34	19	121
Ports	32	17	183
Hospitals, health	29	13	167
Mining	27	17	129
Bridges	26	21	107
Water	20	13	124
Fossil thermal power	16	14	109
Roads	16	11	102
Pipelines	14	9	110
Wind power	13	7	97
Energy transmission	8	4	166
Solar power	1	2	50

SOURCE: FLYVBJERG DATABASE

*Cost overrun was calculated not including inflation and baselined as late in the project cycle as possible, just before the go-ahead (final business case at final investment decision). This means that the numbers in the table are conservative. If inflation had been included and early business cases used as the baseline, cost overrun would be much higher, sometimes several times higher.

APPENDIX B

FURTHER READINGS BY BENT FLYVBJERG

If you're interested in learning more about my research on project leadership, below is a list of recommended readings. Free downloads of the listed articles are available on Social Science Research Network (SSRN), ResearchGate, Academia, arXiv, and Google Scholar. Direct links to SSRN are provided below for each article that had been published at the time of writing this book.

Bent Flyvbjerg, Alexander Budzier, Maria D. Christodoulou, and M. Zottoli, "So You Think Projects Are Unique? How Uniqueness Bias Undermines Project Management," under review.

Bent Flyvbjerg, Alexander Budzier, Mark Keil, Jong Seok Lee, Dirk W. Bester, and Daniel Lunn, "The Empirical Reality of IT Project Cost Overruns: Discovering a Power-Law Distribution," *Journal of Management Information Systems* 39, no. 3 (Fall 2022), https://www.jmis-web.org.

Bent Flyvbjerg, "Heuristics for Masterbuilders: Fast and Frugal Ways to Become a Better Project Leader," *Saïd Business School Working Papers*, University of Oxford, 2022, https://papers.ssrn.com/sol3/papers.cfm?abstract_id=4159984.

Atif Ansar and Bent Flyvbjerg, "How to Solve Big Problems: Bespoke Versus Platform Strategies," *Oxford Review of Economic Policy* 38, no. 2 (2022): 1–31, https://papers.ssrn.com/sol3/papers.cfm?abstract_id=4119492.

Bent Flyvbjerg, "Top Ten Behavioral Biases in Project Management: An Overview," *Project Management Journal* 52, no. 6 (2021): 531–46, https://papers.ssrn.com/sol3/papers.cfm?abstract_id=3979164.

Bent Flyvbjerg, "Make Megaprojects More Modular," *Harvard Business Review* 99, no.6 (November–December 2021): 58–63, https://papers.ssrn.com/sol3/papers.cfm?abstract_id=3937465.

Bent Flyvbjerg and Dirk W. Bester, "The Cost-Benefit Fallacy: Why Cost-

Benefit Analysis Is Broken and How to Fix It," *Journal of Benefit-Cost Analysis* 12, no. 3 (2021): 395–419, https://papers.ssrn.com/sol3/papers.cfm?abstract_id=3918328.

Bent Flyvbjerg, Alexander Budzier, and Daniel Lunn, "Regression to the Tail: Why the Olympics Blow Up," *Environment and Planning A: Economy and Space* 53, no. 2 (March 2021): 233–60, https://papers.ssrn.com/sol3/papers.cfm?abstract_id=3686009.

Bent Flyvbjerg, "Four Ways to Scale Up: Smart, Dumb, Forced, and Fumbled," *Saïd Business School Working Papers*, University of Oxford, 2021, https://papers.ssrn.com/sol3/papers.cfm?abstract_id=3760631.

Bent Flyvbjerg, "The Law of Regression to the Tail: How to Survive Covid-19, the Climate Crisis, and Other Disasters," *Environmental Science and Policy* 114 (December 2020): 614–18, https://papers.ssrn.com/sol3/papers.cfm?abstract_id=3600070.

Bent Flyvbjerg, Atif Ansar, Alexander Budzier, Søren Buhl, Chantal Cantarelli, Massimo Garbuio, Carsten Glenting, Mette Skamris Holm, Dan Lovallo, Daniel Lunn, Eric Molin, Arne Rønnest, Allison Stewart, and Bert van Wee, "Five Things You Should Know About Cost Overrun," *Transportation Research Part A: Policy and Practice* 118 (December 2018): 174–90, https://papers.ssrn.com/sol3/papers.cfm?abstract_id=3248999.

Bent Flyvbjerg and J. Rodney Turner, "Do Classics Exist in Megaproject Management?," *International Journal of Project Management* 36, no. 2 (2018): 334–41, https://papers.ssrn.com/sol3/papers.cfm?abstract_id=3012134.

Bent Flyvbjerg, ed., *The Oxford Handbook of Megaproject Management* (Oxford, UK: Oxford University Press, 2017), https://amzn.to/3OCTZqI.

Bent Flyvbjerg, "Introduction: The Iron Law of Megaproject Management," in *The Oxford Handbook of Megaproject Management*, ed. Bent Flyvbjerg (Oxford, UK: Oxford University Press, 2017), 1–18, https://papers.ssrn.com/sol3/papers.cfm?abstract_id=2742088.

Atif Ansar, Bent Flyvbjerg, Alexander Budzier, and Daniel Lunn, "Does Infrastructure Investment Lead to Economic Growth or Economic Fragility? Evidence from China," *Oxford Review of Economic Policy* 32, no. 3 (Autumn 2016): 360–90, https://papers.ssrn.com/sol3/papers.cfm?abstract_id=2834326.

Bent Flyvbjerg, "The Fallacy of Beneficial Ignorance: A Test of Hirschman's Hiding Hand," *World Development* 84 (May 2016): 176–89, https://papers.ssrn.com/sol3/papers.cfm?abstract_id=2767128.

Atif Ansar, Bent Flyvbjerg, Alexander Budzier, and Daniel Lunn, "Should We Build More Large Dams? The Actual Costs of Hydropower Megaproject Development," *Energy Policy* 69 (March 2014): 43–56, https://papers.ssrn.com/sol3/papers.cfm?abstract_id=2406852.

Bent Flyvbjerg, ed., *Megaproject Planning and Management: Essential Readings*, vols. 1–2 (Cheltenham, UK: Edward Elgar, 2014), https://amzn.to/3kg1g1s.

Bent Flyvbjerg, "What You Should Know About Megaprojects and Why: An Overview," *Project Management Journal* 45, no. 2 (April–May 2014): 6–19, https://papers.ssrn.com/sol3/papers.cfm?abstract_id=2424835. This article was awarded the *PMI Project Management Journal* 2015 Paper of the Year Award.

Bent Flyvbjerg, "How Planners Deal with Uncomfortable Knowledge: The Dubious Ethics of the American Planning Association," *Cities* 32 (June 2013): 157–63; with comments by Ali Modarres, David Thacher, and Vanessa Watson (June 2013), and Richard Bolan and Bent Flyvbjerg (February 2015), https://papers.ssrn.com/sol3/papers.cfm?abstract_id=2278887.

Bent Flyvbjerg, "Quality Control and Due Diligence in Project Management: Getting Decisions Right by Taking the Outside View," *International Journal of Project Management* 31, no. 5 (May 2013): 760–74, https://papers.ssrn.com/sol3/papers.cfm?abstract_id=2229700.

Bent Flyvbjerg, "Why Mass Media Matter and How to Work with Them: Phronesis and Megaprojects," in *Real Social Science: Applied Phronesis*, ed. Bent Flyvbjerg, Todd Landman, and Sanford Schram (Cambridge, UK: Cambridge University Press, 2012), 95–121, https://papers.ssrn.com/sol3/papers.cfm?abstract_id=2278219.

Bent Flyvbjerg and Alexander Budzier, "Why Your IT Project May Be Riskier Than You Think," *Harvard Business Review* 89, no. 9 (2011): 23–25, https://papers.ssrn.com/sol3/papers.cfm?abstract_id=2229735. This article was selected by *Harvard Business Review* as the leading article for its "Ideas Watch" section, featuring the most important new ideas in business and management.

Bent Flyvbjerg, "Survival of the Unfittest: Why the Worst Infrastructure Gets Built, and What We Can Do About It," *Oxford Review of Economic Policy* 25, no. 3 (2009): 344–67, https://papers.ssrn.com/sol3/papers.cfm?abstract_id=2229768.

Bent Flyvbjerg, Massimo Garbuio, and Dan Lovallo, "Delusion and Deception in Large Infrastructure Projects: Two Models for Explaining and Preventing Executive Disaster," *California Management Review* 51, no. 2 (Winter 2009): 170–93, https://papers.ssrn.com/sol3/papers.cfm?abstract_id=2229781.

Bent Flyvbjerg, Nils Bruzelius, and Bert van Wee, "Comparison of Capital Costs per Route-Kilometre in Urban Rail," *European Journal of Transport and Infrastructure Research* 8, no. 1 (March 2008): 17–30, https://papers.ssrn.com/sol3/papers.cfm?abstract_id=2237995.

Bent Flyvbjerg, "Policy and Planning for Large-Infrastructure Projects: Problems, Causes, Cures," *Environment and Planning B: Planning and Design* 34, no. 4 (2007), 578–97, https://papers.ssrn.com/sol3/papers.cfm?abstract_id=2230414. This article was awarded the Association of European Schools of Planning (AESOP) Prize for Best Published Paper, July 2008.

Bent Flyvbjerg, "Cost Overruns and Demand Shortfalls in Urban Rail and

Other Infrastructure," *Transportation Planning and Technology* 30, no. 1 (February 2007): 9–30, https://papers.ssrn.com/sol3/papers.cfm?abstract_id=2230421.

Bent Flyvbjerg, "From Nobel Prize to Project Management: Getting Risks Right," *Project Management Journal* 37, no. 3 (August 2006): 5–15, https://papers.ssrn.com/sol3/papers.cfm?abstract_id=2238013.

Bent Flyvbjerg, "Design by Deception: The Politics of Megaproject Approval," *Harvard Design Magazine*, no. 22 (Spring–Summer 2005): 50–59, https://papers.ssrn.com/sol3/papers.cfm?abstract_id=2238047.

Bent Flyvbjerg, Mette K. Skamris Holm, and Søren L. Buhl, "How (In)accurate Are Demand Forecasts in Public Works Projects? The Case of Transportation," *Journal of the American Planning Association* 71, no. 2 (Spring 2005): 131–46, https://papers.ssrn.com/sol3/papers.cfm?abstract_id=2238050.

Bent Flyvbjerg, Carsten Glenting, and Arne Rønnest, *Procedures for Dealing with Optimism Bias in Transport Planning: Guidance Document* (London: UK Department for Transport, June 2004), https://papers.ssrn.com/sol3/papers.cfm?abstract_id=2278346.

Bent Flyvbjerg, Mette K. Skamris Holm, and Søren L. Buhl, "What Causes Cost Overrun in Transport Infrastructure Projects?," *Transport Reviews* 24, no. 1 (January 2004): 3–18, https://papers.ssrn.com/sol3/papers.cfm?abstract_id=2278352.

Bent Flyvbjerg, Nils Bruzelius, and Werner Rothengatter, *Megaprojects and Risk: An Anatomy of Ambition* (Cambridge, UK: Cambridge University Press, 2003), https://amzn.to/3ELjq4R.

Bent Flyvbjerg, "Delusions of Success: Comment on Dan Lovallo and Daniel Kahneman," *Harvard Business Review* 81, no. 12 (December 2003): 121–22, https://papers.ssrn.com/sol3/papers.cfm?abstract_id=2278359.

Bent Flyvbjerg, Mette K. Skamris Holm, and Søren L. Buhl, "Underestimating Costs in Public Works Projects: Error or Lie?," *Journal of the American Planning Association* 68, no. 3 (Summer 2002): 279–95, https://papers.ssrn.com/sol3/papers.cfm?abstract_id=2278415.

Nils Bruzelius, Bent Flyvbjerg, and Werner Rothengatter, "Big Decisions, Big Risks: Improving Accountability in Mega Projects," *International Review of Administrative Sciences* 64, no. 3 (September 1998): 423–40, https://papers.ssrn.com/sol3/papers.cfm?abstract_id=2719896.

ACKNOWLEDGMENTS

Writing a book is a "Big Thing." As such, it takes teamwork. I wish to thank the many people who made the book possible. It's a big team, so undoubtedly I forgot some, for which I ask forgiveness, but which does not lessen their contribution or my gratitude.

Gerd Gigerenzer, Daniel Kahneman, Benoit Mandelbrot, and Nassim Nicholas Taleb are principal intellectual influences. Nobody understands risk better than they do, and understanding risk is *the* key to understanding big projects. Kahneman and Taleb accepted positions as distinguished research scholars with my group at Oxford, for which I cannot thank them enough. It greatly facilitated intellectual exchange, and you will see their influence throughout the book.

Frank Gehry and Ed Catmull are main practical influences. When Gehry built the Guggenheim Museum Bilbao on time and on budget I knew I had to pick his brain, because if you can build architecture like *that* on time and on budget, you can build *anything* on time and on budget. So why is it so rare, and what is Gehry's secret? Gehry generously agreed to talk, resulting in multiple interviews. Ed Catmull is responsible for an uninterrupted string of Hollywood blockbusters so long (the longest in movie history) that on principle it should be statistically impossible, given that movies are notoriously hit or miss. So how did it happen? Catmull, too, agreed to talk, and I'm grateful to him and Gehry for sharing their time and insights and for facilitating further interviews with members of their teams. Both also kindly accepted invitations to explain their thinking in lectures in my course at Oxford.

The following helpfully shared their experience in additional interviews: Patrick Collison, Morgan Doan, Pete Docter, Simon Douthwaite, David Drake, Anders Eldrup, Sally Forgan, Danny Forster, Paul Gardien, Mike Green, Richard Harper, Robi Kirsic, Bernie Koth, Eddie Kramer, Jim Lasko, Dana Macaulay, Adam Marelli, Ian McAllister, Molly Melching, Manuel Melis, Deb Niven, Don Norman, Dominic Packer, Henrik Poulsen, Alan South, John Storyk, Lou Thompson, Kimberly Dasher Tripp, Ralph Vartabedian, Craig Webb, Andrew Wolstenholme, Ricky Wong, and Micah Zenko. Besides the formal interviews, I'm grateful to the following for their help with further information gathering: Kermit Baker, Elena Bonometti, Scott Gilmore, Jan Haust, Paul Hillier, and Liam Scott.

The book builds on the world's largest database of its kind, with information regarding sixteen thousand–plus projects, big and small. Mette Skamris Holm was key to collecting the first data with me at Aalborg University. Chantal Cantarelli and Bert van Wee became collaborators in further data collection when I was chair at Delft University of Technology. Later, Chantal moved with me to the University of Oxford, where we joined forces with Alexander Budzier, Atif Ansar, and numerous research assistants who became essential in developing the database into what it is today. My work as an external consultant for McKinsey & Company contributed further data from McKinsey clients, for which Jürgen Laartz was consequential. I wish to thank each of my collaborators and our institutions for their help and support in building the database, without which the book would not have been possible.

With data come statistics and statisticians. Their work is not directly visible in the main text, because I wanted to keep it nontechnical. But statisticians have been hard at work in the background ensuring the validity of results. I wish to thank, in particular, Dirk W. Bester, Søren Buhl, Maria Christodoulou, Daniel Lunn, and Mariagrazia Zottoli. Readers with a technical bent can find references to the statistics in the endnotes.

A special thank-you goes to my long-suffering co-author, Dan Gardner, who worked with me for over two years, developing ideas, finding case studies past and present, and helping me tell my story far better than I could have. Dan had to put up with my scholarly nitpicking of every word and sentence. I want to compliment him for never losing his cool in the process and for defending the storyline as vigorously as I defended the scholarship in our writing.

Special thanks also to Alexander Budzier, my alter ego and closest collaborator in megaproject management. Many years ago, we committed to being partners through thick and thin. I hope Alex thinks I've kept my word as well as I think he has his. There is no one I'd rather have by my side when we crunch the numbers or are deep in the "big muddy," trying to turn around some multibillion-dollar project that's gone off its rails, as we did in chapter 6. Alex has helped with everything, from data to ideas to fact-checking.

A writer could not ask for a better agent than Jim Levine. Jim was the first to see the potential of *How Big Things Get Done* when the book was only an idea. Without him the idea would have remained just that. Jim also provided feedback on the writing, made effective edits to the manuscript, and helped nail the title in an exemplary team effort. My gratitude to all the team at Levine Greenberg Rostan Literary Agency. Courtney Paganelli was always encouraging and incredibly helpful in turning the fledgling project into the beginnings of a book.

I'm thankful to everyone at Random House. Talia Krohn and Paul Whitlatch edited the manuscript with vision and insight, much improving the result. Doug Pepper gave highly useful comments. Katie Berry kept the manuscript organized and on schedule. Lynn Anderson masterly copyedited the final draft. Thanks to Robert Siek,

Katie Zilberman, and Fritz Metsch for producing such a beautifully finished book, Jessie Bright for designing the stylish jacket, Jane Farnol for compiling the index, and Cozetta Smith, Dyana Messina, Mason Eng, and Julie Cepler for doing everything possible to help convey the messages within to a wide audience without. Thanks also to David Drake, Gillian Blake, Annsley Rosner, Michelle Giuseffi, Sally Franklin, Allison Fox, and the rest of the publishing team. Nicole Amter expertly put together the book's bibliography.

During the research for the book, I have benefited from insightful conversations with many brilliant mentors and colleagues. Martin Wachs, my doctoral and postdoctoral supervisor, supported every major decision and publication in my academic career, including the present book. Unexpectedly, Marty died in the middle of us fact-checking the California High-Speed Rail case in the introduction, on which he was an expert. I didn't understand why his emails suddenly—and uncharacteristically—stopped. Then I got the tragic news. No one could hope for a better and more generous supervisor and mentor. Marty has left a profound and painful void. Verner C. Petersen taught me the value of fundamental positions in philosophy and social theory for understanding planning and management. Other important interlocutors include Jeremy Adelman, Arun Agrawal, Michele Alacevich, Alan Altshuler, Jørgen Andreasen, Atif Ansar, Dan Ariely, Martin Beniston, Maria Flyvbjerg Bo, Alexander Budzier, Chantal Cantarelli, David Champion, Aaron Clauset, Stewart Clegg, Andrew Davies, Henrik Flyvbjerg, John Flyvbjerg, W. H. Fok, Karen Trapenberg Frick, Hans-Georg Gemünden, Gerd Gigerenzer, Edward Glaeser, Carsten Glenting, Tony Gómez-Ibáñez, The Right Honourable The Lord Hardie, Martina Huemann, Sir Bernard Jenkin, Hans Lauritz Jørgensen, Daniel Kahneman, Mark Keil, Mike Kiernan, Thomas Kniesner, Jonathan Lake, Edgardo Latrubesse, Richard LeBlanc, Jong Seok Lee, Zhi Liu, Dan Lovallo, Gordon McNicoll, Edward Merrow, Ralf Müller, Simon Flyvbjerg Nørrelykke, Juan de Dios Ortúza, Jamie Peck, Morten Rugtved Petersen, Don Pickrell, Kim Pilgaard, Shankar Sankaran, Jens Schmidt, Peter Sestoft, Jonas Söderlund, Benjamin Sovacool, Allison Stewart, Cass Sunstein, Nassim Nicholas Taleb, Philip Tetlock, J. Rodney Turner, Bo Vagnby, Bert van Wee, Graham Winch, and Andrew Zimbalist. Thank you, all.

I also wish to thank the participants in the executive education programs I have taught, including Oxford's MSc in Major Programme Management, the UK Government's Major Projects Leadership Academy, the Hong Kong Government's Major Projects Leadership Programme, and similar programs in the private sector, which have given me invaluable opportunity to test the ideas in the book with more than a thousand top-level, high-caliber business and government executives, in geographies as different as the United States, Europe, Asia, Africa, and Australia. Big thanks also to Atif Ansar, Alexander Budzier, Paul Chapman, Patrick O'Connell, and Andrew White for excellent help in co-founding, co-directing, and co-delivering these programs.

Together with Alexander Budzier I co-founded Oxford Global Projects as an outlet to leverage our academic research in practice and as a source of additional data. It, too, has proven a crucial testing ground for the ideas in the book, and I wish to thank the many clients who invited us to try our data, theories, and methods on their projects. I'm grateful to each member of the OGP team: Rayaheen Adra, Karlene Agard, Simone Andersen, Mike Bartlett, Radhia Benalia, Alexander Budzier, Caitlin Combrinck, Michele Dallachiesa, Gerd Duch, Sam Franzen, Andi Garavaglia, Adam Hede, Andreas Leed, Newton Li, and Caixia Mao.

Funding for the work on the book has come from my endowed chairs: the BT Professorship and Chair of Major Programme Management at the University of Oxford and the Villum Kann Rasmussen Professorship and Chair of Major Program Management at the

IT University of Copenhagen. I wish to thank BT Group, the Villum Foundation, the University of Oxford, and the IT University of Copenhagen for generously sponsoring my research, no strings attached, creating the ideal conditions for independent scholarship.

Gratefulness doesn't even begin to convey what I owe my family and friends for always being there when I need them: Carissa, Maria, Ava, August, Kasper, John, Mikala, Henrik, Olga, Claus, Damon, Finn, Frank, Jeremy, Kim, Niels, Vaughan.

My biggest and warmest thanks go to Carissa Véliz, who was locked down with me each day of writing the book, while completing her own. She has influenced every aspect, from title to content to cover. Dan probably got tired of hearing, "I'll ask Carissa," whenever he and I were unsure or disagreed about something. But she's the wordsmith I trust the most (read her stuff and you'll understand), and the book is significantly better for it. Carissa read the full manuscript in detail from beginning to end, substantially improving the writing. Finally, she helped the two of us pull through the pandemic, despite unexpected heartbreak and being isolated in a foreign country far from our families for what seemed like forever. Words don't suffice to express my admiration and gratitude. Nevertheless, from the bottom of my heart: Thank you, guapa.

NOTES

INTRODUCTION: CALIFORNIA DREAMIN'

1. Ticket price estimates were provided in a range of scenarios, with a low of $68 and a high of $104. The total cost of the project was estimated at between $32.785 billion and $33.625 billion. See California High-Speed Rail Authority, *Financial Plan* (Sacramento: California High-Speed Rail Authority, 1999); California High-Speed Rail Authority, *California High-Speed Train Business Plan* (Sacramento: California High-Speed Rail Authority, 2008); Safe, Reliable High-Speed Passenger Train Bond Act for the 21st Century, AB-3034, 2008, https://leginfo.legislature.ca.gov/faces/billNavClient.xhtml?bill_id=200720080AB3034.
2. California High-Speed Rail Authority, *California High-Speed Rail Program Revised 2012 Business Plan: Building California's Future* (Sacramento: California High-Speed Rail Authority, 2012); California High-Speed Rail Authority, *Connecting California: 2014 Business Plan* (Sacramento: California High-Speed Rail Authority, 2014); California High-Speed Rail Authority, *Connecting and Transforming California: 2016 Business Plan* (Sacramento: California High-Speed Rail Authority, 2016); California High-Speed Rail Authority, *2018 Business Plan* (Sacramento: California High-Speed Rail Authority, 2018); California High-Speed Rail Authority, *2020 Business Plan: Recovery and Transformation* (Sacramento: California High-Speed Rail Authority, 2021); California High-Speed Rail Authority, *2020 Business Plan: Ridership & Revenue Forecasting Report* (Sacramento: California High-Speed Rail Authority, 2021); California High-Speed Rail Authority, *Revised Draft 2020 Business Plan: Capital Cost Basis of Estimate Report* (Sacramento: California High-Speed Rail Authority, 2021).
3. California High-Speed Rail Authority, *Revised Draft 2020 Business Plan: Capital Cost Basis of Estimate Report*.
4. For a full account of the Nepal school project, see Bent Flyvbjerg, "Four Ways to Scale Up: Smart, Dumb, Forced, and Fumbled," *Saïd Business School Working Papers*, Oxford University, 2021.
5. "What Did Nepal Do?," Exemplars in Global Health, 2022, https://www.exemplars.health/topics/stunting/nepal/what-did-nepal-do.

6. The name of the project is the Basic and Primary Education Project (BPEP). I worked in close collaboration with the Danish architect Hans Lauritz Jørgensen, who designed prototypes of schools and classrooms. I planned and programmed the project. Later, a delivery team took over and spent twelve years building the schools. I was offered the opportunity to head the delivery team but respectfully declined because I had decided that my university professorship would be my primary vocation, however much I loved—and love—being involved in hands-on project planning and delivery. I wanted to *really* understand what makes projects tick—at the root-cause level—which would require in-depth university research, in my judgment. So I returned to Denmark and my professorship to carry out that research, first at Aalborg University and later at Delft University of Technology in the Netherlands, the University of Oxford in the United Kingdom, and the IT University of Copenhagen in Denmark.
7. Bent Flyvbjerg, "Introduction: The Iron Law of Megaproject Management," in *The Oxford Handbook of Megaproject Management*, ed. Bent Flyvbjerg (Oxford, UK: Oxford University Press, 2017), 1–18.
8. Joseph E. Stevens, *Hoover Dam: An American Adventure* (Norman: University of Oklahoma Press, 1988); Young Hoon Kwak et al., "What Can We Learn from the Hoover Dam Project That Influenced Modern Project Management?," *International Journal of Project Management* 32 (2014): 256–64.
9. Martin W. Bowman, *Boeing 747: A History* (Barnsley, UK: Pen and Sword Aviation, 2015); Stephen Dowling, "The Boeing 747: The Plane That Shrank the World," BBC, June 19, 2020, https://www.bbc.com/future/article/20180927-the-boeing-747-the-plane-that-shrank-the-world.
10. Cited by Patrick Collison based on personal communication with Tony Fadell at https://patrickcollison.com/fast; Walter Isaacson, *Steve Jobs* (New York: Simon & Schuster, 2011), 384–90.
11. Jason Del Rey, "The Making of Amazon Prime, the Internet's Most Successful and Devastating Membership Program," Vox, May 3, 2019, https://www.vox.com/recode/2019/5/3/18511544/amazon-prime-oral-history-jeff-bezos-one-day-shipping.
12. John Tauranc, *The Empire State Building: The Making of a Landmark* (Ithaca, NY: Cornell University Press, 2014), 153.
13. William F. Lamb, "The Empire State Building," *Architectural Forum* 54, no. 1 (January 1931): 1–7.
14. Empire State Inc., *The Empire State* (New York: Publicity Association, 1931), 21.
15. Carol Willis, *Building the Empire State* (New York: Norton, 1998), 11–12.
16. Tauranc, *The Empire State Building*, 204.
17. Ibid.
18. Benjamin Flowers, *Skyscraper: The Politics and Power of Building New York*

City in the Twentieth Century (Philadelphia: University of Pennsylvania Press, 2009), 14.

1: THINK SLOW, ACT FAST

1. To triangulate inside information and support my memory of events, I have relied on the following sources: Shani Wallis, "Storebaelt Calls on Project Moses for Support," *TunnelTalk,* April 1993, https://www.tunneltalk.com /Denmark-Apr1993-Project-Moses-called-on-to-support-Storebaelt -undersea-rail-link.php; Shani Wallis, "Storebaelt—The Final Chapters," *TunnelTalk,* May 1995, https://www.tunneltalk.com/Denmark-May1995 -Storebaelt-the-final-chapters.php; "Storebaelt Tunnels, Denmark," Constructive Developments, https://sites.google.com/site/constructivedevelop ments/storebaelt-tunnels.
2. De af Folketinget Valgte Statsrevisorer [National Audit Office of Denmark], *Beretning om Storebæltsforbindelsens økonomi,* beretning 4/97 (Copenhagen: Statsrevisoratet, 1998); Bent Flyvbjerg, "Why Mass Media Matter and How to Work with Them: Phronesis and Megaprojects," in *Real Social Science: Applied Phronesis,* eds. Bent Flyvbjerg, Todd Landman, and Sanford Schram (Cambridge, UK: Cambridge University Press, 2012), 95–121.
3. Walter Williams, *Honest Numbers and Democracy* (Washington, DC: Georgetown University Press, 1998).
4. For examples of studies that got the data wrong, see Bent Flyvbjerg et al., "Five Things You Should Know About Cost Overrun," *Transportation Research Part A: Policy and Practice* 118 (December 2018): 174–90.
5. My main collaborator in collecting the first data set of 258 projects was Mette K. Skamris Holm, at the time a doctoral student at Aalborg University and co-author of the main publications about these data. Mette went on to have a brilliant career in planning practice. At the time of writing, she is the city engineer of Aalborg municipality, Denmark.
6. Bent Flyvbjerg, Mette K. Skamris Holm, and Søren L. Buhl, "Underestimating Costs in Public Works Projects: Error or Lie?," *Journal of the American Planning Association* 68, no. 3 (Summer 2002): 279–95; Bent Flyvbjerg, Mette K. Skamris Holm, and Søren L. Buhl, "What Causes Cost Overrun in Transport Infrastructure Projects?," *Transport Reviews* 24, no. 1 (January 2004): 3–18; Bent Flyvbjerg, Mette K. Skamris Holm, and Søren L. Buhl, "How (In)accurate Are Demand Forecasts in Public Works Projects? The Case of Transportation," *Journal of the American Planning Association* 71, no. 2 (Spring 2005): 131–46.
7. Michael Wilson, "Study Finds Steady Overruns in Public Projects," *The New York Times,* July 11, 2002.
8. Here and elsewhere in this book, cost overruns are measured in real terms

(that is, not including inflation), and with a baseline in the final business case (that is, *not* in the early outline or draft business case). This means that the overruns reported are conservative; that is, low. If inflation were included and if the baseline were set in earlier business cases, the overruns would be much higher—sometimes several times higher. In mathematical terms, cost overrun is measured in percent as $O = (C_a/C_e - 1) \times 100$, where O = percentage overrun; C_a = actual outturn cost; C_e = estimated cost at the time of the final investment decision (aka the date of decision to build or final business case), with all costs measured in constant (real) prices. For more detail about how cost overrun is measured and the pitfalls of such measurement, see Flyvbjerg et al., "Five Things You Should Know About Cost Overrun."
9. Bent Flyvbjerg and Alexander Budzier, "Why Your IT Project May Be Riskier Than You Think," *Harvard Business Review* 89, no. 9 (September 2011): 23–25.
10. For an overview, see Appendix A.
11. Bent Flyvbjerg and Dirk W. Bester, "The Cost-Benefit Fallacy: Why Cost-Benefit Analysis Is Broken and How to Fix It," *Journal of Benefit-Cost Analysis* 12, no. 3 (2021): 395–419.
12. Marion van der Kraats, "BER Boss: New Berlin Airport Has Money Only Until Beginning of 2022," *Aviation Pros*, November 1, 2021, https://www.aviationpros.com/airports/news/21244678/ber-boss-new-berlin-airport-has-money-only-until-beginning-of-2022.
13. Bent Flyvbjerg, "Introduction: The Iron Law of Megaproject Management," in *The Oxford Handbook of Megaproject Management*, ed. Bent Flyvbjerg (Oxford, UK: Oxford University Press, 2017), 1–18.
14. Max Roser, Cameron Appel, and Hannah Ritchie, "Human Height," *Our World in Data*, May 2019, https://ourworldindata.org/human-height.
15. The average adult male is 175 centimeters (5 feet, 9 inches) tall. The tallest adult male is 272 centimeters (8 feet, 11 inches) tall. At the time of writing, the wealthiest person in the world was Jeff Bezos, with a net worth of $197.8 billion; average per capita wealth globally was $63,100.
16. See also Bent Flyvbjerg et al., "The Empirical Reality of IT Project Cost Overruns: Discovering a Power-Law Distribution," forthcoming in *Journal of Management Information Systems* 39, no. 3 (Fall 2022).
17. For the mathematically/statistically inclined reader: In probability theory and statistics, kurtosis is a standard measure of the "tailedness" of the probability distribution of a real-valued random variable. The Gaussian (normal) distribution has a kurtosis of 3. Probability distributions with a kurtosis lower than 3 have thinner tails than the Gaussian, which is itself considered thin-tailed. Probability distributions with a kurtosis larger than 3 are considered fat-tailed. The higher above 3 the kurtosis is for a distribution (called "excess kurtosis"), the more fat-tailed the distribution is considered to be. The mathematician Benoit Mandelbrot found a kurtosis of 43.36 in

a pioneering study of daily variations in the Standard & Poor's 500 index between 1970 and 2001—14.5 times more fat-tailed than the Gaussian—which he found alarmingly high in terms of financial risk; see Benoit B. Mandelbrot and Richard L. Hudson, *The (Mis)behavior of Markets* (London: Profile Books, 2008), 96. But Mandelbrot's finding is not particularly high when compared with the kurtosis I have found for percentage cost overruns in information technology projects, which is 642.51, or 214 times more fat-tailed than the Gaussian, or in water projects, with a kurtosis of 182.44. In fact, for the twenty-plus project types for which I have data, only a handful have a kurtosis for cost overrun that indicates a normal or near-normal distribution (the results are similar for schedule overruns and benefit shortfalls, albeit with fewer data). A large majority of project types has a kurtosis higher than 3—often much higher—indicating fat-tailed and very-fat-tailed distributions. Statistics and decision theory further talk about "kurtosis risk," which is the risk that results when a statistical model assumes the normal (or near-normal) distribution but is applied to observations that have a tendency to occasionally be much further (in terms of number of standard deviations) from the average than is expected for a normal distribution. Project management scholarship and practice largely ignore kurtosis risk, which is unfortunate given the extreme levels of kurtosis documented above and which is a root cause of why this type of management so often goes so systematically and spectacularly wrong.

18. Bent Flyvbjerg and Alexander Budzier, "Why Your IT Project May Be Riskier Than You Think."
19. Ibid.
20. "Former SCANA CEO Sentenced to Two Years for Defrauding Ratepayers in Connection with Failed Nuclear Construction Program," US Department of Justice, October 7, 2021, https://www.justice.gov/usao-sc/pr/former-scana-ceo-sentenced-two-years-defrauding-ratepayers-connection-failed-nuclear.
21. *Restoration Home*, season 3, episode 8, BBC, https://www.bbc.co.uk/programmes/b039glq7.
22. Alex Christian, "The Untold Story of the Big Boat That Broke the World," *Wired*, June 22, 2021, https://www.wired.co.uk/article/ever-given-global-supply-chain.
23. Motoko Rich, Stanley Reed, and Jack Ewing, "Clearing the Suez Canal Took Days. Figuring Out the Costs May Take Years," *The New York Times*, March 31, 2021.
24. Charles Perrow, *Normal Accidents: Living with High-Risk Technologies*, updated edition (Princeton, NJ: Princeton University Press, 1999).
25. Henning Larsen, *De skal sige tak! Kulturhistorisk testamente om Operaen* (Copenhagen: People's Press, 2009), 14.
26. Maria Abi-Habib, Oscar Lopez, and Natalie Kitroeff, "Construction Flaws

Led to Mexico City Metro Collapse, Independent Inquiry Shows," *The New York Times*, June 16, 2021; Oscar Lopez, "Faulty Studs Led to Mexico City Metro Collapse, Attorney General Says," *The New York Times*, October 14, 2021.
27. Natalie Kitroeff et al., "Why the Mexico City Metro Collapsed," *The New York Times*, June 13, 2021.
28. Ed Catmull, *Creativity, Inc.: Overcoming the Unseen Forces That Stand in the Way of True Inspiration* (New York: Random House, 2014), 115.
29. Like so many wise words ascribed to Abraham Lincoln, Winston Churchill, Mark Twain, and other notables, this quotation might not be accurate; see https://quoteinvestigator.com/2014/03/29/sharp-axe/.
30. Author interview with Louis Thompson, April 22, 2020. Here and elsewhere in the book, an "author interview" is an interview carried out by one or both of the authors; that is, by Bent Flyvbjerg, Dan Gardner, or both.

2: THE COMMITMENT FALLACY

1. Steve Vogel, *The Pentagon: A History* (New York: Random House, 2007), 11.
2. Ibid., 41.
3. Ibid., 76.
4. Ibid., 49.
5. Strategic misrepresentation is sometimes also called political bias, strategic bias, power bias, or the Machiavelli factor. This bias is a rationalization in which the end justifies the means. The strategy (e.g., to achieve funding) dictates the bias (e.g., make a project look good on paper). Strategic misrepresentation can be traced to agency problems and political-organizational pressures; for instance, competition for scarce funds or jockeying for position. Strategic misrepresentation is deliberate deception, and as such it is lying, per definition; see Bent Flyvbjerg, "Top Ten Behavioral Biases in Project Management: An Overview," *Project Management Journal* 52, no. 6 (December 2021): 531–46; Lawrence R. Jones and Kenneth J. Euske, "Strategic Misrepresentation in Budgeting," *Journal of Public Administration Research and Theory* 1, no. 4 (1991): 437–60; Wolfgang Steinel and Carsten K. W. De Dreu, 2004, "Social Motives and Strategic Misrepresentation in Social Decision Making," *Journal of Personality and Social Psychology* 86, no. 3 (March 1991): 419–34; Ana Guinote and Theresa K. Vescio, eds., *The Social Psychology of Power* (New York: Guilford Press, 2010).
6. Dan Lovallo and Daniel Kahneman, "Delusions of Success: How Optimism Undermines Executives' Decisions," *Harvard Business Review* 81, no. 7 (July 2003), 56–63; Bent Flyvbjerg, "Delusions of Success: Comment on Dan Lovallo and Daniel Kahneman," *Harvard Business Review* 81, no. 12 (December 2003): 121–22.
7. In his 2011 bestseller, *Thinking, Fast and Slow*, Kahneman would write,

"Errors in the initial budget are not always innocent. The authors of unrealistic plans are often driven by the desire to get the plan approved—whether by their superiors or by a client—supported by the knowledge that projects are rarely abandoned unfinished merely because of overruns in costs or completion times" (pp. 250–51). That is clearly not a description of psychological cognitive bias, which is innocent per definition, but of political bias, specifically strategic misrepresentation aimed at getting projects under way. For a more full account of my discussions with Daniel Kahneman about power bias and strategic misrepresentation, see Flyvbjerg, "Top Ten Behavioral Biases in Project Management."

8. Flyvbjerg, "Top Ten Behavioral Biases in Project Management."
9. Optimism is a well-documented cognitive bias. It is the tendency for individuals to be overly bullish about the outcomes of planned actions. The neuroscientist Sharot Tali calls it "one of the greatest deceptions of which the human mind is capable." Whereas strategic misrepresentation is deliberate, optimism bias is nondeliberate. In the grip of optimism, people, including experts, are unaware that they are optimistic. They make decisions based on an ideal vision of the future rather than on a rational weighting of gains, losses, and probabilities. They overestimate benefits and underestimate costs. They involuntarily spin scenarios of success and overlook the potential for mistakes and miscalculations. As a result, plans are unlikely to deliver as expected in terms of benefits and costs. See Tali Sharot, *The Optimism Bias: A Tour of the Irrationally Positive Brain* (New York: Pantheon, 2011), xv; Daniel Kahneman, *Thinking, Fast and Slow* (New York: Farrar, Straus and Giroux, 2011), 255; Flyvbjerg, "Top Ten Behavioral Biases in Project Management."
10. Iain A. McCormick, Frank H. Walkey, and Dianne E. Green, "Comparative Perceptions of Driver Ability—A Confirmation and Expansion," *Accident Analysis & Prevention* 18, no. 3 (June 1986): 205–8.
11. Arnold C. Cooper, Carolyn Y. Woo, and William C. Dunkelberg, "Entrepreneurs' Perceived Chances for Success," *Journal of Business Venturing* 3, no. 2 (Spring 1988): 97–108.
12. Neil D. Weinstein, Stephen E. Marcus, and Richard P. Moser, "Smokers' Unrealistic Optimism About Their Risk," *Tobacco Control* 14, no. 1 (February 2005): 55–59.
13. Kahneman, *Thinking, Fast and Slow*, 257.
14. Keith E. Stanovich and Richard F. West, "Individual Differences in Reasoning: Implications for the Rationality Debate," *Behavioral and Brain Sciences* 23, no. 5 (2000): 645–65.
15. Gerd Gigerenzer, Peter M. Todd, and the ABC Research Group, *Simple Heuristics That Make Us Smart* (Oxford, UK: Oxford University Press, 1999); Gerd Gigerenzer, Ralph Hertwig, and Thorsten Pachur, eds., *Heuristics: The Foundations of Adaptive Behavior* (Oxford, UK: Oxford University

Press, 2011); Gerd Gigerenzer and Wolfgang Gaissmaier, "Heuristic Decision Making," *Annual Review of Psychology* 62, no. 1 (2011): 451–82.
16. Gary Klein, *Sources of Power: How People Make Decisions* (Cambridge, MA: MIT Press, 1999).
17. The planning fallacy is a subcategory of optimism bias that arises from individuals producing plans and estimates that are unrealistically close to best-case scenarios. The term was originally coined by Daniel Kahneman and Amos Tversky to describe the tendency for people to underestimate task completion times. Roger Buehler and his colleagues continued working following this definition. Later, the concept was broadened to cover the tendency for people to, on the one hand, underestimate costs, schedules, and risks for planned actions and, on the other, overestimate benefits and opportunities for those actions. Because the original narrow and later broader concepts are so fundamentally different in the scope they cover, with Cass Sunstein I suggested the term "planning fallacy writ large" for the broader concept, to avoid confusing the two. See Daniel Kahneman and Amos Tversky, "Intuitive Prediction: Biases and Corrective Procedures," in *Studies in the Management Sciences: Forecasting*, vol. 12, eds. Spyros Makridakis and S. C. Wheelwright (Amsterdam: North Holland, 1979), 315; Roger Buehler, Dale Griffin, and Heather MacDonald, "The Role of Motivated Reasoning in Optimistic Time Predictions," *Personality and Social Psychology Bulletin* 23, no. 3 (March 1997): 238–47; Roger Buehler, Dale Wesley Griffin, and Michael Ross, "Exploring the 'Planning Fallacy': Why People Underestimate Their Task Completion Times," *Journal of Personality and Social Psychology* 67, no. 3 (September 1994): 366–81; Bent Flyvbjerg and Cass R. Sunstein, "The Principle of the Malevolent Hiding Hand; or, The Planning Fallacy Writ Large," *Social Research* 83, no. 4 (Winter 2017): 979–1004.
18. Douglas Hofstadter, *Gödel, Escher, Bach: An Eternal Golden Braid* (New York: Basic Books, 1979).
19. Roger Buehler, Dale Griffin, and Johanna Peetz, "The Planning Fallacy: Cognitive, Motivational, and Social Origins," *Advances in Experimental Social Psychology* 43 (2010): 1–62.
20. Dale Wesley Griffin, David Dunning, and Lee Ross, "The Role of Construal Processes in Overconfident Predictions About the Self and Others," *Journal of Personality and Social Psychology* 59, no. 6 (January 1991): 1128–39; Ian R. Newby-Clark et al., "People Focus on Optimistic Scenarios and Disregard Pessimistic Scenarios While Predicting Task Completion Times," *Journal of Experimental Psychology: Applied* 6, no. 3 (October 2000): 171–82.
21. "Leadership Principles," Amazon, https://www.amazon.jobs/en/principles.
22. Francesca Gino and Bradley Staats, "Why Organizations Don't Learn," *Harvard Business Review* 93, no. 10 (November 2015): 110–18.
23. Availability bias is the tendency to overweigh whatever comes to mind. Availability is influenced by the recency of memories and by how unusual

or emotionally charged they may be, with more recent, more unusual, and more emotional memories being more easily recalled. Powerful individuals have been shown to be more susceptible to availability bias than individuals who are not powerful. The causal mechanism seems to be that powerful individuals are affected more strongly by ease of retrieval than by the content they retrieve because they are more likely to "go with the flow" and trust their intuition than individuals who are not powerful. See Mario Weick and Ana Guinote, "When Subjective Experiences Matter: Power Increases Reliance on the Ease of Retrieval," *Journal of Personality and Social Psychology* 94, no. 6 (June 2008): 956–70; Flyvbjerg, "Top Ten Behavioral Biases in Project Management."

24. Jean Nouvel, interview about DR-Byen in *Weekendavisen* (Copenhagen), January 16, 2009, 4.
25. Willie Brown, "When Warriors Travel to China, Ed Lee Will Follow," *San Francisco Chronicle*, July 27, 2013.
26. Personal communication, author's archives.
27. Ibid.
28. George Radwanski, "Olympics Will Show Surplus Mayor Insists," *The Gazette*, January 30, 1973.
29. Brown, "When Warriors Travel to China, Ed Lee Will Follow."
30. Elia Kazan, *A Life* (New York: Da Capo Press, 1997), 412–13.
31. Steven Bach, *Final Cut: Art, Money, and Ego in the Making of* Heaven's Gate, *the Film That Sank United Artists* (New York: Newmarket Press, 1999), 23.
32. Bent Flyvbjerg and Allison Stewart, "Olympic Proportions: Cost and Cost Overrun at the Olympics, 1960–2012," *Saïd Business School Working Papers*, University of Oxford, 2012.
33. Escalation of commitment is the tendency to justify increased investment in a decision based on the cumulative prior investment, despite new evidence suggesting that the decision may be wrong and additional costs will not be offset by additional benefits. Escalation of commitment applies to individuals, groups, and whole organizations. It was first described by Barry M. Staw in 1976 with later work by Joel Brockner, Barry Staw, Dustin J. Sleesman et al., and Helga Drummond. Economists use related terms like *sunk-cost fallacy* (Arkes and Blumer, 1985) and *lock-in* (Cantarelli et al., 2010) to describe similar phenomena. Escalation of commitment is captured in popular expressions such as "Throwing good money after bad" and "In for a penny, in for a pound." In its original definition, escalation of commitment is unreflected and nondeliberate. As with other cognitive biases, people don't know that they are subject to the bias. However, once you understand the mechanism, it may be used deliberately. See Barry M. Staw, "Knee-Deep in the Big Muddy: A Study of Escalating Commitment to a Chosen Course of Action," *Organizational Behavior and Human Resources* 16, no. 1 (1976): 27–44; Joel Brockner, "The Escalation of Commitment to a Failing Course

of Action: Toward Theoretical Progress," *Academy of Management Review* 17, no. 1 (1992): 39–61; Barry M. Staw, "The Escalation of Commitment: An Update and Appraisal," in *Organizational Decision Making*, ed. Zur Shapira (Cambridge, UK: Cambridge University Press, 1997), 191–215; Dustin J. Sleesman et al., "Cleaning up the Big Muddy: A Meta-analytic Review of the Determinants of Escalation of Commitment," *Academy of Management Journal* 55, no. 3 (2012): 541–62; Helga Drummond, "Is Escalation Always Irrational?," originally published in *Organization Studies* 19, no. 6 (1998), cited in *Megaproject Planning and Management: Essential Readings*, vol. 2, ed. Bent Flyvbjerg (Cheltenham, UK: Edward Elgar, 2014), 291–309; Helga Drummond, "Megaproject Escalation of Commitment: An Update and Appraisal," in *The Oxford Handbook of Megaproject Management*, ed. Bent Flyvbjerg (Oxford, UK: Oxford University Press, 2017), 194–216; Flyvbjerg, "Top Ten Behavioral Biases in Project Management."
34. Sleesman et al., "Cleaning Up the Big Muddy."
35. Richard H. Thaler, *Misbehaving: How Economics Became Behavioural* (London: Allen Lane, 2015), 20.
36. Vogel, *The Pentagon*, 24.
37. Bent Flyvbjerg, Massimo Garbuio, and Dan Lovallo, "Delusion and Deception in Large Infrastructure Projects: Two Models for Explaining and Preventing Executive Disaster," *California Management Review* 51, no. 2 (Winter 2009): 170–93.
38. Vogel, *The Pentagon*, 102.
39. A classic finding of social psychology is that people try to be at least somewhat consistent in their words and deeds, so if we make a commitment—particularly a public commitment—we tend to subsequently behave in ways consistent with that commitment; see Rosanna E. Guadagno and Robert B. Cialdini, "Preference for Consistency and Social Influence: A Review of Current Research Findings," *Social Influence* 5, no. 3 (2010): 152–63; Robert B. Cialdini, *Influence: The Psychology of Persuasion*, new and expanded edition (New York: Harper Business, 2021), 291–362. Publicly committing to complete a process before drawing conclusions can thus be a helping hand in keeping an open mind.

3: THINK FROM RIGHT TO LEFT

1. Author interview with Frank Gehry, March 5, 2021.
2. Academy of Achievement, "Frank Gehry, Academy Class of 1995, Full Interview," YouTube, July 19, 2017, https://www.youtube.com/watch?v=wTElCmNkkKc.
3. Paul Goldberger, *Building Art: The Life and Work of Frank Gehry* (New York: Alfred A. Knopf, 2015), 290–94.
4. Ibid., 290.

5. Ibid., 303. The success in Bilbao was so significant that it gave rise to the phrase "Bilbao effect" to describe economic revitalization resulting from the creation of a spectacular new building. But what happened in Bilbao only repeated what the Sydney Opera House had first done in Sydney, a precedent that was very much on the minds of Basque officials, who explicitly asked Gehry to replicate it. So the phenomenon might be better called the "Sydney effect." Whatever its name, it is rare. Many cities have tried to replicate it, but outside Sydney and Bilbao, the record has generally been one of disappointment.
6. Jason Farago, "Gehry's Quiet Interventions Reshape the Philadelphia Museum," *The New York Times*, May 30, 2021.
7. John B. Robinson, "Futures Under Glass: A Recipe for People Who Hate to Predict," *Futures* 22, no. 8 (1990): 820–42.
8. Peter H. Gleick et al., "California Water 2020: A Sustainable Vision," Pacific Institute, May 1995, http://s3-us-west-2.amazonaws.com/ucldc-nuxeo-ref-media/dd359729-560b-4899-aaa2-1944b7a42e5b.
9. Steve Jobs's full comments, which were prompted by a tough question from the audience, can be seen in the following video: 258t, "Steve Jobs Customer Experience," YouTube, October 16, 2015, https://www.youtube.com/watch?v=r2O5qKZlI50.
10. Steven Levy, "20 Years Ago, Steve Jobs Built the 'Coolest Computer Ever.' It Bombed," *Wired*, July 24, 2020, https://www.wired.com/story/20-years-ago-steve-jobs-built-the-coolest-computer-ever-it-bombed/.
11. Colin Bryar and Bill Carr, *Working Backwards: Insights, Stories, and Secrets from Inside Amazon* (New York: St. Martin's Press, 2021), 98–105; Charles O'Reilly and Andrew J. M. Binns, "The Three Stages of Disruptive Innovation: Idea Generation, Incubation, and Scaling," *California Management Review* 61, no. 3 (May 2019): 49–71.
12. Author interview with Ian McAllister, November 12, 2020.
13. Bryar and Carr, *Working Backwards*, 106–9.
14. Ibid., 158–60.
15. Brad Stone, *Amazon Unbound: Jeff Bezos and the Invention of a Global Empire* (New York: Simon & Schuster, 2021), 40–41.
16. Robert A. Caro, *Working: Researching, Interviewing, Writing* (New York: Vintage Books, 2019), 197–99. From an interview originally published in *Paris Book Review*, Spring 2016.

4: PIXAR PLANNING

1. "World Heritage List: Sydney Opera House," UNESCO, https://whc.unesco.org/en/list/166.
2. Cristina Bechtler, *Frank O. Gehry/Kurt W. Forster* (Ostfildern-Ruit: Hatje Cantz, 1999), 23.

3. Matt Tyrnauer, "Architecture in the Age of Gehry," *Vanity Fair,* June 30, 2010.
4. Paul Goldberger, *Building Art: The Life and Work of Frank Gehry* (New York: Alfred A. Knopf, 2015), 299; Bent Flyvbjerg, "Design by Deception: The Politics of Megaproject Approval," *Harvard Design Magazine,* no. 22 (Spring–Summer 2005): 50–59.
5. Paul Israel, *Edison: A Life of Invention* (New York: John Wiley & Sons, 1998), 167–77.
6. For more on positive and negative learning curves, see Bent Flyvbjerg, "Four Ways to Scale Up: Smart, Dumb, Forced, and Fumbled," *Saïd Business School Working Papers,* University of Oxford, 2021.
7. Peter Murray, *The Saga of the Sydney Opera House* (London: Routledge, 2003), 7–8.
8. Flyvbjerg, "Design by Deception."
9. At the time, engineers concluded that Utzon's original design of the shells could not be built. Decades later, Frank Gehry's team showed that it could in fact have been built if Gehry's CATIA 3D design model had been available to Utzon and his team. The root problem was not that Utzon's design was unbuildable but that the technology to design and build it had not yet been developed.
10. Philip Drew, *The Masterpiece: Jørn Utzon, a Secret Life* (South Yarra, Victoria, Australia: Hardie Grant Books, 2001).
11. It is often claimed that Jørn Utzon was not invited to the Sydney Opera House opening ceremony. It's a good story, which is probably why it persists, including on Wikipedia ("Sydney Opera House," accessed July 9, 2022). But it is false. Utzon was invited. He declined, however, giving as his reason that his attendance might cause embarrassment by reopening the controversy over the building, which would be unfortunate, given the presence of Queen Elizabeth. The opening should be an occasion for joy and celebration, not antagonism, Utzon argued. He also wanted to avoid the media and knew that if he went to Sydney that would be impossible. He explained that under the circumstances not showing up was the most diplomatic thing he could do (Drew, *The Masterpiece,* 432–33). Declining the invitation might have miffed the hosts, however. During my research, I interviewed staff at the Sydney Opera House. They told me that for decades after the opening they had been instructed not to mention Utzon's name when they gave tours of the building (which happens several times a day). Instead, Peter Hall, the Australian architect hired to finish the building, was named as the architect. Only in the 1990s, almost thirty years after Utzon had left Australia, did the world wake up to the neglect and suddenly start showering him with prizes, including the Wolf Prize in Israel, the Sonning Prize in Denmark, and the Pritzker Architecture Prize in the United States. Eventually, a kind of reconciliation was arrived at

when the opera house authorities invited Utzon to prepare design guidelines for future work on the building and Utzon accepted the invitation in August 1999 on the condition that his son Jan Utzon represent him in Australia; see ibid., xiv–xv.
12. Goldberger, *Building Art*, 291–92.
13. CATIA stands for computer-aided three-dimensional interactive application. It is a software suite for computer-aided design (CAD), computer-aided manufacturing (CAM), computer-aided engineering (CAE), 3D modeling, and product lifecycle management (PLM) developed by the French company Dassault Systèmes. It is used in a range of industries, including aerospace and defense. It was adapted to architecture on the initiative of Frank Gehry and his practice. Gehry later renamed his adaption "Digital Project."
14. For a photo of the Vitra Design Museum with the spiral staircase at the back of the building, see https://bit.ly/3n7hrAH.
15. "Looking Back at Frank Gehry's Building-Bending Feats," *PBS NewsHour*, September 11, 2015, https://www.pbs.org/newshour/show/frank-gehry; author interview with Craig Webb, April 23, 2021.
16. "The Seven-Beer Snitch," *The Simpsons*, April 3, 2005.
17. Goldberger, *Building Art*, 377–78.
18. Personal communication with Frank Gehry, author's archives.
19. Architectural Videos, "Frank Gehry Uses CATIA for His Architecture Visions," YouTube, November 2, 2011, https://www.youtube.com/watch?v=UEn53Wr6380.
20. Author interview with Pete Docter, January 7, 2021.
21. Ibid.
22. Sophia Kunthara, "A Closer Look at Theranos' Big-Name Investors, Partners, and Board as Elizabeth Holmes' Criminal Trial Begins," *Crunchbase News*, September 14, 2021, https://news.crunchbase.com/news/theranos-elizabeth-holmes-trial-investors-board/.
23. John Carreyrou, *Bad Blood: Secrets and Lies in a Silicon Valley Startup* (New York: Alfred A. Knopf, 2018), 299; *U.S. v. Elizabeth Holmes, et al.*, https://www.justice.gov/usao-ndca/us-v-elizabeth-holmes-et-al.
24. Leonid Rozenblit and Frank Keil, "The Misunderstood Limits of Folk Science: An Illusion of Explanatory Depth," *Cognitive Science* 26, no. 5 (2002): 521–62; Rebecca Lawson, "The Science of Cycology: Failures to Understand How Everyday Objects Work," *Memory & Cognition* 34, no. 8 (2006): 1667–75.
25. Eric Ries, *The Lean Startup* (New York: Currency, 2011).
26. United States Congress, House Committee on Science and Astronautics, "1974 NASA Authorization Hearings," 93rd Congress, first session, on H.R. 4567, US Government Printing Office, 1, 271.
27. Author interview with Pete Docter, January 7, 2021.

5: ARE YOU EXPERIENCED?

1. Aristotle, *The Nicomachean Ethics*, translated by J. A. K. Thomson, revised with notes and appendices by Hugh Tredennick, introduction and bibliography by Jonathan Barnes (Harmondsworth, UK: Penguin Classics, 1976).
2. Author interview with Lou Thompson, chairman of the California High-Speed Rail Peer Review Group, June 4, 2020.
3. Lee Berthiaume, "Skyrocketing Shipbuilding Costs Continue as Estimate Puts Icebreaker Price at $7.25B," *The Canadian Press*, December 16, 2021.
4. The Danish name for the Danish Court Administration is Domstolsstyrelsen. I was on its board of directors, which holds ultimate responsibility for running the courts.
5. Uniqueness bias was originally identified by psychologists as the tendency of individuals to see themselves as more singular than they actually are; e.g., singularly healthy, clever, or attractive. In project planning and management, I first used the term in my 2014 paper "What You Should Know About Megaprojects and Why" in *Project Management Journal*, where I defined uniqueness bias as the tendency of planners and managers to see their projects as singular. It is a general bias, but it turns out to be particularly rewarding as an object of study in project management because project planners and managers are systematically primed to see their projects as unique; see Bent Flyvbjerg, "What You Should Know About Megaprojects and Why: An Overview," *Project Management Journal* 45, no. 2 (April–May 2014): 6–19; Bent Flyvbjerg, "Top Ten Behavioral Biases in Project Management: An Overview," *Project Management Journal* 52, no. 6 (2021), 531–46; Bent Flyvbjerg, Alexander Budzier, Maria D. Christodoulou, and M. Zottoli, "So You Think Projects Are Unique? How Uniqueness Bias Undermines Project Management," under review.
6. Marvin B. Lieberman and David B. Montgomery, "First-Mover Advantages," *Strategic Management Journal* 9, no. 51 (Summer 1988): 41–58.
7. Peter N. Golder and Gerard J. Tellis, "Pioneer Advantage: Marketing Logic or Marketing Legend?," *Journal of Marketing Research* 30, no. 2 (May 1993): 158–70.
8. Fernando F. Suarez and Gianvito Lanzolla, "The Half-Truth of First-Mover Advantage," *Harvard Business Review* 83, no. 4 (April 2005): 121–27; Marvin Lieberman, "First-Mover Advantage," in *Palgrave Encyclopedia of Strategic Management*, eds. Mie Augier and David J. Teece (London: Palgrave Macmillan, 2018), 559–62.
9. *Oxford Dictionary of Quotations*, 8th ed., ed. Elizabeth Knowles (New York: Oxford University Press, 2014), 557.
10. Bent Flyvbjerg, Alexander Budzier, and Daniel Lunn, "Regression to the

Tail: Why the Olympics Blow Up," *Environment and Planning A: Economy and Space* 53, no. 2 (March 2021): 233–60.
11. Ibid.
12. Ashish Patel, Paul A. Bosela, and Norbert J. Delatte, "1976 Montreal Olympics: Case Study of Project Management Failure," *Journal of Performance of Constructed Facilities* 27, no. 3 (2013): 362–69.
13. Ibid.
14. For photos and contemporary news reports, see Andy Riga, "Montreal Olympic Photo Flashback: Stadium Was Roofless at 1976 Games," *Montreal Gazette*, July 21, 2016.
15. Brendan Kelly, "Olympic Stadium Architect Remembered as a Man of Vision," *Montreal Gazette*, October 3, 2019.
16. Rafael Sacks and Rebecca Partouche, "Empire State Building Project: Archetype of 'Mass Construction,'" *Journal of Construction Engineering and Management* 136, no. 6 (June 2010): 702–10.
17. William F. Lamb, "The Empire State Building; Shreve, Lamb & Harmon, Architects: VII. The General Design," *Architectural Forum* 54, no. 1 (January 1931), 1–7.
18. Mattias Jacobsson and Timothy L. Wilson, "Revisiting the Construction of the Empire State Building: Have We Forgotten Something?," *Business Horizons* 61, no. 1 (October 2017): 47–57; John Tauranac, *The Empire State Building: The Making of a Landmark* (Ithaca, NY: Cornell University Press, 2014), 204.
19. Carol Willis, *Form Follows Finance: Skyscrapers and Skylines in New York and Chicago* (Princeton, NJ: Princeton Architectural Press, 1995), 95.
20. Catherine W. Bishir, "Shreve and Lamb (1924–1970s)," North Carolina Architects & Builders: A Biographical Dictionary, 2009, https://ncarchitects.lib.ncsu.edu/people/P000414.
21. Michael Polanyi, *The Tacit Dimension* (Chicago: University of Chicago Press, 1966), 4.
22. Malcolm Gladwell, *Blink: The Power of Thinking Without Thinking* (New York: Back Bay Books, 2007), 1–5.
23. Psychologists have long tended to divide into two seemingly contradictory schools of thought on intuition. One school, known as "heuristics and biases" and led by Daniel Kahneman, relies mostly on laboratory experiments to show how the fast thinking of intuition can mislead. The other, known as "naturalistic decision making" (NDM), studies how experienced people make decisions in workplaces and has shown that intuition can be an excellent basis for judgments—like an experienced nurse who senses something is wrong with a newborn baby even though instruments and protocols suggest that the baby is fine. The psychologist Gary Klein is the dean of the latter school. In 2009, Kahneman and Klein published a joint

paper that concluded that the two schools are actually in fundamental agreement. They also outlined the conditions required for skilled intuition to develop. See Daniel Kahneman and Gary Klein, "Conditions for Intuitive Expertise: A Failure to Disagree," *American Psychologist* 64, no. 6 (September 2009): 515–26. For an overview of naturalistic decision making and the research on skilled intuition, see Gary Klein, "A Naturalistic Decision-Making Perspective on Studying Intuitive Decision Making," *Journal of Applied Research in Memory and Cognition* 4, no. 3 (September 2015): 164–68; see also Gary Klein, *Sources of Power: How People Make Decisions* (Cambridge, MA: MIT Press, 1999).

24. It should be emphasized that the cost and schedule overruns on the Walt Disney Concert Hall were not due to Frank Gehry's lack of planning, although he was often blamed. Gehry was forced off the Disney Concert Hall project after the design development phase, when the client decided to give the project to an executive architect it thought would be better at producing construction documents and doing construction administration. The executive architect failed, which was a main cause of the delays and overruns on the Disney Concert Hall. In fact, when Gehry was later brought back in, he delivered the Disney Concert Hall on budget, compared with the budget estimated at the start of construction, according to Gehry's biographer Paul Goldberger and Stephen Rountree, president of Music Center, Los Angeles, and owner of the Disney Concert Hall. See Paul Goldberger, *Building Art: The Life and Work of Frank Gehry* (New York: Alfred A. Knopf, 2015), 322; Stephen D. Rountree, "Letter to the Editor, Jan Tuchman, Engineering News Record," Music Center, Los Angeles, April 1, 2010.

The Walt Disney Concert Hall has a special place in Frank Gehry's career as his near nemesis and as the project that taught him how to protect his designs from being undermined by politics and business. The Disney Concert Hall was Gehry's "near-Utzon experience," in the sense that it threatened to undo his career, as the Sydney Opera House undid Utzon's. There was a major difference, however, that saved Gehry, but only just: When trouble hit Gehry, he could not flee back home as Utzon had, because he was home already. He lived and worked in Los Angeles, just a few miles down the freeway from the Disney Concert Hall. As a consequence, when the project went wrong, he became a pariah in his own hometown. For years he was hammered by the local press. He could not go out without being accosted by people, who would blame him for the Disney Concert Hall debacle or express their sympathy with his unhappy fate, both of which equally annoyed Gehry. "They were all out to get me here [in Los Angeles] because I'm the local guy," he later explained in an interview, "so they started a barrage coming at me" (quoted in Frank Gehry, *Gehry Talks: Architecture + Process*, ed. Mildred Friedman [London: Thames & Hudson,

2003], 114). Almost ten years after the fact, Gehry still called that period the "darkest times" of his life and said, "I have a lot of wounds from the process"; see Frank O. Gehry, "Introduction," in *Symphony: Frank Gehry's Walt Disney Concert Hall*, ed. Gloria Gerace (New York: Harry N. Abrams, 2003), 15. The nadir came in 1997, when after nine years of work on the Disney Concert Hall, the political and business leaders in charge tried to oust Gehry and have someone else complete his designs and drawings. That was the final straw. For a while Gehry thought the project was over as far as he was concerned, and he considered leaving Los Angeles altogether.

However, Walt Disney's widow, Lillian Disney, was a main sponsor of the project, and the Disney family now stepped in with its power and money on the side of Gehry. The Disney Concert Hall had turned into a scandal, to be sure, but after the dust settled, Gehry's position in the project had been strengthened and he was at last in charge of design and the final drawings. The Disney family's spokesperson, Lillian and Walt Disney's daughter Diane Disney Miller, issued a statement saying, "We promised Los Angeles a Frank Gehry building, and that's what we intend to deliver"; see Richard Koshalek and Dana Hutt, "The Impossible Becomes Possible: The Making of Walt Disney Concert Hall," in *Symphony*, page 57. Unlike Utzon in Sydney, Gehry had powerful supporters in Los Angeles who defended him when the attacks got out of hand. That ultimately saved him and his designs for the Disney Concert Hall.

But Gehry was also lucky regarding his timing. His lowest point with the Disney Concert Hall happened to coincide with his rise to international superstardom with the opening in 1997 of the Guggenheim Museum in Bilbao, Spain. That building was immediately and globally recognized as a sensation in modern design, moving architecture to new levels of artistic expression, as mentioned in the main text. Because of the controversy and delays with the Disney Concert Hall, although the Guggenheim Bilbao was started three years after the Disney Concert Hall, it was completed six years before it. The Guggenheim Bilbao therefore forced the issue with political and business leaders in Los Angeles, with local media, and with the general public that if Gehry could build world-class architecture on time and budget in faraway Bilbao, perhaps he could do the same at home in Los Angeles. Gehry was finally given the responsibility for completing the Disney Concert Hall, and there were no new cost overruns and scandals on the $274 million project from the time his office took charge until completion in 2003. Just as important, the Walt Disney Concert Hall was instantly and broadly recognized as "the most astonishing masterpiece of public architecture ever built in Los Angeles"; see Koshalek and Hutt, "The Impossible Becomes Possible," 58.

So is all well that ends well? This is the conventional view of scandal in architecture. After all, the finished building will typically remain for a century or more, whereas the hardships and scandals that went into its making will soon be forgotten. People fall, buildings stand. From this point of view, projects such as the Walt Disney Concert Hall and the Sydney Opera House are successes despite the turmoil and grief they involved. Not to Gehry, however. Here, too, he is unconventional. His lesson from the Disney Concert Hall was *Never again!* He was uncomfortably aware that luck and circumstance had saved him from the fate of Utzon. Never again would he risk his livelihood and that of his partners. Never again would he endure the abuse and "darkness" he had been subjected to by the Disney Concert Hall. During the long gestation process of the hall, Gehry came to see that it is both unintelligent and unnecessary to take the kind of risks and accept the kind of mistreatment he had. Cost overruns, delays, controversy, reputational damage, and placing one's career and business at risk are not inevitable ingredients in building a masterpiece, Gehry learned. Slowly—blow by blow at the Disney Concert Hall, triumph by triumph in Bilbao and elsewhere—it dawned on Gehry that there is a different way to organize design and construction, where he would stay in control instead of becoming marginalized and "infantilized," as he calls it. Gehry coined a term for the new setup he eventually developed: "the organization of the artist," put in print for the first time in *Harvard Design Magazine;* see Bent Flyvbjerg, "Design by Deception: The Politics of Megaproject Approval," *Harvard Design Magazine,* no. 22 (Spring–Summer 2005): 50–59. Gehry has used this setup on every project since the Disney Concert Hall to deliver sublime architecture on time and on budget.

25. Aristotle, *The Nicomachean Ethics,* translated by J. A. K. Thomson, revised with notes and appendices by Hugh Tredennick, introduction and bibliography by Jonathan Barnes (Harmondsworth, UK: Penguin Classics, 1976), 1144b33–1145a11. For a more extensive account of the importance of *phronesis* in human knowledge and action, see Bent Flyvbjerg, *Making Social Science Matter: Why Social Inquiry Fails and How It Can Succeed Again* (Cambridge, UK: Cambridge University Press, 2001).

6: SO YOU THINK YOUR PROJECT IS UNIQUE?

1. I did my work on XRL with a core team consisting of Professor Tsung-Chung Kao, Dr. Alexander Budzier, and myself, assisted by a wider team of MTR experts. The work is reported in Bent Flyvbjerg and Tsung-Chung Kao with Alexander Budzier, "Report to the Independent Board Committee on the Hong Kong Express Rail Link Project," in MTR Independent Board Committee, *Second Report by the Independent Board Committee on the Express Rail Link Project* (Hong Kong: MTR, 2014), A1–A122.
2. Robert Caro, *Working: Researching, Interviewing, Writing* (New York: Vintage Books, 2019), 71–77.

3. Ibid., 74.
4. Ibid., 72.
5. Ibid., 76–77.
6. Anchoring is the tendency to rely too heavily, or "anchor," on one piece of information when making decisions. The human brain will anchor on almost anything, as illustrated in the main text, whether random numbers, previous experience, or false information. It has proven difficult to avoid this. Therefore, the most effective way of dealing with anchoring seems to be not to avoid it but to make sure the brain anchors in relevant information before making decisions; e.g., in base rates that are pertinent to the decision at hand. This advice is similar to recommending that gamblers know the objective odds of the game they play to increase their chances of winning and limit their losses. It is sound advice but often goes unheeded. See Timothy D. Wilson et al., "A New Look at Anchoring Effects: Basic Anchoring and Its Antecedents," *Journal of Experimental Psychology: General* 125, no. 4 (1996): 387–402; Nicholas Epley and Thomas Gilovich, "The Anchoring-and-Adjustment Heuristic: Why the Adjustments Are Insufficient," *Psychological Science* 17, no. 4 (2006): 311–18; Joseph P. Simmons, Robyn A. LeBoeuf, and Leif D. Nelson, "The Effect of Accuracy Motivation on Anchoring and Adjustment: Do People Adjust from Provided Anchors?," *Journal of Personality and Social Psychology* 99, no. 6 (2010): 917–32; Bent Flyvbjerg, "Top Ten Behavioral Biases in Project Management: An Overview," *Project Management Journal* 52, no. 6 (2021): 531–46.
7. Amos Tversky and Daniel Kahneman, "Judgment Under Uncertainty: Heuristics and Biases," *Science* 185, no. 4157 (1974): 1124–31; see also Gretchen B. Chapman and Eric J. Johnson, "Anchoring, Activation, and the Construction of Values," *Organizational Behavior and Human Decision Processes* 79, no. 2 (1999): 115–53; Drew Fudenberg, David K. Levine, and Zacharias Maniadis, "On the Robustness of Anchoring Effects in WTP and WTA Experiments," *American Economic Journal: Microeconomics* 4, no. 2 (2012): 131–45; Wilson et al., "A New Look at Anchoring Effects"; Epley and Gilovich, "The Anchoring-and-Adjustment Heuristic."
8. Daniel Kahneman and Amos Tversky, "Intuitive Prediction: Biases and Corrective Procedures," *Studies in Management Sciences* 12 (1979): 318.
9. Flyvbjerg, "Top Ten Behavioral Biases in Project Management"; Bent Flyvbjerg, Alexander Budzier, Maria D. Christodoulou, and M. Zottoli, "So You Think Projects Are Unique? How Uniqueness Bias Undermines Project Management," under review. See also Jerry Suls and Choi K. Wan, "In Search of the False Uniqueness Phenomenon: Fear and Estimates of Social Consensus," *Journal of Personality and Social Psychology* 52 (1987): 211–17; Jerry Suls, Choi K. Wan, and Glenn S. Sanders, "False Consensus and False Uniqueness in Estimating the Prevalence of Health-Protective Behaviors," *Journal of Applied Social Psychology* 18 (1988): 66–79; George R. Goethals,

David M. Messick, and Scott Allison, "The Uniqueness Bias: Studies in Constructive Social Comparison," in *Social Comparison: Contemporary Theory and Research*, eds. Jerry Suls and T. A. Wills (Hillsdale, NJ: Erlbaum, 1991), 149–76.

10. Secretary of Defense Donald Rumsfeld used the term *unknown unknowns* at a US Department of Defense (DoD) news briefing on February 12, 2002. See "DoD News Briefing: Secretary Rumsfeld and Gen. Myers," US Department of Defense, February 12, 2002, https://archive.ph/20180320091111/http://archive.defense.gov/Transcripts/Transcript.aspx?TranscriptID=2636#selection-401.0-401.53.

11. Bent Flyvbjerg, Carsten Glenting, and Arne Kvist Rønnest, *Procedures for Dealing with Optimism Bias in Transport Planning: Guidance Document* (London: UK Department for Transport, 2004); Bent Flyvbjerg, "From Nobel Prize to Project Management: Getting Risks Right," *Project Management Journal* 37, no. 3 (August 2006): 5–15.

12. The development and use of reference-class forecasting in UK government projects is documented in the following publications: HM Treasury, *The Green Book: Appraisal and Evaluation in Central Government*, Treasury Guidance (London: TSO, 2003); HM Treasury, *Supplementary Green Book Guidance: Optimism Bias* (London: HM Treasury, 2003); Flyvbjerg et al., *Procedures for Dealing with Optimism Bias in Transport Planning*; Ove Arup and Partners Scotland, *Scottish Parliament, Edinburgh Tram Line 2 Review of Business Case* (West Lothian, Scotland: Ove Arup and Partners, 2004); HM Treasury, *The Orange Book. Management of Risk: Principles and Concepts* (London: HM Treasury, 2004); UK Department for Transport, *The Estimation and Treatment of Scheme Costs: Transport Analysis Guidance*, TAG Unit 3.5.9, October 2006; UK Department for Transport, *Changes to the Policy on Funding Major Projects* (London: Department for Transport); UK National Audit Office, 2009, "Note on Optimism Bias," Lords Economic Affairs Committee Inquiry on Private Finance and Off-Balance Sheet Funding, November 2009; HM Treasury, *The Green Book: Appraisal and Evaluation in Central Government* (2003 edition with 2011 amendments) (London: HM Treasury, 2011); UK National Audit Office, NAO, *Over-optimism in Government Projects* (London: UK National Audit Office, 2013); HM Treasury, "Supplementary Green Book Guidance: Optimism Bias," April 2013, https://assets.publishing.service.gov.uk/government/uploads/system/uploads/attachment_data/file/191507/Optimism_bias.pdf; HM Treasury, "Early Financial Cost Estimates of Infrastructure Programmes and Projects and the Treatment of Uncertainty and Risk," March 26, 2015; Bert De Reyck et al., "Optimism Bias Study: Recommended Adjustments to Optimism Bias Uplifts," UK Department for Transport, https://assets.publishing.service.gov.uk/government/uploads/system/uploads/attachment_data/file

/576976/dft-optimism-bias-study.pdf; UK Infrastructure and Projects Authority, *Improving Infrastructure Delivery: Project Initiation Routemap* (London: Crown, 2016); Bert De Reyck et al., "Optimism Bias Study: Recommended Adjustments to Optimism Bias Uplifts," update, Department for Transport, London, 2017; HM Treasury, *The Green Book: Central Government Guidance on Appraisal and Evaluation* (London: Crown, 2018); HM Treasury, *The Orange Book. Management of Risk: Principles and Concepts* (London: HM Treasury, 2019); HM Treasury, *The Green Book: Central Government Guidance on Appraisal and Evaluation* (London: HM Treasury, 2020). Preliminary research showed that RCF worked. In 2006, the UK government made the new forecasting method mandatory on all big transport infrastructure projects; see UK Department for Transport, *The Estimation and Treatment of Scheme Costs: Transport Analysis Guidance*, TAG Unit 3.5.9, 2006; UK Department for Transport, *Changes to the Policy on Funding Major Projects* (London: Department for Transport, 2006); UK Department for Transport and Oxford Global Projects, *Updating the Evidence Behind the Optimism Bias Uplifts for Transport Appraisals: 2020 Data Update to the 2004 Guidance Document "Procedures for Dealing with Optimism Bias in Transport Planning"* (London: UK Department for Transport, 2020).

13. Transport- og Energiministeriet [Danish Ministry for Transport and Energy], *Aktstykke om nye budgetteringsprincipper* [Act on New Principles for Budgeting], Aktstykke nr. 16, Finansudvalget, Folketinget, Copenhagen, October 24, 2006; Transport- og Energiministeriet, "Ny anlægsbudgettering på Transportministeriets område, herunder om økonomistyrings–model og risikohåndtering for anlægsprojekter," Copenhagen, November 18, 2008; Danish Ministry of Transport, Building, and Housing, *Hovednotatet for Ny Anlægsbudgettering: Ny anlægsbudgettering på Transport-, Bygnings- og Boligministeriets område, herunder om økonomistyringsmodel og risikohåndtering for anlægsprojekter* (Copenhagen: Danish Ministry of Transport, Building, and Housing, 2017).

14. National Research Council, *Metropolitan Travel Forecasting: Current Practice and Future Direction*, Special Report no. 288 (Washington, DC: Committee for Determination of the State of the Practice in Metropolitan Area Travel Forecasting and Transportation Research Board, 2007); French Ministry of Transport, *Ex-Post Evaluation of French Road Projects: Main Results* (Paris: French Ministry of Transport, 2007); Bent Flyvbjerg, Chikeung Hon, and Wing Huen Fok, "Reference-Class Forecasting for Hong Kong's Major Roadworks Projects," *Proceedings of the Institution of Civil Engineers* 169, no. CE6 (November 2016): 17–24; Australian Transport and Infrastructure Council, *Optimism Bias* (Canberra: Commonwealth of Australia, 2018); New Zealand Treasury, *Better Business Cases: Guide to Developing a Detailed Business Case* (Wellington, NZ: Crown, 2018); Irish

Department of Public Expenditure and Reform, *Public Spending Code: A Guide to Evaluating, Planning and Managing Public Investment* (Dublin: Irish Department of Public Expenditure and Reform, 2019).

15. Jordy Batselier and Mario Vanhoucke, "Practical Application and Empirical Evaluation of Reference-Class Forecasting for Project Management," *Project Management Journal* 47, no. 5 (2016): 36; further documentation of RCF accuracy can be found in Li Liu and Zigrid Napier, "The Accuracy of Risk-Based Cost Estimation for Water Infrastructure Projects: Preliminary Evidence from Australian Projects," *Construction Management and Economics* 28, no. 1 (2010): 89–100; Li Liu, George Wehbe, and Jonathan Sisovic, "The Accuracy of Hybrid Estimating Approaches: A Case Study of an Australian State Road and Traffic Authority," *The Engineering Economist* 55, no. 3 (2010): 225–45; Byung-Cheol Kim and Kenneth F. Reinschmidt, "Combination of Project Cost Forecasts in Earned Value Management," *Journal of Construction Engineering and Management* 137, no. 11 (2011): 958–66; Robert F. Bordley, "Reference-Class Forecasting: Resolving Its Challenge to Statistical Modeling," *The American Statistician* 68, no. 4 (2014): 221–29; Omotola Awojobi and Glenn P. Jenkins, "Managing the Cost Overrun Risks of Hydroelectric Dams: An Application of Reference-Class Forecasting Techniques," *Renewable and Sustainable Energy Reviews* 63 (September 2016): 19–32; Welton Chang et al., "Developing Expert Political Judgment: The Impact of Training and Practice on Judgmental Accuracy in Geopolitical Forecasting Tournaments," *Judgment and Decision Making* 11, no. 5 (September 2016): 509–26; Jordy Batselier and Mario Vanhoucke, "Improving Project Forecast Accuracy by Integrating Earned Value Management with Exponential Smoothing and Reference-Class Forecasting," *International Journal of Project Management* 35, no. 1 (2017): 28–43.
16. Daniel Kahneman, *Thinking, Fast and Slow* (New York: Farrar, Straus and Giroux, 2011), 251.
17. If you think your planned project will be affected by more and bigger unknown unknowns than the projects in the reference class, you add contingencies, building in buffers of time or money; again, this is anchoring and adjustment. For example, if climate change is increasing flooding risk, that may not be reflected in the reference-class data because they are historical; therefore your adjustment must be larger than the reference class indicates. If you think your project will be less affected than the reference class, you subtract. But be warned: This will reintroduce subjective judgment to the mix, which risks reintroducing optimism bias. Careful, self-critical analysis—and data—are essential.
18. See chapter 1 and Bent Flyvbjerg, "Quality Control and Due Diligence in Project Management: Getting Decisions Right by Taking the Outside View," *International Journal of Project Management* 31, no. 5 (May 2013): 760–74.

19. Kahneman, *Thinking, Fast and Slow*, 245–47.
20. Bent Flyvbjerg, Nils Bruzelius, and Werner Rothengatter, *Megaprojects and Risk: An Anatomy of Ambition* (Cambridge, UK: Cambridge University Press, 2003).
21. Statens Offentlige Utredninger (SOU), *Betalningsansvaret för kärnavfallet* (Stockholm: Statens Offentlige Utredninger, 2004), 125.
22. Bent Flyvbjerg, "The Law of Regression to the Tail: How to Survive Covid-19, the Climate Crisis, and Other Disasters," *Environmental Science and Policy* 114 (December 2020): 614–18. For the mathematically and statistically inclined reader: A power law distribution with an alpha value of 1 or lower has an infinite (nonexistent) mean. If the alpha value is 2 or lower, variance is infinite (nonexistent), resulting in unstable sample means, making forecasting impossible. As a conservative heuristic, Nassim Nicholas Taleb and his colleagues recommend considering variables with an alpha value of 2.5 or less as not forecastable in practice. For such variables, the sample mean will be too unstable and will require too much data for forecasts to be reliable or even practical. To illustrate, they mention the fact that 10^{14} observations would be needed for the sample mean of a Pareto 80/20 distribution, with an alpha value of 1.13, to be as reliable as the sample mean of just thirty observations from a Gaussian (normal) distribution; see Nassim Nicholas Taleb, Yaneer Bar-Yam, and Pasquale Cirillo, "On Single Point Forecasts for Fat-Tailed Variables," *International Journal of Forecasting* 38 (2022): 413–22. In short, for fat-tailed phenomena, cost-benefit analysis, risk assessment, and other forecasting will be neither reliable nor practical.
23. Project planners and scholars have generally been trained to assume that project performance follows regression to the mean. This is unfortunate, because the data do not support the assumption; project performance in fact follows regression to the tail for many kinds of projects; see Flyvbjerg, "The Law of Regression to the Tail." Project planners and managers must therefore understand regression to the tail in order to deliver their projects successfully.

    Sir Francis Galton coined the term *regression to the mean*—or *regression towards mediocrity*, as he originally called it; see Francis Galton, "Regression Towards Mediocrity in Hereditary Stature," *The Journal of the Anthropological Institute of Great Britain and Ireland* 15 (1886), 246–63. It is now a widely used concept in statistics and statistical modeling, describing how measurements of a sample mean will tend toward the population mean when done in sufficient numbers, although there may be large variations in individual measurements. Galton illustrated his principle by the example that parents who are tall tend to have children who grow up to be shorter than their parents, closer to the mean of the population, and vice versa for short parents. Today we know that Galton's example is flawed, because the height of a child is not statistically independent of the height of its parents, due to genetics unknown to Galton. Nevertheless, we understand what Galton was trying to prove, and it turns out that he was right. In a statistically more correct example of Galton's principle, with statistically independent events, a roulette wheel with a 50:50 chance of red or black can show red five times in a row—in fact, it will do this in 3 percent of any five consecutive spins of the wheel—yet the odds are 50:50 for red versus black in ensuing spins. Therefore, the more spins of the wheel that are done, the closer the outcome will be to 50:50 red to black, even when one starts with five consecutive reds. When done in large numbers, the average outcome of spins regresses to its expected mean as the number is increased, no matter what the starting point was.

There is nothing as practical as a theory that is correct. Regression to the mean has been proven mathematically for many types of statistics, and it is highly useful in health, insurance, and schools, on factory floors, in casinos, and in risk management; e.g., for flight safety. Much of statistics and statistical modeling builds on regression to the mean, including the law of large numbers, sampling, standard deviations, and conventional tests of statistical significance. Anyone who has done a basic statistics course has been trained in regression to the mean, whether they are aware of it or not. But regression to the mean presupposes that a population mean exists. For some random events of great consequence, this is not the case.

For example, the size distributions of earthquakes, floods, wildfires, pandemics, wars, and terrorist attacks have no population mean, or the mean is ill defined due to infinite variance. In other words, mean and variance do not exist. Regression to the mean is a meaningless concept for such phenomena, whereas regression to the tail is meaningful and consequential. A distribution must have a nonvanishing probability density toward infinity (or minus infinity) for regression to the tail to occur in data sampled from it. This nonvanishing probability density toward infinity looks like a tail on a graph of the distribution. Regression to the tail occurs only for distributions with infinite variance. The frequency of new extremes and the amount by which a new extreme exceeds the previous extreme indicate whether the underlying distribution that data are sampled from has an expected value and finite variance, or infinite variance and hence no well-defined expected value. In the latter case, "regression to the mean" means regression to infinity; i.e., there *is* no mean value in the conventional sense. Ever better attempts to estimate the mean with conventional methods (i.e., by the mean values of a sample) will yield ever larger values, which is to say values in the tail.

I have named this phenomenon—that events appear in the tail in sufficient size and frequency for the mean *not* to converge—"the law of regression to the tail"; see Flyvbjerg, 2020, "The Law of Regression to the Tail." The law depicts a situation with extreme events, and no matter how extreme

the most extreme event is, there will always be an event even more extreme. It is only a matter of time (or a larger sample) until it appears. Earthquake size is an archetypical example of a phenomenon that follows the law of regression to the tail. So are forest fires and floods. But the law applies not only to extreme natural and social phenomena. My data show that it applies to everyday project planning and management, too, from ordinary IT projects to Olympic Games to nuclear power plants and big dams; see Bent Flyvbjerg et al., "The Empirical Reality of IT Project Cost Overruns: Discovering a Power-Law Distribution," accepted for publication in *Journal of Management Information Systems* 39, no. 3 (Fall 2022); Bent Flyvbjerg, Alexander Budzier, and Daniel Lunn, 2021, "Regression to the Tail: Why the Olympics Blow Up," *Environment and Planning A: Economy and Space* 53, no. 2 (March 2021): 233–60. Or to put the matter differently: Project planning and management behave like extreme natural and social phenomena, although planners and managers largely ignore this and treat projects as if they abide by regression to the mean, which in and of itself goes a long way toward explaining the dismal performance of most projects.
24. This is where the standard 10 to 15 percent contingency that is found in much conventional project management comes from. It builds on the assumption of a normal distribution. But this assumption is typically not met in reality, as explained in the main text. The assumption is therefore generally misguided.
25. Flyvbjerg, "The Law of Regression to the Tail."
26. HS2 was under construction at the time of writing.
27. "Exploring Our Past, Preparing for the Future," HS2, 2022, https://www.hs2.org.uk/building-hs2/archaeology/.
28. *Journal of the House of Representatives of the United States*, 77th Congress, Second Session, January 5, 1942 (Washington, DC: US Government Printing Office), 6.
29. Author interview with Jim Lasko, June 3, 2020; Hal Dardick, "Ald. Burke Calls Great Chicago Fire Festival a 'Fiasco,'" *Chicago Tribune*, October 6, 2014.
30. Statistical tests ensured that only projects that were statistically similar in terms of cost and schedule overruns were included. See full account in Bent Flyvbjerg et al., "Report to the Independent Board Committee on the Hong Kong Express Rail Link Project," in MTR Independent Board Committee, *Second Report by the Independent Board Committee on the Express Rail Link Project* (Hong Kong: MTR, 2014), A1–A122.
31. The highest level of insurance against overrun a client has ever asked my team and me to model is 95 percent, which resulted in humongous contingencies. This is because the marginal cost of insurance increases with the level of insurance. The client wanted to be *really* safe for political reasons. Under normal circumstances, I do not recommend insurance above approx-

imately 80 percent for big stand-alone projects such as XRL, because it's simply too expensive and the funds an organization sets aside for contingencies cannot be used for more productive purposes elsewhere in the organization. For portfolio managers who are responsible for many projects I recommend an even lower level, closer to the mean in the reference class, because the losses on some projects in the portfolio can then be offset by gains on others.

32. Hong Kong Development Bureau, Project Cost Management Office, and Oxford Global Projects, *AI in Action: How The Hong Kong Development Bureau Built the PSS, an Early-Warning-Sign System for Public Works Projects* (Hong Kong: Development Bureau, 2022).

7: CAN IGNORANCE BE YOUR FRIEND?

1. Author interview with Eddie Kramer, May 25, 2020.
2. Author interviews with John Storyk, May 28 and June 2, 2020.
3. Electric Lady Studios, https://electricladystudios.com.
4. *Restoration Home,* season 3, episode 8, BBC, https://www.bbc.co.uk/programmes/b039glq7.
5. Albert O. Hirschman, "The Principle of the Hiding Hand," *The Public Interest,* no. 6 (Winter 1967), 10–23.
6. Malcolm Gladwell, "The Gift of Doubt: Albert O. Hirschman and the Power of Failure," *The New Yorker,* June 17, 2013; Cass R. Sunstein, "An Original Thinker of Our Time," *The New York Review of Books,* May 23, 2013, 14–17.
7. Albert O. Hirschman, *Development Projects Observed,* 3rd ed. (Washington, DC: Brookings Institution, 2015).
8. Michele Alacevich, "Visualizing Uncertainties; or, How Albert Hirschman and the World Bank Disagreed on Project Appraisal and What This Says About the End of 'High Development Theory,'" *Journal of the History of Economic Thought* 36, no. 2 (June 2014): 157.
9. Hirschman was explicit that he saw the described behavior and the Hiding Hand as typical and as a "general principle of action." See Hirschman, *Development Projects Observed,* 1, 3, 7, 13; and "The Principle of the Hiding Hand," *The Public Interest,* 13.
10. This is the story as related by Hirschman. In fact, the paper mill in Bangladesh and several other projects that Hirschman described as successes, saved by the Hiding Hand, turned out to be disasters. The mill operated at a loss throughout the 1970s, becoming a drag on the national economy instead of the boost Hirschman had predicted just years before. The Paz del Río steel mill in Colombia is another example of a major project admired by Hirschman in which the Hiding Hand triggered financial disaster instead of creative solutions. Finally, Nigeria's three-hundred-mile-long

Bornu Railway catalyzed an ethnic conflict that led to secession and a tragic civil war, with hunger and starvation and killings in breakaway Biafra from 1967 to 1970. Privately, it disturbed Hirschman that he had failed to see that a project he had just studied and pronounced a success could have such disastrous consequences so shortly after. But curiously, nowhere does this failure or the fact that project outcomes seemed to run counter to the principle of the Hiding Hand cause Hirschman to critically assess and revise the principle, not even when he wrote a new preface to a later edition of *Development Projects Observed* or when a group of prominent scholars invited him to reflect on the principle. For the full story, with full references, see Bent Flyvbjerg, "The Fallacy of Beneficial Ignorance: A Test of Hirschman's Hiding Hand," *World Development* 84 (April 2016): 176–89.
11. Peter Biskind, *Easy Riders, Raging Bulls* (London: Bloomsbury, 1998), 264–77.
12. Hirschman, *Development Projects Observed*, 1, 3, 7, 13; Hirschman, "The Principle of the Hiding Hand."
13. Flyvbjerg, "The Fallacy of Beneficial Ignorance."
14. Daniel Kahneman, *Thinking, Fast and Slow* (New York: Farrar, Straus and Giroux, 2011), 255.
15. Joseph Campbell, *The Hero with a Thousand Faces* (San Francisco: New World Library, 2008).
16. Bent Flyvbjerg, "Design by Deception: The Politics of Megaproject Approval," *Harvard Design Magazine*, no. 22 (Spring–Summer 2005): 50–59. The term *one-building architect* is used to designate architects known for mainly one building. Utzon did design other buildings than the Sydney Opera House, some of which were built, especially in his home country, Denmark. But they were minor compared with the Sydney Opera House. Internationally (and in Denmark), Utzon is known almost exclusively for the Sydney Opera House. I've asked the question "Can you name a building other than the Sydney Opera House that Jørn Utzon designed?" of at least a thousand people in my lectures on the subject. Very few can, and they are almost always Danish or professional architects or both.
17. Kristin Byron, Deborah Nazarian, and Shalini Khazanchi, "The Relationships Between Stressors and Creativity: A Meta-Analysis Examining Competing Theoretical Models," *Journal of Applied Psychology* 95, no. 1 (2010): 201–12.

8: A SINGLE, DETERMINED ORGANISM

1. Joseph E. Stevens, *Hoover Dam: An American Adventure* (Norman: University of Oklahoma Press, 1988); Michael Hiltzik, *Colossus: Hoover Dam and the Making of the American Century* (New York: Free Press, 2010).
2. Bent Flyvbjerg and Alexander Budzier, *Report for the Commission of Inquiry*

Respecting the Muskrat Falls Project (St. John's, Province of Newfoundland and Labrador, Canada: Muskrat Falls Inquiry, 2018); Richard D. LeBlanc, *Muskrat Falls: A Misguided Project*, 6 vols. (Province of Newfoundland and Labrador, Canada: Commission of Inquiry Respecting the Muskrat Falls Project, 2020).

3. Author interviews with Andrew Wolstenholme, May 27, 2020, May 28, 2021, and January 14, 2022.
4. Andrew Davies, David Gann, and Tony Douglas, "Innovation in Megaprojects: Systems Integration at London Heathrow Terminal 5," *California Management Review* 51, no. 2 (Winter 2009): 101–25.
5. "Your 'Deadline' Won't Kill You: Or Will It?," Merriam-Webster, https://www.merriam-webster.com/words-at-play/your-deadline-wont-kill-you.
6. That change allowed another T5 innovation: rehearsal. When construction of the main terminal building at an airport in Hong Kong suffered a long delay, impacting the entire project, T5 managers decided that they would take the many workers who would erect the T5 main building and the components the workers would assemble to a site in the English countryside. There they practiced the assembly. That rehearsal led to the discovery of challenges and the development of solutions long before the real assembly at Heathrow. It wasn't cheap. But the cost was a fraction of what it would have been if the problems had first surfaced at the worksite and delayed the project.
7. "Rethinking Construction: The Report of the Construction Task Force to the Deputy Prime Minister, John Prescott, on the Scope for Improving the Quality and Efficiency of UK Construction," Constructing Excellence, 1998, https://constructingexcellence.org.uk/wp-content/uploads/2014/10/rethinking_construction_report.pdf.
8. See in particular self-determination theory, the dominant theory of motivation in modern psychology; Richard M. Ryan and Edward L. Deci, *Self-determination Theory: Basic Psychological Needs in Motivation, Development, and Wellness* (New York: Guilford Press, 2017); Marylène Gagné and Edward L. Deci, "Self-determination Theory and Work Motivation," *Journal of Organizational Behavior* 26, no. 4 (2005): 331–62. Consider also the famous natural experiment of the General Motors–Toyota NUMMI joint venture: In the 1970s, a GM plant in Fremont, California, was notorious for being the worst GM had. Productivity and quality were rock bottom. Morale was so low that employees intentionally sabotaged cars. GM closed the plant in 1982. Toyota, which had no North American manufacturing capability at the time, proposed a joint venture that would see the plant reopen and operate using the same machinery and mostly the same workers. But Toyota would manage using its methods, which famously respected and empowered workers. Morale soared; absenteeism and turnover plunged. Production quality improved dramatically, and productivity soared so much

that output doubled while the cost per vehicle declined by $750. See Christopher Roser, *"Faster, Better, Cheaper" in the History of Manufacturing: From the Stone Age to Lean Manufacturing and Beyond* (Boca Raton, FL: CRC Press, 2017), 1–5, 336–39; Paul S. Adler, "Time-and-Motion Regained," *Harvard Business Review* 71, no. 1(January–February 1993): 97–108.
9. Author interview with Richard Harper, September 12, 2021.
10. Davies, Gann, and Douglas, "Innovation in Megaprojects: Systems Integration at London Heathrow Terminal 5," 101–25.
11. Amy Edmondson, *The Fearless Organization: Creating Psychological Safety in the Workplace for Learning, Innovation, and Growth* (New York: Wiley, 2018); Alexander Newman, Ross Donohue, and Nathan Eva, "Psychological Safety: A Systematic Review of the Literature," *Human Resource Management Review* 27, no. 3 (September 2015): 521–35. Research at Google found that psychological safety was a distinguishing feature of teams that outperformed others; see Charles Duhigg, "What Google Learned from Its Quest to Build the Perfect Team," *The New York Times Magazine*, February 25, 2016.
12. "Heathrow Terminal 5 Named 'World's Best' At Skytrax Awards," *International Airport Review*, March 28, 2019, https://www.internationalairportreview.com/news/83710/heathrow-worlds-best-skytrax/.
13. James Daley, "Owner and Contractor Embark on War of Words over Wembley Delay," *The Independent*, September 22, 2011; "Timeline: The Woes of Wembley Stadium," *Manchester Evening News*, February 15, 2007; Ben Quinn, "253m Legal Battle over Wembley Delays," *The Guardian*, March 16, 2008.

9: WHAT'S YOUR LEGO?

1. Hiroko Tabuchi, "Japan Strains to Fix a Reactor Damaged Before Quake," *The New York Times*, June 17, 2011, https://www.nytimes.com/2011/06/18/world/asia/18japan.html; "Japan to Abandon Troubled Fast Breeder Reactor," February 7, 2014, Phys.org, https://phys.org/news/2014-02-japan-abandon-fast-breeder-reactor.html.
2. "Japanese Government Says Monju Will Be Scrapped," *World Nuclear News*, December 22, 2016, https://www.world-nuclear-news.org/NP-Japanese-government-says-Monju-will-be-scrapped-2212164.html.
3. Yoko Kubota, "Fallen Device Retrieved from Japan Fast-Breeder Reactor," Reuters, June 24, 2011, https://www.reuters.com/article/us-japan-nuclear-monju-idUSTRE75N0H320110624; "Falsified Inspections Suspected at Monju Fast-Breeder Reactor," *The Japan Times*, April 11, 2014; "More Maintenance Flaws Found at Monju Reactor," *The Japan Times*, March 26, 2015; Jim Green, "Japan Abandons Monju Fast Reactor: The Slow Death of a Nuclear Dream," *The Ecologist*, October 6, 2016.

4. "Monju Prototype Reactor, Once a Key Cog in Japan's Nuclear Energy Policy, to Be Scrapped," *The Japan Times*, December 21, 2016; "Japan Cancels Failed $9bn Monju Nuclear Reactor," BBC, December 21, 2016, https://www.bbc.co.uk/news/world-asia-38390504.
5. "Japanese Government Says Monju Will Be Scrapped."
6. For the full story of Monju and other nuclear power plants, see Bent Flyvbjerg, "Four Ways to Scale Up: Smart, Dumb, Forced, and Fumbled," *Saïd Business School Working Papers*, University of Oxford, 2021.
7. Note that despite being fast we did *not* fast-track the Nepalese schools. Fast tracking means that construction is begun before designs are complete. It is dangerous, as we saw in the story of Jørn Utzon and the construction of the Sydney Opera House. See Terry Williams, Knut Samset, and Kjell Sunnevåg, eds., *Making Essential Choices with Scant Information: Front-End Decision Making in Major Projects* (London: Palgrave Macmillan, 2009).
8. Ramesh Chandra, *Encyclopedia of Education in South Asia*, vol. 6: *Nepal* (Delhi: Kalpaz Publications, 2014); Harald O. Skar and Sven Cederroth, *Development Aid to Nepal: Issues and Options in Energy, Health, Education, Democracy, and Human Rights* (Richmond, Surrey: Routledge Curzon Press, 2005); Alf Morten, Yasutami Shimomure, and Annette Skovsted Hansen, *Aid Relationships in Asia: Exploring Ownership in Japanese and Nordic Aid* (London: Palgrave Macmillan, 2008); Angela W. Little, *Education for All and Multigrade Teaching: Challenges and Opportunities* (Dordrecht: Springer, 2007); S. Wal, *Education and Child Development* (New Delhi: Sarup and Sons, 2006); Flyvbjerg, "Four Ways to Scale Up: Smart, Dumb, Forced, and Fumbled."
9. James H. Brown and Geoffrey B. West, eds., *Scaling in Biology* (Oxford, UK: Oxford University Press, 2000); Geoffrey West, *Scale: The Universal Laws of Life and Death in Organisms, Cities, and Companies* (London: Weidenfeld and Nicolson, 2017); Knut Schmidt-Nielsen, *Scaling: Why Is Animal Size So Important?* (Cambridge, UK: Cambridge University Press, 1984).
10. Author interview with Mike Green, June 5, 2020.
11. Benoit B. Mandelbrot, *Fractals and Scaling in Finance* (New York: Springer, 1997).
12. Erin Tallman, "Behind the Scenes at China's Prefab Hospitals Against Coronavirus," *E-Magazine* by Medical Expo, March 5, 2020, https://emag.medicalexpo.com/qa-behind-the-scenes-of-chinas-prefab-hospitals-against-coronavirus/.
13. Author interview with Ricky Wong, deputy head of Hong Kong's Civil Engineering Office, September 16, 2021.
14. I wish to thank Carissa Véliz for alerting me to Sears Modern Homes as an early and excellent example of modularity in housing and construction. The Sears archives are located at http://www.searsarchives.com/homes/index

.htm. See also #HGTV, "What It's Like to Live in a Sears Catalog Home," YouTube, May 13, 2018, https://www.youtube.com/watch?v=3kb24gwnZ18.
15. Author interview with Mike Green, June 5, 2020.
16. Dan Avery, "Warren Buffett to Offer a Fresh Approach on Modular Construction," *Architectural Digest,* May 20, 2021; author interviews with Danny Forster, January 4 and 27, 2021.
17. Steven Levy, "One More Thing: Inside Apple's Insanely Great (or Just Insane) New Mothership," *Wired,* May 16, 2017, https://www.wired.com/2017/05/apple-park-new-silicon-valley-campus/.
18. Leif Lia et al., "The Current Status of Hydropower Development and Dam Construction in Norway," *Hydropower & Dams* 22, no. 3 (2015); "Country Profile Norway," International Hydropower Association, https://www.hydropower.org/country-profiles/norway.
19. Tom Randall, "Tesla Flips the Switch on the Gigafactory," Bloomberg, January 4, 2017, https://www.bloomberg.com/news/articles/2017-01-04/tesla-flips-the-switch-on-the-gigafactory; Sean Whaley, "Tesla Officials Show Off Progress at Gigafactory in Northern Nevada," *Las Vegas Review-Journal,* March 20, 2016; Seth Weintraub, "Tesla Gigafactory Tour Roundup and Tidbits: 'This Is the Coolest Factory in the World,'" *Electrek,* July 28, 2016, https://electrek.co/2016/07/28/tesla-gigafactory-tour-roundup-and-tidbits-this-is-the-coolest-factory-ever/.
20. Atif Ansar and Bent Flyvbjerg, "How to Solve Big Problems: Bespoke Versus Platform Strategies," *Oxford Review of Economic Policy* 38, no. 2 (2022): 338–68.
21. Flyvbjerg, "Four Ways to Scale Up"; Fitz Tepper, "Satellite Maker Planet Labs Acquires BlackBridge's Geospatial Business," *TechCrunch,* July 15, 2015, https://techcrunch.com/2015/07/15/satellite-maker-planet-labs-acquires-blackbridges-geospatial-business/; Freeman Dyson, "The Green Universe: A Vision," *The New York Review of Books,* October 13, 2016, 4–6; Carissa Véliz, *Privacy Is Power: Why and How You Should Take Back Control of Your Data* (London: Bantam, 2020), 154.
22. Today I teach my students, many of whom are executives in charge of big projects, to tunnel like Madrid, should they ever find themselves leading a rail, road, water, or other project requiring extensive tunneling. For most, treating tunnels as Lego comes as an epiphany, because tunneling, like other digging, is conventionally seen as archetypically bespoke. I have literally had students walk straight out of my class on the Madrid Metro and place a call to order additional boring machines for their projects. Each machine typically costs between $20 million and $40 million, depending on size and type, which is cheap, considering the time and money multiple machines save.
23. Author interview with Manuel Melis, March 3, 2021; Manuel Melis, "Building a Metro: It's Easier Than You Think," *International Railway Jour-*

nal, April 2002, 16–19; Bent Flyvbjerg, "Make Megaprojects More Modular," *Harvard Business Review* 99, no. 6 (November–December 2021): 58–63; Manuel Melis, *Apuntes de introducción al proyecto y ponstrucción de túneles y metros en suelos y rocas blandas o muy rotas: la constricción del Metro de Madrid y la M-30* (Madrid: Politécnica, 2011).

24. Marc Levinson, *The Box: How the Shipping Container Made the World Smaller and the World Economy Bigger* (Princeton, NJ: Princeton University Press, 2016).

25. In mathematical/statistical terms, the degree of fat-tailedness was measured by the alpha-value of a power law fit to the cost overrun data for each project type. Projects with an alpha value of four or below were considered fat-tailed. Similar results were found for schedule and benefits. These conclusions apply to my current data set. With my team, I'm constantly growing the data, and results may change as more data are collected. The results should be considered preliminary in this sense.

26. Bent Flyvbjerg, ed., *The Oxford Handbook of Megaproject Management* (New York: Oxford University Press, 2017); Thomas Frey, "Megaprojects Set to Explode to 24% of Global GDP Within a Decade," *Future of Construction,* February 10, 2017, https://futureofconstruction.org/blog/megaprojects-set-to-explode-to-24-of-global-gdp-within-a-decade.

27. Kaamil Ahmed, "Ending World Hunger by 2030 Would Cost $330 Billion, Study Finds," *The Guardian,* October 13, 2020. Using the conservative numbers from Flyvbjerg, *Oxford Handbook of Megaproject Management* (2017)—that is, $6 trillion to $9 trillion per year—a 5 percent cost cut would equal savings of $300 billion to $450 billion per year. Using Frey's "Megaprojects Set to Explode" (2017) number—$22 trillion invested per year—the savings would be $1.1 trillion per year. With a 30 percent cost cut, the savings would be $1.8 trillion to $2.7 trillion and $6.6 trillion, respectively. And finally, at 80 percent, which assumes significant technological innovation, some of which is already happening, the savings would be $4.8 trillion to $7.2 trillion per year and $17.6 trillion per year for the Flyvbjerg and Frey numbers, respectively. These numbers do not include increases in the efficiency of benefits delivery, which would add further substantial gains on top of the cost savings.

28. The diagram is adapted from Michael Barnard, "A Decade of Wind, Solar, and Nuclear in China Shows Clear Scalability Winners," CleanTechnica, September 5, 2021, https://cleantechnica.com/2021/09/05/a-decade-of-wind-solar-nuclear-in-china-shows-clear-scalability-winners/, updated with data from 2021 at "Renewable Capacity Statistics 2021," International Renewable Energy Agency, https://www.irena.org/-/media/Files/IRENA/Agency/Publication/2021/Apr/IRENA_RE_Capacity_Statistics_2021.pdf.

29. Joanne Liou, "What Are Small Modular Reactors (SMRs)?," International

Atomic Energy Agency, November 4, 2021, https://www.iaea.org/newscenter/news/what-are-small-modular-reactors-smrs.
30. Bill Gates, "How We'll Invent the Future: Ten Breakthrough Technologies, 2019," *MIT Technology Review*, March–April 2019, 8–10; Reuters, "Bill Gates and Warren Buffett to Build New Kind of Nuclear Reactor in Wyoming," *The Guardian*, June 3, 2021.
31. Nadja Popovich and Winston Choi-Schagrin, "Hidden Toll of the Northwest Heat Wave: Hundreds of Extra Deaths," *The New York Times*, August 11, 2021.
32. Andrea Woo, "Nearly 600 People Died in BC Summer Heat Wave, Vast Majority Seniors: Coroner," *The Globe and Mail*, November 1, 2021.
33. "Climate Change and Health," World Health Organization, October 30, 2021, https://www.who.int/news-room/fact-sheets/detail/climate-change-and-health.
34. IPCC, "Summary for Policymakers" in *Climate Change 2021: The Physical Science Basis. Contribution of Working Group I to the Sixth Assessment Report of the Intergovernmental Panel on Climate Change*, eds. V. Masson-Delmotte et al. (Cambridge, UK: Cambridge University Press, 2021), 23.
35. Bent Flyvbjerg, "The Law of Regression to the Tail: How to Survive Covid-19, the Climate Crisis, and Other Disasters," *Environmental Science and Policy* 114 (December 2020): 614–18.
36. *Net Zero by 2050: A Roadmap for the Global Energy Sector*, International Energy Agency, May 2021, https://www.iea.org/reports/net-zero-by-2050.
37. Electrification is one of two dominant megatrends in the world today. Digitalization is the other, and it is interesting to compare the two. Both trends are delivered through tens of thousands of projects, big and small, year in and year out, decade after decade, in every area of the world. However, there is a fundamental difference between the two trends and the two types of projects in terms of performance and management. Electrification projects, not including nuclear and hydroelectric power projects, are at one end of the scale, with high-quality performance and management in terms of cost and schedule overruns that are few and small. Digitalization projects are at the other end of the scale, with low-quality performance in terms of cost and schedule overruns, which tend to be huge and unpredictable. In my analysis, low-quality project management—and *not* problems with digital technology—is *the* key problem for current digitalization. It's the elephant in the room for all things digital, widely ignored despite being hugely costly and wasteful. In contrast, high-quality project management is key to the massive global success of electrification, especially for wind power, solar power, batteries, and transmission. This is fortunate, because if we quickly scale up the current trend for well-managed electrification, we might just save ourselves from the worst of the climate crisis, as explained in the main text. In any case, IT project managers have much to learn from their col-

leagues in electrification. See Bent Flyvbjerg et al., "The Empirical Reality of IT Project Cost Overruns: Discovering a Power-Law Distribution," *Journal of Management Information Systems* 39, no. 3 (Fall 2022).
38. "Pathway to Critical and Formidable Goal of Net-Zero Emissions by 2050 Is Narrow but Brings Huge Benefits, According to IEA Special Report," International Energy Agency (IEA), May 18, 2021, https://www.iea.org /news/pathway-to-critical-and-formidable-goal-of-net-zero-emissions-by -2050-is-narrow-but-brings-huge-benefits.
39. Author interview with Anders Eldrup, July 13, 2021.
40. Author interview with Henrik Poulsen, June 29, 2021.
41. "Making Green Energy Affordable: How the Offshore Wind Energy Industry Matured—and What We Can Learn from It," Ørsted, June 2019, https://orsted.com/-/media/WWW/Docs/Corp/COM/explore/Making -green-energy-affordable-June-2019.pdf.
42. Heather Louise Madsen and John Parm Ulhøi, "Sustainable Visioning: Re-framing Strategic Vision to Enable a Sustainable Corporate Transformation," *Journal of Cleaner Production* 288 (March 2021): 125602.
43. "Share of Electricity Production by Source," *Our World in Data*, https:// ourworldindata.org/grapher/share-elec-by-source.
44. In addition to traditional business spin-offs, there have been big financial spin-offs, for instance, Copenhagen Infrastructure Partners (CIP), founded in 2012 in collaboration with PensionDanmark, the largest labor market pension company in Denmark and one of the first direct institutional investors in offshore wind projects globally. Today, CIP is a major global infrastructure investment fund with offices around the world, working side by side with Ørsted in enabling the transition to a low-carbon energy system.

CODA: ELEVEN HEURISTICS FOR BETTER PROJECT LEADERSHIP

1. Oxford English Dictionary 2022: full entry, https://www.oed.com/view /Entry/86554?isAdvanced=false&result=1&rskey=WrJUIh&.
2. Gerd Gigerenzer, Ralph Hertwig, and Thorsten Pachur, eds., *Heuristics: The Foundations of Adaptive Behavior* (Oxford, UK: Oxford University Press, 2011).
3. Today, two main schools exist in thinking about heuristics. The first focuses on "positive heuristics," defined as heuristics that help people make better decisions, such as the recognition heuristic and the take-the-best heuristic; see Gerd Gigerenzer and Daniel G. Goldstein, "Reasoning the Fast and Frugal Way: Models of Bounded Rationality," *Psychological Review* 103, no. 4 (1996): 650–69; Gerd Gigerenzer, "Models of Ecological Rationality: The Recognition Heuristic," *Psychological Review* 109, no. 1 (2002): 75–90. Gerd Gigerenzer is the leading proponent of this school. The second school concentrates on "negative heuristics," defined as heuristics that trip up peo-

ple, violating basic laws of rationality and logic; e.g., the availability heuristic and the anchoring heuristic; see Amos Tversky and Daniel Kahneman, "Availability: A Heuristic for Judging Frequency and Probability," *Cognitive Psychology* 5, no. 2 (September 1973): 207–32; Daniel Kahneman, "Reference Points, Anchors, Norms, and Mixed Feelings," *Organizational Behavior and Human Decision Processes* 51, no. 2 (1992): 296–312. Daniel Kahneman and Amos Tversky are the leading exponents of this school. Both schools have demonstrated their relevance in impressive detail. Important disagreements exist between the two, to be sure; see Gerd Gigerenzer, "The Bias Bias in Behavioral Economics," *Review of Behavioral Economics* 5, nos. 3–4 (December 2018): 303–36; Daniel Kahneman and Gary Klein, "Conditions for Intuitive Expertise: A Failure to Disagree," *American Psychologist* 64, no. 6 (2009): 515–26. But they are best understood as complementary models for understanding different aspects of heuristics, not as competing models for explaining the same thing. In short, you need to understand both schools of thought to fully understand the role of heuristics in human adaptive behavior, which is to understand human existence. Chapter 2 covered central aspects of negative heuristics, their impact on decision making, and how they may be mitigated. This coda focuses on positive heuristics and especially on how they pertain to successfully leading and delivering projects.
4. For a longer and more detailed list of my heuristics, including deeper explanations of what heuristics are, why they work, and how to tease them out, with more examples, see Bent Flyvbjerg, "Heuristics for Masterbuilders: Fast and Frugal Ways to Become a Better Project Leader," *Saïd Business School Working Papers*, University of Oxford, 2022.
5. Ed Catmull, *Creativity, Inc: Overcoming the Unseen Forces That Stand in the Way of True Inspiration* (New York: Random House, 2014), 315.
6. medianwandel, "WWDC 1997: Steve Jobs About Apple's Future," YouTube, October 19, 2011, https://www.youtube.com/watch?v=qyd0tP0SK6o.

BIBLIOGRAPHY

258t. 2015. "Steve Jobs Customer Experience." YouTube, October 16. https://www.youtube.com/watch?v=r2O5qKZlI50.
Aaltonen, Kirsi, and Jaakko Kujala. 2010. "A Project Lifecycle Perspective on Stakeholder Influence Strategies in Global Projects." *Scandinavian Journal of Management* 26 (4): 381–97.
Abi-Habib, Maria, Oscar Lopez, and Natalie Kitroeff. 2021. "Construction Flaws Led to Mexico City Metro Collapse, Independent Inquiry Shows." *The New York Times*, June 16.
Academy of Achievement. 2017. "Frank Gehry, Academy Class of 1995, Full Interview." YouTube, July 18. https://www.youtube.com/watch?v=wTElCmNkkKc.
Adelman, Jeremy. 2013. *Worldly Philosopher: The Odyssey of Albert O. Hirschman*. Princeton, NJ: Princeton University Press.
Adler, Paul S. 1993. "Time-and-Motion Regained." *Harvard Business Review* 17 (1): 97–108.
Aguinis, Herman. 2014. "Revisiting Some 'Established Facts' in the Field of Management." *Business Research Quarterly* 17 (1): 2–10.
Ahmed, Kaamil. 2020. "Ending World Hunger by 2030 Would Cost $330 Billion, Study Finds." *The Guardian*, October 13.
Alacevich, Michele. 2007. "Early Development Economics Debates Revisited." *Policy Research Working Paper* no. 4441. Washington, DC: World Bank.
Alacevich, Michele. 2014. "Visualizing Uncertainties, or How Albert Hirschman and the World Bank Disagreed on Project Appraisal and What This Says About the End of 'High Development Theory.'" *Journal of the History of Economic Thought* 36 (2): 157.
Albalate, Daniel, and Germa Bel. 2014. *The Economics and Politics of High-Speed Rail*. New York: Lexington Books.
Alho, Juha M. 1992. "The Accuracy of Environmental Impact Assessments: Skew Prediction Errors." *Ambio* 21 (4): 322–23.
Altshuler, Alan, and David Luberoff. 2003. *Mega-Projects: The Changing Politics of Urban Public Investment*. Washington, DC: Brookings Institution.
Alvares, Claude, and Ramesh Billorey. 1988. *Damning the Narmada: India's*

Greatest Planned Environmental Disaster. Penang: Third World Network and Asia-Pacific People's Environment Network, APPEN.
Amazon. 2022. "Leadership Principles." https://www.amazon.jobs/en/principles.
Ambrose, Stephen E. 2000. *Nothing Like It in the World: The Men Who Built the Transcontinental Railroad, 1863–1869.* New York: Touchstone.
Anderson, Cameron, and Adam D. Galinsky. 2006. "Power, Optimism, and Risk-Taking." *European Journal of Social Psychology* 36 (4): 511–36.
Andranovich, Greg, Matthew J. Burbank, and Charles H. Heying. 2001. "Olympic Cities: Lessons Learned from Mega-Event Politics." *Journal of Urban Affairs* 23 (2): 113–31.
Andriani, Pierpaolo, and Bill McKelvey. 2007. "Beyond Gaussian Averages: Redirecting International Business and Management Research Toward Extreme Events and Power Laws." *Journal of International Business Studies* 38 (7): 1212–30.
Andriani, Pierpaolo, and Bill McKelvey. 2009. "Perspective—from Gaussian to Paretian Thinking: Causes and Implications of Power Laws in Organizations." *Organization Science* 20 (6): 1053–71.
Andriani, Pierpaolo, and Bill McKelvey. 2011. "From Skew Distributions to Power-Law Science." In *Complexity and Management,* eds. P. Allen, S. Maguire, and Bill McKelvey. Los Angeles: Sage, 254–73.
Anguera, Ricard. 2006. "The Channel Tunnel: An Ex Post Economic Evaluation." *Transportation Research Part A* 40 (4): 291–315.
Ansar, Atif, and Bent Flyvbjerg. 2022. "How to Solve Big Problems: Bespoke Versus Platform Strategies." *Oxford Review of Economic Policy* 38 (2): 338–68.
Ansar, Atif, Bent Flyvbjerg, Alexander Budzier, and Daniel Lunn. 2014. "Should We Build More Large Dams? The Actual Costs of Hydropower Megaproject Development." *Energy Policy* 69: 43–56.
Ansar, Atif, Bent Flyvbjerg, Alexander Budzier, and Daniel Lunn. 2016. "Does Infrastructure Investment Lead to Economic Growth or Economic Fragility? Evidence from China." *Oxford Review of Economic Policy* 32 (3): 360–90.
Ansar, Atif, Bent Flyvbjerg, Alexander Budzier, and Daniel Lunn. 2017. "Big Is Fragile: An Attempt at Theorizing Scale." In *The Oxford Handbook of Megaproject Management,* ed. Bent Flyvbjerg. Oxford, UK: Oxford University Press, 60–95.
Anthopoulos, Leonidas, Christopher G. Reddick, Irene Giannakidou, and Nikolaos Mavridis. 2016. "Why E-Government Projects Fail? An Analysis of the healthcare.gov Website." *Government Information Quarterly* 33 (1): 161–73.
Architectural Videos. "Frank Gehry Uses CATIA for His Architecture Visions." YouTube, November 1, 2011. https://www.youtube.com/watch?v=UEn53Wr6380.

Aristotle. 1976. *The Nicomachean Ethics.* Translated by J. A. K. Thomson, revised with notes and appendices by Hugh Tredennick. Introduction and bibliography by Jonathan Barnes. Harmondsworth, UK: Penguin Classics.

Arkes, Hal R., and Catherine Blumer. 1985. "The Psychology of Sunk Cost." *Organizational Behavior and Human Decision Processes* 35 (1): 124–40.

Arup, Ove, and Partners Scotland. 2004. *Scottish Parliament, Edinburgh Tram Line 2: Review of Business Case.* West Lothian, UK: Ove Arup and Partners.

Australian Transport and Infrastructure Council. 2018. *Optimism Bias.* Canberra: Commonwealth of Australia.

Avery, Dan. 2021. "Warren Buffett to Offer a Fresh Approach on Modular Construction." *Architectural Digest,* May 20. https://www.architecturaldigest.com/story/warren-buffett-offer-fresh-approach-modular-construction.

Awojobi, Omotola, and Glenn P. Jenkins. 2016. "Managing the Cost Overrun Risks of Hydroelectric Dams: An Application of Reference-Class Forecasting Techniques." *Renewable and Sustainable Energy Reviews* 63 (September): 19–32.

Baade, Robert A., and Victor A. Matheson. 2004. "The Quest for the Cup: Assessing the Economic Impact of the World Cup." *Regional Studies* 38 (4): 343–54.

Baade, Robert A., and Victor A. Matheson. 2016. "Going for the Gold: The Economics of the Olympics." *Journal of Economic Perspectives* 30 (2): 201–18.

Bach, Steven. 1999. *Final Cut: Art, Money, and Ego in the Making of Heaven's Gate, the Film That Sank United Artists.* New York: Newmarket Press.

Backwell, Ben. 2018. *Wind Power: The Struggle for Control of a New Global Industry.* London: Routledge.

Baham, Cory, Rudy Hirschheim, Andres A. Calderon, and Victoria Kisekka. 2017. "An Agile Methodology for the Disaster Recovery of Information Systems Under Catastrophic Scenarios." *Journal of Management Information Systems* 34 (3): 633–63.

Bain, Susan. 2005. *Holyrood: The Inside Story.* Edinburgh: Edinburgh University Press.

Bak, Per. 1996. *How Nature Works: The Science of Self-Organized Criticality.* New York: Springer Science & Business Media.

Bak, Per, Chao Tang, and Kurt Wiesenfeld. 1988. "Self-Organized Criticality: An Explanation of the 1/f Noise." *Physical Review Letters* 59 (4): 381.

Bak, Per, Chao Tang, and Kurt Wiesenfeld. 1988. "Self-Organized Criticality." *Physical Review A* 38 (1): 364–74.

Bakker, Karen. 1999. "The Politics of Hydropower: Developing the Mekong." *Political Geography* 18 (2): 209–32.

Baldwin, Carliss Y., and Kim B. Clark. 2000. *Design Rules: The Power of Modularity.* Cambridge, MA: MIT Press.

Bar-Hillel, Maya. 1980. "The Base-Rate Fallacy in Probability Judgments." *Acta Psychologica* 44 (3): 211–33.

Barabási, Albert-László. 2005. "The Origin of Bursts and Heavy Tails in Human Dynamics." *Nature* 435: 207–11.
Barabási, Albert-László. 2014. *Linked: How Everything Is Connected to Everything Else and What It Means for Business, Science, and Everyday Life.* New York: Basic Books.
Barabási, Albert-László, and Réka Albert. 1999. "Emergence of Scaling in Random Networks." *Science* 286 (5439): 509–12.
Barabási, Albert-László, Kwang-Il Goh, and Alexei Vazquez. 2005. Reply to Comment on "The Origin of Bursts and Heavy Tails in Human Dynamics." arXiv preprint. arXiv:physics/0511186.
Barnard, Michael. 2021. "A Decade of Wind, Solar, and Nuclear in China Shows Clear Scalability Winners." *CleanTechnica*, September 5. https://cleantechnica.com/2021/09/05/a-decade-of-wind-solar-nuclear-in-china-shows-clear-scalability-winners/.
Barthiaume, Lee. 2021. "Skyrocketing Shipbuilding Costs Continue as Estimate Puts Icebreaker Price at $7.25 Bill." *The Canadian Press*, December 16.
Bartlow, James. 2000. "Innovation and Learning in Complex Offshore Construction Projects." *Research Policy* 29 (7): 973–89.
Batselier, Jordy. 2016. *Empirical Evaluation of Existing and Novel Approaches for Project Forecasting and Control.* Doctoral dissertation. Ghent, Belgium: University of Ghent.
Batselier, Jordy, and Mario Vanhoucke. 2016. "Practical Application and Empirical Evaluation of Reference-Class Forecasting for Project Management." *Project Management Journal* 47 (5): 36.
Batselier, Jordy, and Mario Vanhoucke. 2017. "Improving Project Forecast Accuracy by Integrating Earned Value Management with Exponential Smoothing and Reference-Class Forecasting." *International Journal of Project Management* 35 (1): 28–43.
BBC. 2013. *Restoration Home.* Season 3, episode 8. BBC, August 21. https://www.youtube.com/watch?v=_NDaO42j_KQ.
BBC. 2016. "Japan Cancels Failed $9bn Monju Nuclear Reactor." BBC, December 21. https://www.bbc.co.uk/news/world-asia-38390504.
Bechtler, Cristina, ed. 1999. *Frank O. Gehry/Kurt W. Forster.* Ostfildern-Ruit, Germany: Cantz.
Bernstein, Peter L. 2005. *Wedding of the Waters: The Erie Canal and the Making of a Great Nation.* New York: W. W. Norton.
Billings, Stephen B., and J. Scott Holladay. 2012. "Should Cities Go for the Gold? The Long-Term Impacts of Hosting the Olympics." *Economic Inquiry* 50 (3): 754–72.
Billington, David P., and Donald C. Jackson. 2006. *Big Dams of the New Deal Era: A Confluence of Engineering and Politics.* Norman: University of Oklahoma Press.

Bishir, Catherine W. 2009. "Shreve and Lamb." In *North Carolina Architects and Builders: A Biographical Dictionary*. Raleigh: North Carolina State University Libraries, https://ncarchitects.lib.ncsu.edu/people/P000414.

Biskind, Peter. 1998. *Easy Riders, Raging Bulls: How the Sex-Drugs-and-Rock 'n' Roll Generation Saved Hollywood*. London: Bloomsbury Publishing.

Bizony, Piers. 2006. *The Man Who Ran the Moon: James Webb, JFK, and the Secret History of Project Apollo*. Cambridge, UK: Icon Books.

Boisot, Max, and Bill McKelvey. 2011. "Connectivity, Extremes, and Adaptation: A Power-Law Perspective of Organizational Effectiveness." *Journal of Management Inquiry* 20 (2): 119–33.

Bok, Sissela. 1999. *Lying: Moral Choice in Public and Private Life*. New York: Vintage.

Bordley, Robert F. 2014. "Reference-Class Forecasting: Resolving Its Challenge to Statistical Modeling." *The American Statistician* 68 (4): 221–29.

Boudet, Hilary Schaffer, and Leonard Ortolano. 2010. "A Tale of Two Sitings: Contentious Politics in Liquefied Natural Gas Facility Siting in California." *Journal of Planning Education and Research* 30 (1): 5–21.

Bovens, Mark, and Paul 't Hart. 1996. *Understanding Policy Fiascoes*. New Brunswick, NJ: Transaction Publishers.

Bowman, Martin W. 2015. *Boeing 747: A History*. Barnsley, UK: Pen and Sword Aviation.

Box, George E. P. 1976. "Science and Statistics." *Journal of the American Statistical Association* 71 (356): 791–99.

Brockner, Joel. 1992. "The Escalation of Commitment to a Failing Course of Action: Toward Theoretical Progress." *Academy of Management Review* 17 (1): 39–61.

Brooks, Frederick P. 1995. *The Mythical Man-Month: Essays on Software Engineering*, 2nd ed. Reading, MA: Addison-Wesley.

Brown, James H., and Geoffrey B. West, eds. 2000. *Scaling in Biology*. Oxford, UK: Oxford University Press.

Brown, Willie. 2013. "When Warriors Travel to China, Ed Lee Will Follow." *San Francisco Chronicle*, July 27.

Bryar, Colin, and Bill Carr. 2021. *Working Backwards: Insights, Stories, and Secrets from Inside Amazon*. New York: St. Martin's Press.

Buckley, Ralf C. 1990. "Environmental Audit: Review and Guidelines." *Environment and Planning Law Journal* 7 (2): 127–41.

Buckley, Ralf C. 1991. "Auditing the Precision and Accuracy of Environmental Impact Predictions in Australia." *Environmental Monitoring and Assessment* 18 (1): 1–23.

Buckley, Ralf C. 1991. "How Accurate Are Environmental Impact Predictions?" *Ambio* 20 (3–4): 161–62, with "Response to Comment by J. M. Alho," 21 (4): 323–24.

Budzier, Alexander, and Bent Flyvbjerg. 2011. "Double Whammy: How ICT Projects Are Fooled by Randomness and Screwed by Political Intent." *Saïd Business School Working Papers*. Oxford, UK: University of Oxford.
Budzier, Alexander, and Bent Flyvbjerg. 2013. "Making Sense of the Impact and Importance of Outliers in Project Management Through the Use of Power Laws." *Proceedings of IRNOP* [International Research Network on Organizing by Projects] 11: 1–28.
Budzier, Alexander, Bent Flyvbjerg, Andi Garavaglia, and Andreas Leed. 2018. *Quantitative Cost and Schedule Risk Analysis of Nuclear Waste Storage*. Oxford, UK: Oxford Global Projects.
Buehler, Roger, Dale Griffin, and Heather MacDonald. 1997. "The Role of Motivated Reasoning in Optimistic Time Predictions." *Personality and Social Psychology Bulletin* 23 (3): 238–47.
Buehler, Roger, Dale Griffin, and Johanna Peetz. 2010. "The Planning Fallacy: Cognitive, Motivational, and Social Origins." *Advances in Experimental Social Psychology* 43: 1–62.
Buehler, Roger, Dale Griffin, and Michael Ross. 1994. "Exploring the 'Planning Fallacy': Why People Underestimate Their Task Completion Times." *Journal of Personality and Social Psychology* 67 (3): 366–81.
Byron, Kristin, Deborah Nazarian, and Shalini Khazanchi. 2010. "The Relationships Between Stressors and Creativity: A Meta-analysis Examining Competing Theoretical Models." *Journal of Applied Psychology* 95 (1): 201–12.
California High-Speed Rail Authority. 1999. *Financial Plan*. Sacramento: California High-Speed Rail Authority.
California High-Speed Rail Authority. 2008. *California High-Speed Train Business Plan*. Sacramento: California High-Speed Rail Authority.
California High-Speed Rail Authority. 2012. *California High-Speed Rail Program, Revised 2012 Business Plan: Building California's Future*. Sacramento: California High-Speed Rail Authority.
California High-Speed Rail Authority. 2014. *Connecting California: 2014 Business Plan*. Sacramento: California High-Speed Rail Authority.
California High-Speed Rail Authority. 2016. *Connecting and Transforming California: 2016 Business Plan*. Sacramento: California High-Speed Rail Authority.
California High-Speed Rail Authority. 2018. *2018 Business Plan*. Sacramento: California High-Speed Rail Authority.
California High-Speed Rail Authority. 2021. *2020 Business Plan: Recovery and Transformation*. Sacramento: California High-Speed Rail Authority.
California High-Speed Rail Authority. 2021. *2020 Business Plan: Ridership and Revenue Forecasting Report*. Sacramento: California High-Speed Rail Authority.
California High-Speed Rail Authority. 2021. *Revised Draft 2020 Business Plan:*

Capital Cost Basis of Estimate Report. Sacramento: California High-Speed Rail Authority.
California Legislative Information. 2008. *Safe, Reliable High-Speed Passenger Train Bond Act for the 21st Century.* Assembly Bill no. 3034. California Legislative Information. https://leginfo.legislature.ca.gov/faces/billNavClient.xhtml?bill_id=200720080AB3034.
Campbell, Joseph. 2008. *The Hero with a Thousand Faces.* San Francisco: New World Library.
Campion-Awwad, Oliver, Alexander Hayton, Leila Smith, and Mark Vuaran. 2014. *The National Programme for IT in the NHS: A Case History.* Cambridge, UK: University of Cambridge.
Cantarelli, Chantal C., Bent Flyvbjerg, and Søren L. Buhl. 2012. "Geographical Variation in Project Cost Performance: The Netherlands Versus Worldwide." *Journal of Transport Geography* 24: 324–31.
Cantarelli, Chantal C., Bent Flyvbjerg, Eric J. E. Molin, and Bert van Wee. 2010. "Cost Overruns in Large-Scale Transportation Infrastructure Projects: Explanations and Their Theoretical Embeddedness." *European Journal of Transport and Infrastructure Research* 10 (1): 5–18.
Cantarelli, Chantal C., Bent Flyvbjerg, Bert van Wee, and Eric J. E. Molin. 2010. "Lock-in and Its Influence on the Project Performance of Large-Scale Transportation Infrastructure Projects: Investigating the Way in Which Lock-in Can Emerge and Affect Cost Overruns." *Environment and Planning B: Planning and Design* 37 (5): 792–807.
Cantarelli, Chantal C., Eric J. E. Molin, Bert van Wee, and Bent Flyvbjerg. 2012. "Characteristics of Cost Overruns for Dutch Transport Infrastructure Projects and the Importance of the Decision to Build and Project Phases." *Transport Policy* 22: 49–56.
Carreyrou, John. 2018. *Bad Blood: Secrets and Lies in a Silicon Valley Startup.* New York: Alfred A. Knopf.
Caro, Robert. 1975. *The Power Broker: Robert Moses and the Fall of New York.* New York: Vintage.
Caro, Robert A. 2019. *Working: Researching, Interviewing, Writing.* New York: Vintage.
Carson, Thomas L. 2006. "The Definition of Lying." *Noûs* 40 (2): 284–306.
Catmull, Ed. 2014. *Creativity, Inc.: Overcoming the Unseen Forces That Stand in the Way of True Inspiration.* New York: Random House.
CBC News. 1999. "Jean Drapeau Dead." CBC News, August 13. https://www.cbc.ca/news/canada/jean-drapeau-dead-1.185985.
Chandler, Alfred D. 1990. *Scale and Scope: Dynamics of Industrial Capitalism,* new ed. Cambridge, MA: Harvard University Press.
Chandra, Ramesh. 2014. *Encyclopedia of Education in South Asia,* vol. 6. Delhi: Gyan Publishing House.

Chang, Welton, Eva Chen, Barbara Mellers, and Philip Tetlock. 2016. "Developing Expert Political Judgment: The Impact of Training and Practice on Judgmental Accuracy in Geopolitical Forecasting Tournaments." *Judgment and Decision Making* 11 (5): 509–26.

Chapman, Gretchen B., and Eric J. Johnson. 1999. "Anchoring, Activation, and the Construction of Values." *Organizational Behavior and Human Decision Processes* 79 (2): 115–53.

Charest, Paul. 1995. "Aboriginal Alternatives to Megaprojects and Their Environmental and Social Impacts." *Impact Assessment* 13 (4): 371–86.

Christian, Alex. 2021. "The Untold Story of the Big Boat That Broke the World." *Wired*, June 22. https://www.wired.co.uk/article/ever-given-global-supply-chain.

Christoffersen, Mads, Bent Flyvbjerg, and Jørgen Lindgaard Pedersen. 1992. "The Lack of Technology Assessment in Relation to Big Infrastructural Decisions." In *Technology and Democracy: The Use and Impact of Technology Assessment in Europe. Proceedings from the 3rd European Congress on Technology Assessment.* Copenhagen, 54–75.

Cialdini, Robert B. 2021. *Influence, New and Expanded: The Psychology of Persuasion.* New York: Harper Business.

Clark, Gordon L., and Neil Wrigley. 1995. "Sunk Costs: A Framework for Economic Geography." *Transactions of the Institute of British Geographers* 20 (2): 204–23.

Clauset, Aaron, Cosma R. Shalizi, and Mark E. J. Newman. 2009. "Power-Law Distributions in Empirical Data." *SIAM Review* 51 (4): 661–703.

Clauset, Aaron, Maxwell Young, and Kristian S. Gleditsch. 2007. "On the Frequency of Severe Terrorist Events." *Journal of Conflict Resolution* 51 (1): 58–87.

Collingridge, David. 1992. *The Management of Scale: Big Organizations, Big Decisions, Big Mistakes.* London: Routledge.

Collins, Jeffrey. 2020. "Former Executive Faces Prison Time in SC Nuclear Debacle." Associated Press, November 25.

Conboy, Kieran. 2010. "Project Failure en Masse: A Study of Loose Budgetary Control in ISD Projects." *European Journal of Information Systems* 19 (3): 273–87.

Construction Task Force. 1998. "Rethinking Construction—The Egan Report." London: Dept. of the Environment, Transport, and the Regions. Constructing Excellence. https://constructingexcellence.org.uk/wp-content/uploads/2014/10/rethinking_construction_report.pdf.

Constructive Developments. 2022. "Storebaelt Tunnels, Denmark." Constructive Developments. https://sites.google.com/site/constructivedevelopments/storebaelt-tunnels.

Cooper, Arnold C., Carolyn Y. Woo, and William C. Dunkelberg. 1988. "Entrepreneurs' Perceived Chances for Success." *Journal of Business Venturing* 3 (2): 97–108.

Cullinane, Kevin, and Mahim Khanna. 2000. "Economies of Scale in Large Containerships: Optimal Size and Geographical Implications." *Journal of Transport Geography* 8 (3): 181–95.

Czerlinski, Jean, Gerd Gigerenzer, and Daniel G. Goldstein. 1999. "How Good Are Simple Heuristics?" In *Simple Heuristics That Make Us Smart*, eds. Gerd Gigerenzer, Peter M. Todd, and ABC Research Group. Oxford, UK: Oxford University Press, 97–118.

Daley, James. 2011. "Owner and Contractor Embark on War of Words over Wembley Delay." *The Independent*, September 22.

Danish Ministry of Transport and Energy, Transport- og Energiministeriet. 2006. *Aktstykke 16: Orientering om nye budgetteringsprincipper for anlægsprojekter*. Copenhagen: Finansudvalget, Folketinget, November 2.

Danish Ministry of Transport and Energy, Transport- og Energiministeriet. 2008. *Ny anlægsbudgettering på Transportministeriets område, herunder om økonomistyringsmodel og risikohåndtering for anlægsprojekter*. Copenhagen: Transportministeriet, November 18.

Danish Ministry of Transport, Building and Housing, Transport-, Bygnings- og Boligministeriet. 2017. *Hovednotat for ny anlægsbudgettering: Ny anlægsbudgettering på Transport-, Bygnings- og Boligministeriets område. Herunder om økonomistyringsmodel og risikohåndtering for anlægsprojekter*. Copenhagen: Transport -, Bygnings- og Boligministeriet.

Dantata, Nasiru A., Ali Touran, and Donald C. Schneck. 2006. "Trends in US Rail Transit Project Cost Overrun." *Transportation Research Board Annual Meeting*. Washington, DC: National Academies.

Dardick, Hal. 2014. "Ald. Burke Calls Great Chicago Fire Festival a 'Fiasco.'" *Chicago Tribune*, October 6.

Davies, Andrew, David Gann, and Tony Douglas. 2009. "Innovation in Megaprojects: Systems Integration at London Heathrow Terminal 5." *California Management Review* 51 (2): 101–25.

Davies, Andrew, and Michael Hobday. 2005. *The Business of Projects: Managing Innovation in Complex Products and Systems*. Cambridge, UK: Cambridge University Press.

De Bruijn, Hans, and Martijn Leijten. 2007. "Megaprojects and Contested Information." *Transportation Planning and Technology* 30 (1): 49–69.

De Reyck, Bert, Yael Grushka-Cockayne, Ioannis Fragkos, and Jeremy Harrison. 2015. *Optimism Bias Study: Recommended Adjustments to Optimism Bias Uplifts*. London: Department for Transport.

De Reyck, Bert, Yael Grushka-Cockayne, Ioannis Fragkos, and Jeremy Harrison. 2017. *Optimism Bias Study—Recommended Adjustments to Optimism Bias Uplifts*, update. London: Department for Transport.

DeGroot, Gerard. 2008. *Dark Side of the Moon: The Magnificent Madness of the American Lunar Quest*. London: Vintage.

Del Cerro Santamaría, Gerardo. 2017. "Iconic Urban Megaprojects in a Global

Context: Revisiting Bilbao." In *The Oxford Handbook of Megaproject Management*, ed. Bent Flyvbjerg. Oxford, UK: Oxford University Press, 497–518.

Delaney, Kevin J., and Rick Eckstein. 2003. *Public Dollars, Private Stadiums: The Battle over Building Sports Stadiums*. New Brunswick, NJ: Rutgers University Press.

Del Rey, Jason. 2019. "The Making of Amazon Prime, the Internet's Most Successful and Devastating Membership Program." Vox, May 3. https://www.vox.com/recode/2019/5/3/18511544/amazon-prime-oral-history-jeff-bezos-one-day-shipping.

Detter, Dag, and Stefan Fölster. 2015. *The Public Wealth of Nations*. New York: Palgrave.

Dipper, Ben, Carys Jones, and Christopher Wood. 1998. "Monitoring and Post-auditing in Environmental Impact Assessment: A Review." *Journal of Environmental Planning and Management* 41 (6): 731–47.

Doig, Jameson W. 2001. *Empire on the Hudson: Entrepreneurial Vision and Political Power at the Port of New York Authority*. New York: Columbia University Press.

Dowling, Stephen. 2020. "The Boeing 747: The Plane That Shrank the World." BBC, June 19. https://www.bbc.com/future/article/20180927-the-boeing-747-the-plane-that-shrank-the-world.

Drew, Philip. 2001. *The Masterpiece: Jørn Utzon, a Secret Life*. South Yarra, Victoria, Australia: Hardie Grant Books.

Drummond, Helga. 2014. "Is Escalation Always Irrational?" In *Megaproject Planning and Management: Essential Readings*, vol. 2, ed. Bent Flyvbjerg. Cheltenham, UK: Edward Elgar, 291–309. Originally published in *Organization Studies* 19 (6).

Drummond, Helga. 2017. "Megaproject Escalation of Commitment: An Update and Appraisal." In *The Oxford Handbook of Megaproject Management*, ed. Bent Flyvbjerg. Oxford, UK: Oxford University Press, 194–216.

Duflo, Esther, and Rohini Pande. 2007. "Dams." *The Quarterly Journal of Economics* 122: 601–46.

Duhigg, Charles. 2016. "What Google Learned from Its Quest to Build the Perfect Team." *The New York Times Magazine*, February 25.

Dyson, Freeman. 2016. "The Green Universe: A Vision." *The New York Review of Books*, October 13, 4–6.

Edmondson, Amy. 2018. *The Fearless Organization: Creating Psychological Safety in the Workplace for Learning, Innovation, and Growth*. Hoboken, NJ: John Wiley & Sons.

Eisenhardt, Kathleen M. 1989. "Agency Theory: An Assessment and Review." *Academy of Management Review* 14 (1): 57–74.

Electric Lady Studios. http://electricladystudios.com.

Emmons, Debra L., Robert E. Bitten, and Claude W. Freaner. 2007. "Using

Historical NASA Cost and Schedule Growth to Set Future Program and Project Reserve Guidelines." *2007 IEEE Aerospace Conference*, 1–16.

Empire State Inc. 1931. *Empire State: A History.* New York: Publicity Association.

Epley, Nicholas, and Thomas Gilovich. 2006. "The Anchoring-and-Adjustment Heuristic: Why the Adjustments Are Insufficient." *Psychological Science* 17 (4): 311–18.

Escobar-Rangel, Lina, and François Lévêque. 2015. "Revisiting the Cost Escalation Curse of Nuclear Power: New Lessons from the French Experience." *Economics of Energy and Environmental Policy* 4 (2): 103–26.

Essex, Stephen, and Brian Chalkley. 2004. "Mega–Sporting Events in Urban and Regional Policy: A History of the Winter Olympics." *Planning Perspectives* 19 (2): 201–32.

Esty, Benjamin C. 2004. "Why Study Large Projects? An Introduction to Research on Project Finance." *European Financial Management* 10 (2): 213–24.

Ethiraj, Sendil K., and Danial A. Levinthal. 2004. "Modularity and Innovation in Complex Systems." *Management Science* 50 (2): 159–73.

EU Commission. 1996. *Guidelines for the Construction of a Transeuropean Transport Network,* EU Bulletin L228. Brussels: EU Commission.

European Court of Auditors. 2014. *EU-Funded Airport Infrastructures: Poor Value for Money.* European Court of Auditors. https://www.eca.europa.eu/Lists/ECADocuments/SR14_21/Q_JAB14021ENC.pdf.

Exemplars in Global Health. 2022. *What Did Nepal Do?* Exemplars in Global Health. https://www.exemplars.health/topics/stunting/nepal/what-did-nepal-do.

Fabricius, Golo, and Marion Büttgen. 2015. "Project Managers' Overconfidence: How Is Risk Reflected in Anticipated Project Success?" *Business Research* 8 (2): 239–63.

Fainstein, Susan S. 2008. "Mega-Projects in New York, London and Amsterdam." *International Journal of Urban and Regional Research* 32 (4): 768–85.

Fallis, Don. 2009. "What Is Lying?" *The Journal of Philosophy* 106 (1): 29–56.

Farago, Jason. 2021. "Gehry's Quiet Interventions Reshape the Philadelphia Museum." *The New York Times,* May 30.

Farmer, J. Doyne, and John Geanakoplos. 2008. *Power Laws in Economics and Elsewhere.* Santa Fe, NM: Santa Fe Institute.

Fearnside, Philip M. 1994. "The Canadian Feasibility Study of the Three Gorges Dam Proposed for China's Yangzi River: A Grave Embarrassment to the Impact Assessment Profession." *Impact Assessment* 12 (1): 21–57.

Feynman, Richard P. 2007. "Richard P. Feynman's Minority Report to the Space Shuttle Challenger Inquiry." In Feynman, *The Pleasure of Finding Things Out.* New York: Penguin, 151–69.

Feynman, Richard P. 2007. "Mr. Feynman Goes to Washington: Investigating the Space Shuttle *Challenger* Disaster." In Feynman, *What Do You Care What Other People Think? Further Adventures of a Curious Character.* New York: Penguin, 113–237.

Flowers, Benjamin. 2009. *Skyscraper: The Politics and Power of Building New York City in the Twentieth Century.* Philadelphia: University of Pennsylvania Press.

Flyvbjerg, Bent. 1998. *Rationality and Power: Democracy in Practice.* Chicago: University of Chicago Press.

Flyvbjerg, Bent. 2001. *Making Social Science Matter: Why Social Inquiry Fails and How It Can Succeed Again.* Cambridge, UK: Cambridge University Press.

Flyvbjerg, Bent. 2003. "Delusions of Success: Comment on Dan Lovallo and Daniel Kahneman." *Harvard Business Review* 81 (12): 121–22.

Flyvbjerg, Bent. 2005. "Design by Deception: The Politics of Megaproject Approval." *Harvard Design Magazine* 22 (Spring/Summer): 50–59.

Flyvbjerg, Bent. 2005. "Measuring Inaccuracy in Travel Demand Forecasting: Methodological Considerations Regarding Ramp Up and Sampling." *Transportation Research A* 39 (6): 522–30.

Flyvbjerg, Bent. 2006. "From Nobel Prize to Project Management: Getting Risks Right." *Project Management Journal* 37 (3): 5–15.

Flyvbjerg, Bent. 2009. "Survival of the Unfittest: Why the Worst Infrastructure Gets Built, and What We Can Do About It." *Oxford Review of Economic Policy* 25 (3): 344–67.

Flyvbjerg, Bent. 2012. "Why Mass Media Matter and How to Work with Them: Phronesis and Megaprojects." In *Real Social Science: Applied Phronesis*, eds. Bent Flyvbjerg, Todd Landman, and Sanford Schram. Cambridge, UK: Cambridge University Press, 95–121.

Flyvbjerg, Bent. 2013. "Quality Control and Due Diligence in Project Management: Getting Decisions Right by Taking the Outside View." *International Journal of Project Management* 31 (5): 760–74.

Flyvbjerg, Bent. 2014. "What You Should Know About Megaprojects and Why: An Overview." *Project Management Journal* 45 (2): 6–19.

Flyvbjerg, Bent, ed. 2014. *Planning and Managing Megaprojects: Essential Readings.* Vols. 1–2. Cheltenham, UK: Edward Elgar.

Flyvbjerg, Bent. 2016, "The Fallacy of Beneficial Ignorance: A Test of Hirschman's Hiding Hand." *World Development* 84 (April): 176–89.

Flyvbjerg, Bent. 2017. "Introduction: The Iron Law of Megaproject Management." In *The Oxford Handbook of Megaproject Management*, ed. Bent Flyvbjerg. Oxford, UK: Oxford University Press, 1–18.

Flyvbjerg, Bent. 2018. "Planning Fallacy or Hiding Hand: Which Is the Better Explanation?" *World Development* 103 (March): 383–86.

Flyvbjerg, Bent. 2020. "The Law of Regression to the Tail: How to Survive Covid-19, the Climate Crisis, and Other Disasters." *Environmental Science and Policy* 114 (December): 614–18.

Flyvbjerg, Bent. 2021. "Four Ways to Scale Up: Smart, Dumb, Forced, and Fumbled." *Saïd Business School Working Papers*. Oxford, UK: University of Oxford.

Flyvbjerg, Bent. 2021. "Make Megaprojects More Modular." *Harvard Business Review* 99 (6): 58–63.

Flyvbjerg, Bent. 2021. "Top Ten Behavioral Biases in Project Management: An Overview." *Project Management Journal* 52 (6): 531–46.

Flyvbjerg, Bent. 2022. "Heuristics for Masterbuilders: Fast and Frugal Ways to Become a Better Project Leader." *Saïd Business School Working Papers*, Oxford, UK: University of Oxford.

Flyvbjerg, Bent, Atif Ansar, Alexander Budzier, Søren Buhl, Chantal Cantarelli, Massimo Garbuio, Carsten Glenting, Mette Skamris Holm, Dan Lovallo, Daniel Lunn, Eric Molin, Arne Rønnest, Allison Stewart, and Bert van Wee. 2018. "Five Things You Should Know About Cost Overrun." *Transportation Research Part A: Policy and Practice* 118 (December): 174–90.

Flyvbjerg, Bent, and Dirk W. Bester. 2021. "The Cost-Benefit Fallacy: Why Cost-Benefit Analysis Is Broken and How to Fix It." *Journal of Benefit-Cost Analysis* 12 (3): 395–419.

Flyvbjerg, Bent, Nils Bruzelius, and Werner Rothengatter. 2003. *Megaprojects and Risk: An Anatomy of Ambition*. Cambridge, UK: Cambridge University Press.

Flyvbjerg, Bent, and Alexander Budzier. 2011. "Why Your IT Project May Be Riskier Than You Think." *Harvard Business Review* 89 (9): 23–25.

Flyvbjerg, Bent, and Alexander Budzier. 2018. *Report for the Commission of Inquiry Respecting the Muskrat Falls Project*. St. John's, Province of Newfoundland and Labrador, Canada: Muskrat Falls Inquiry.

Flyvbjerg, Bent, Alexander Budzier, Maria D. Christodoulou, and M. Zottoli. Under review. "So You Think Projects Are Unique? How Uniqueness Bias Undermines Project Management."

Flyvbjerg, Bent, Alexander Budzier, Mark Keil, Jong Seok Lee, Dirk W. Bester, and Daniel Lunn. 2022. "The Empirical Reality of IT Project Cost Overruns: Discovering a Power-Law Distribution." Forthcoming in *Journal of Management Information Systems* 39 (3).

Flyvbjerg, Bent, Alexander Budzier, and Daniel Lunn. 2021. "Regression to the Tail: Why the Olympics Blow Up." *Environment and Planning A: Economy and Space* 53 (2): 233–60.

Flyvbjerg, Bent, Massimo Garbuio, and Dan Lovallo. 2009. "Delusion and Deception in Large Infrastructure Projects: Two Models for Explaining and Preventing Executive Disaster." *California Management Review* 51 (2): 170–93.

Flyvbjerg, Bent, Carsten Glenting, and Arne Rønnest. 2004. *Procedures for Dealing with Optimism Bias in Transport Planning: Guidance Document*. London: UK Department for Transport.

Flyvbjerg, Bent, Mette K. Skamris Holm, and Søren L. Buhl. 2002. "Underestimating Costs in Public Works Projects: Error or Lie?" *Journal of the American Planning Association* 68 (3): 279–95.
Flyvbjerg, Bent, Mette K. Skamris Holm, and Søren L. Buhl. 2004. "What Causes Cost Overrun in Transport Infrastructure Projects?" *Transport Reviews* 24 (1): 3–18.
Flyvbjerg, Bent, Mette K. Skamris Holm, and Søren L. Buhl. 2005. "How (In)accurate Are Demand Forecasts in Public Works Projects? The Case of Transportation." *Journal of the American Planning Association* 71 (2): 131–46.
Flyvbjerg, Bent, Chi-keung Hon, and Wing Huen Fok. 2016. "Reference-Class Forecasting for Hong Kong's Major Roadworks Projects." *Proceedings of the Institution of Civil Engineers* 169 (CE6): 17–24.
Flyvbjerg, Bent, and Tsung-Chung Kao, with Alexander Budzier. 2014. *Report to the Independent Board Committee on the Hong Kong Express Rail Link Project.* Hong Kong: MTR, A1–A122.
Flyvbjerg, Bent, Todd Landman, and Sanford Schram, eds. 2012. *Real Social Science: Applied Phronesis.* Cambridge, UK: Cambridge University Press.
Flyvbjerg, Bent, and Allison Stewart. 2012. "Olympic Proportions: Cost and Cost Overrun at the Olympics, 1960–2012." *Saïd Business School Working Papers.* Oxford, UK: University of Oxford.
Flyvbjerg, Bent, and Cass R. Sunstein. 2017. "The Principle of the Malevolent Hiding Hand; or, The Planning Fallacy Writ Large." *Social Research* 83 (4): 979–1004.
Fox Broadcasting Company. 2005. "The Seven-Beer Snitch." *The Simpsons.* Season 16, episode 14, April 3.
French Ministry of Transport. 2007. *Ex-Post Evaluation of French Road Projects: Main Results.* Paris: French Ministry of Transport.
Frey, Thomas. 2017. "Megaprojects Set to Explode to 24% of Global GDP Within a Decade." *Future of Construction,* February 10. https://futureofconstruction.org/blog/megaprojects-set-to-explode-to-24-of-global-gdp-within-a-decade/.
Frick, Karen T. 2008. "The Cost of the Technological Sublime: Daring Ingenuity and the New San Francisco–Oakland Bay Bridge." In *Decision-Making on Mega-Projects: Cost–Benefit Analysis, Planning, and Innovation,* eds. Hugo Priemus, Bent Flyvbjerg, and Bert van Wee. Cheltenham, UK: Edward Elgar, 239–62.
Fudenberg, Drew, David K. Levine, and Zacharias Maniadis. 2012. "On the Robustness of Anchoring Effects in WTP and WTA Experiments." *American Economic Journal: Microeconomics* 4 (2): 131–45.
Gabaix, Xavier. 2009. "Power Laws in Economics and Finance." *Annual Review of Economics* 1: 255–94.

Gaddis, Paul O. 1959. "The Project Manager." *Harvard Business Review* 37 (3): 89–99.
Gagné, Marylène, and Edward L. Deci. 2005. "Self-determination Theory and Work Motivation." *Journal of Organizational Behavior* 26 (4): 331–62.
Galton, Francis. 1886. "Regression Towards Mediocrity in Hereditary Stature." *The Journal of the Anthropological Institute of Great Britain and Ireland* 15: 246–63.
Garbuio, Massimo, and Gloria Gheno. 2021. "An Algorithm for Designing Value Propositions in the IoT Space: Addressing the Challenges of Selecting the Initial Class in Reference Class Forecasting." *IEEE Transactions on Engineering Management* 99: 1–12.
Gardner, Dan. 2009. *Risk: The Science and Politics of Fear.* London: Virgin Books.
Gardner, Dan. 2010. *Future Babble: Why Expert Predictions Fail and Why We Believe Them Anyway.* London: Virgin Books.
Garud, Raghu, Arun Kumaraswamy, and Richard N. Langlois. 2003. *Managing in the Modular Age: Architectures, Networks, and Organizations.* Oxford, UK: Blackwell Publishers.
Gasper, Des. 1986. "Programme Appraisal and Evaluation: The Hiding Hand and Other Stories." *Public Administration and Development* 6 (4): 467–74.
Gates, Bill. 2019. "How We'll Invent the Future: 10 Breakthrough Technologies." *MIT Technology Review,* February 27. https://www.technologyreview.com/2019/02/27/103388/bill-gates-how-well-invent-the-future/.
Gehry, Frank O. 2003. *Gehry Talks: Architecture + Process,* ed. Mildred Friedmann. London: Thames & Hudson.
Gehry, Frank O. 2003. "Introduction." In *Symphony: Frank Gehry's Walt Disney Concert Hall,* ed. Gloria Gerace. New York: Harry N. Abrams.
Gellert, Paul, and Barbara Lynch. 2003. "Mega-Projects as Displacements." *International Social Science Journal* 55, no. 175: 15–25.
Genus, Audley. 1997. "Managing Large-Scale Technology and Inter-organizational Relations: The Case of the Channel Tunnel." *Research Policy* 26 (2): 169–89.
Giezen, Mendel. 2012. "Keeping It Simple? A Case Study into the Advantages and Disadvantages of Reducing Complexity in Mega Project Planning." *International Journal of Project Management* 30 (7): 781–90.
Gigerenzer, Gerd. 2002. "Models of Ecological Rationality: The Recognition Heuristic." *Psychological Review* 109 (1): 75–90.
Gigerenzer, Gerd. 2014. *Risk Savvy: How to Make Good Decisions.* London: Allen Lane.
Gigerenzer, Gerd. 2018. "The Bias Bias in Behavioral Economics." *Review of Behavioral Economics* 5 (3–4): 303–36.
Gigerenzer, Gerd. 2021. "Embodied Heuristics." *Frontiers in Psychology* 12 (September): 1–12.

Gigerenzer, Gerd, and Henry Brighton. 2011. "Homo Heuristicus: Why Biased Minds Make Better Inferences." In *Heuristics: The Foundations of Adaptive Behavior*, eds. Gerd Gigerenzer, Ralph Hertwig, and Thorsten Pachur. Oxford, UK: Oxford University Press, 2–27.

Gigerenzer, Gerd, and Wolfgang Gaissmaier. 2011. "Heuristic Decision Making." *Annual Review of Psychology* 62 (1): 451–82.

Gigerenzer, Gerd, and Daniel G. Goldstein. 1996. "Reasoning the Fast and Frugal Way: Models of Bounded Rationality." *Psychological Review* 103 (4): 650–69.

Gigerenzer, Gerd, Ralph Hertwig, and Thorsten Pachur, eds. 2011. *Heuristics: The Foundations of Adaptive Behavior*. Oxford, UK: Oxford University Press.

Gigerenzer, Gerd, Peter M. Todd, and the ABC Research Group. 1999. *Simple Heuristics That Make Us Smart*. Oxford, UK: Oxford University Press.

Gil, Nuno, Marcela Miozzo, and Silvia Massini. 2011. "The Innovation Potential of New Infrastructure Development: An Empirical Study of Heathrow Airport's T5 Project." *Research Policy* 41 (2): 452–66.

Gilovich, Thomas, Dale Griffin, and Daniel Kahneman, eds. 2002. *Heuristics and Biases: The Psychology of Intuitive Judgment*. Cambridge, UK: Cambridge University Press.

Gino, Francesca, and Bradley Staats. 2015. "Why Organizations Don't Learn." *Harvard Business Review* 93 (10): 110–18.

Gladwell, Malcolm. 2007. *Blink: The Power of Thinking Without Thinking*. New York: Back Bay Books.

Gladwell, Malcolm. 2013. "The Gift of Doubt: Albert O. Hirschman and the Power of Failure." *The New Yorker*, June 17.

Gleick, Peter, Santos Gomez, Penn Loh, and Jason Morrison. 1995. "California Water 2020: A Sustainable Vision." Oakland, CA: Pacific Institute.

Goel, Rajnish K., Bhawani Singh, and Jian Zhao. 2012. *Underground Infrastructures: Planning, Design, and Construction*. Waltham, MA: Butterworth-Heinemann.

Goethals, George R., David M. Messick, and Scott T. Allison. 1991. "The Uniqueness Bias: Studies in Constructive Social Comparison." In *Social Comparison: Contemporary Theory and Research*, eds. Jerry Suls and T. A. Wills. Hillsdale, NJ: Erlbaum, 149–76.

Goldberger, Paul. 2015. *Building Art: The Life and Work of Frank Gehry*. New York: Alfred A. Knopf.

Goldblatt, David. 2016. *The Games: A Global History of the Olympics*. London: Macmillan.

Golder, Peter N., and Gerard J. Tellis. 1993. "Pioneer Advantage: Marketing Logic or Marketing Legend?" *Journal of Marketing Research* 30 (2): 158–70.

Goldstein, Daniel G., and Gerd Gigerenzer. 1999. "The Recognition Heuristic: How Ignorance Makes Us Smart." In *Simple Heuristics That Make Us Smart*, eds. Gerd Gigerenzer, Peter M. Todd, and the ABC Research Group. Oxford, UK: Oxford University Press, 37–58.

Gordon, Christopher M. 1994. "Choosing Appropriate Construction Contracting Method." *Journal of Construction Engineering and Management* 120 (1): 196–211.

Green, Jim. 2016. "Japan Abandons Monju Fast Reactor: The Slow Death of a Nuclear Dream." *The Ecologist*, October 6.

Griffin, Dale W., David Dunning, and Lee Ross. 1990. "The Role of Construal Processes in Overconfident Predictions About the Self and Others." *Journal of Personality and Social Psychology* 59 (6): 1128–39.

Griffith, Saul. 2021. *Electrify: An Optimist's Playbook for Our Clean Energy Future*. Cambridge, MA: MIT Press.

Grubler, Arnulf. 2010. "The Costs of the French Nuclear Scale-up: A Case of Negative Learning by Doing." *Energy Policy* 38 (9): 5174–88.

Guadagno, Rosanna E., and Robert B. Cialdini. 2010. "Preference for Consistency and Social Influence: A Review of Current Research Findings." *Social Influence* 5 (3): 152–63.

Guinote, Ana. 2017. "How Power Affects People: Activating, Wanting, and Goal Seeking." *Annual Review of Psychology* 68 (1): 353–81.

Guinote, Ana, and Theresa K. Vescio, eds. 2010. *The Social Psychology of Power*. New York: Guilford Press.

Gumbel, Emil J. 2004. *Statistics of Extremes*. Mineola, NY: Dover Publications.

Hall, Peter. 1980. *Great Planning Disasters*. Harmondsworth, UK: Penguin Books.

Hall, Peter. Undated. *Great Planning Disasters Revisited*, paper. London: Bartlett School.

Henderson, P. D. 1977. "Two British Errors: Their Probable Size and Some Possible Lessons." *Oxford Economic Papers* 29 (2): 159–205.

Hendy, Jane, Barnaby Reeves, Naomi Fulop, Andrew Hutchings, and Cristina Masseria. 2005. "Challenges to Implementing the National Programme for Information Technology (NPfIT): A Qualitative Study." *The BMJ* 331 (7512): 331–36.

HGTV. 2018. "What It's Like to Live in a Sears Catalog Home." YouTube, May 13. https://www.youtube.com/watch?v=3kb24gwnZ18.

Hiltzik, Michael A. 2010. *Colossus: Hoover Dam and the Making of the American Century*. New York: Free Press.

Hiroko, Tabuchi. 2011. "Japan Strains to Fix a Reactor Damaged Before Quake." *The New York Times*, June 17.

Hirschman, Albert O. 1967. "The Principle of the Hiding Hand." *The Public Interest*, no. 6 (Winter): 10–23.

Hirschman, Albert O. 2014. *Development Projects Observed* (Brookings Classic), 3rd ed., with new foreword by Cass R. Sunstein and new afterword by Michele Alacevich. Washington, DC: Brookings Institution.

HM Treasury. 2003. *The Green Book: Appraisal and Evaluation in Central Government.* London: The Stationery Office (TSO).
HM Treasury. 2003. *Supplementary Green Book Guidance: Optimism Bias.* London: The Stationery Office (TSO).
HM Treasury. 2004. *The Orange Book. Management of Risk: Principles and Concepts.* London: The Stationery Office (TSO).
HM Treasury. 2011. *The Green Book: Appraisal and Evaluation in Central Government*, 2003 edition with 2011 amendments. London: The Stationery Office (TSO).
HM Treasury. 2013. *Green Book Supplementary Guidance: Optimism Bias.* London: The Stationery Office (TSO).
HM Treasury. 2015. *Early Financial Cost Estimates of Infrastructure Programmes and Projects and the Treatment of Uncertainty and Risk.* Update, March 26. London: The Stationery Office (TSO).
HM Treasury. 2018. *The Green Book: Central Government Guidance on Appraisal and Evaluation.* London: The Stationery Office (TSO).
HM Treasury. 2019. *The Orange Book. Management of Risk: Principles and Concepts.* London: The Stationery Office (TSO).
HM Treasury. 2020. *The Green Book: Central Government Guidance on Appraisal and Evaluation.* London: The Stationery Office (TSO).
Hobday, Mike. 1998. "Product Complexity, Innovation and Industrial Organisation." *Research Policy* 26 (6): 689–710.
Hodge, Graeme A., and Carsten Greve. 2009. "PPPs: The Passage of Time Permits a Sober Reflection." *Institute of Economic Affairs* 29 (1): 33–39.
Hodge, Graeme A., and Carsten Greve. 2017. "On Public-Private Partnership Performance: A Contemporary Review." *Public Works Management and Policy* 22 (1): 55–78.
Hofstadter, Douglas R. 1979. *Gödel, Escher, Bach: An Eternal Golden Braid.* New York: Basic Books.
Hong, Byoung H., Kyoun E. Lee, and Jae W. Lee. 2007. "Power Law in Firms Bankruptcy." *Physics Letters A* 361: 6–8.
Hong Kong Development Bureau, Project Cost Management Office, and Oxford Global Projects. 2022. *AI in Action: How the Hong Kong Development Bureau Built the PSS, an Early-Warning-Sign System for Public Work Projects.* Hong Kong: Development Bureau.
Horne, John. 2007. "The Four 'Knowns' of Sports Mega Events." *Leisure Studies* 26 (1): 81–96.
HS2, Ltd. "Exploring Our Past, Preparing for the Future." https://www.hs2.org.uk/building-hs2/archaeology/.
Hughes, Thomas P. 2000. *Rescuing Prometheus: Four Monumental Projects That Changed the Modern World.* New York: Vintage.
International Airport Review. 2019. "Heathrow Terminal 5 Named 'World's Best' at Skytrax Awards." *International Airport Review*, March 28. https://

www.internationalairportreview.com/news/83710/heathrow-worlds-best
-skytrax/.
International Energy Agency (IEA). 2021. *Net Zero by 2050: A Roadmap for the Global Energy Sector.* Paris: IEA, May. https://www.iea.org/reports/net-zero
-by-2050.
International Energy Agency (IEA). 2021. *Pathway to Critical and Formidable Goal of Net-Zero Emissions by 2050 Is Narrow but Brings Huge Benefits.* Paris: IEA, May 18. https://www.iea.org/news/pathway-to-critical-and
-formidable-goal-of-net-zero-emissions-by-2050-is-narrow-but-brings
-huge-benefits.
International Hydropower Association (IHA). 2019. "Country Profile: Norway." IHA. https://www.hydropower.org/country-profiles/norway.
International Renewable Energy Agency (IRENA). 2021. *Renewable Capacity Statistics 2021.* IRENA, March. https://www.irena.org/publications/2021
/March/Renewable-Capacity-Statistics-2021.
IPCC. 2021. "Summary for Policymakers." In *Climate Change 2021: The Physical Science Basis. Contribution of Working Group I to the Sixth Assessment Report of the Intergovernmental Panel on Climate Change,* eds. V. Masson-Delmotte, P. Zhai, A. Pirani, S. L. Connors, C. Péan, S. Berger, N. Caud, Y. Chen, L. Goldfarb, M. I. Gomis, M. Huang, K. Leitzell, E. Lonnoy, J.B.R. Matthews, T. K. Maycock, T. Waterfield, O. Yelekçi, R. Yu, and B. Zhou. Cambridge, UK: Cambridge University Press.
Irish Department of Public Expenditure and Reform. 2019. *Public Spending Code: A Guide to Evaluating, Planning and Managing Public Investment.* Dublin: Department of Public Expenditure and Reform.
Isaacson, Walter. 2011. *Steve Jobs.* New York: Simon & Schuster.
Israel, Paul. 1998. *Edison: A Life of Invention.* Hoboken, NJ: John Wiley and Sons.
Jacobsson, Mattias, and Timothy L. Wilson. 2018. "Revisiting the Construction of the Empire State Building: Have We Forgotten Something?" *Business Horizons* 61 (1): 47–57.
The Japan Times. 2014. "Falsified Inspections Suspected at Monju Fast-Breeder Reactor." *The Japan Times,* April 11.
The Japan Times. 2015. "More Maintenance Flaws Found at Monju Reactor." *The Japan Times,* March 26.
The Japan Times. 2016. "Monju Prototype Reactor, Once a Key Cog in Japan's Nuclear Energy Policy, to Be Scrapped." *The Japan Times,* December 21.
Jensen, Henrik J. 1998. *Self-Organized Criticality: Emergent Complex Behavior in Physical and Biological Systems.* Cambridge, UK: Cambridge University Press.
Jones, Lawrence R., and Kenneth J. Euske. 1991. "Strategic Misrepresentation in Budgeting." *Journal of Public Administration Research and Theory* 1 (4): 437–60.

Josephson, Paul R. 1995. "Projects of the Century in Soviet History: Large-Scale Technologies from Lenin to Gorbachev." *Technology and Culture* 36 (3): 519–59.
Journal of the House of Representatives of the United States. 1942. 77th Congress, 2nd Session, January 5. Washington, DC: US Government Printing Office, 6.
Jørgensen, Magne, and Kjetil Moløkken-Østvold. 2006. "How Large Are Software Cost Overruns? A Review of the 1994 CHAOS Report." *Information and Software Technology* 48 (4): 297–301.
Kahneman, Daniel. 1992. "Reference Points, Anchors, Norms, and Mixed Feelings." *Organizational Behavior and Human Decision Processes* 51 (2): 296–312.
Kahneman, Daniel. 1994. "New Challenges to the Rationality Assumption." *Journal of Institutional and Theoretical Economics* 150 (1): 18–36.
Kahneman, Daniel. 2011. *Thinking, Fast and Slow.* New York: Farrar, Straus and Giroux.
Kahneman, Daniel, and Gary Klein. 2009. "Conditions for Intuitive Expertise: A Failure to Disagree." *American Psychologist* 64 (6): 515–26.
Kahneman, Daniel, and Dan Lovallo. 1993. "Timid Choices and Bold Forecasts: A Cognitive Perspective on Risk Taking." *Management Science* 39 (1): 17–31.
Kahneman, Daniel, and Dan Lovallo. 2003. "Response to Bent Flyvbjerg." *Harvard Business Review* 81 (12): 122.
Kahneman, Daniel, Dan Lovallo, and Olivier Sibony. 2011. "Before You Make That Big Decision." *Harvard Business Review* 89 (6): 51–60.
Kahneman, Daniel, Olivier Sibony, and Cass R. Sunstein. 2021. *Noise: A Flaw in Human Judgment.* London: William Collins.
Kahneman, Daniel, Paul Slovic, and Amos Tversky, eds. 1982. *Judgment Under Uncertainty: Heuristics and Biases.* Cambridge, UK: Cambridge University Press.
Kahneman, Daniel, and Amos Tversky. 1979. "Intuitive Prediction: Biases and Corrective Procedures." In *Studies in the Management Sciences: Forecasting,* vol. 12, eds. Spyros Makridakis and S. C. Wheelwright. Amsterdam: North Holland, 313–27.
Kahneman, Daniel, and Amos Tversky. 1979. "Prospect Theory: An Analysis of Decisions Under Risk." *Econometrica* 47: 313–27.
Kain, John F. 1990. "Deception in Dallas: Strategic Misrepresentation in Rail Transit Promotion and Evaluation." *Journal of the American Planning Association* 56 (2): 184–96.
Kazan, Elia. 1997. *A Life.* New York: Da Capo.
Keil, Mark, Joan Mann, and Arun Rai. 2000. "Why Software Projects Escalate: An Empirical Analysis and Test of Four Theoretical Models." *MIS Quarterly* 24 (4): 631–64.
Keil, Mark, and Ramiro Montealegre. 2000. "Cutting Your Losses: Extricating

Your Organization When a Big Project Goes Awry." *Sloan Management Review* 41 (3): 55–68.

Keil, Mark, Arun Rai, and Shan Liu. 2013. "How User Risk and Requirements Risk Moderate the Effects of Formal and Informal Control on the Process Performance of IT Projects." *European Journal of Information Systems* 22 (6): 650–72.

Kelly, Brendan. 2019. "Olympic Stadium Architect Remembered as a Man of Vision." *Montreal Gazette*, October 3.

Kim, Byung-Cheol, and Kenneth F. Reinschmidt. 2011. "Combination of Project Cost Forecasts in Earned Value Management." *Journal of Construction Engineering and Management* 137 (11): 958–66.

King, Anthony, and Ivor Crewe. 2013. *The Blunders of Our Governments*. London: Oneworld Publications.

Kitroeff, Natalie, Maria Abi-Habib, James Glanz, Oscar Lopez, Weiyi Cai, Evan Grothjan, Miles Peyton, and Alejandro Cegarra. 2021. "Why the Mexico City Metro Collapsed." *The New York Times*, June 13.

Klein, Gary. 2007. "Performing a Project Premortem." *Harvard Business Review* 85 (9): 18–19.

Knowles, Elizabeth, ed. 2014. *Oxford Dictionary of Quotations*, 8th ed. New York: Oxford University Press, 557.

Koch-Weser, Iacob N. 2013. *The Reliability of China's Economic Data: An Analysis of National Output*. Washington, DC: US-China Economic and Security Review Commission, US Congress.

Koshalek, Richard, and Dana Hutt. 2003. "The Impossible Becomes Possible: The Making of Walt Disney Concert Hall." In *Symphony: Frank Gehry's Walt Disney Concert Hall*, ed. Gloria Gerace. New York: Harry N. Abrams.

Krapivsky, Paul, and Dmitri Krioukov. 2008. "Scale-Free Networks as Preasymptotic Regimes of Superlinear Preferential Attachment." *Physical Review E* 78 (2): 1–11.

Krugman, Paul. 2000. "How Complicated Does the Model Have to Be?" *Oxford Review of Economic Policy* 16 (4): 33–42.

Kubota, Yoko. 2011. "Fallen Device Retrieved from Japan Fast-Breeder Reactor." Reuters, June 24. https://www.reuters.com/article/us-japan-nuclear-monju-idUSTRE75N0H320110624.

Kunthara, Sophia. 2014. "A Closer Look at Theranos' Big-Name Investors, Partners, and Board as Elizabeth Holmes' Criminal Trial Begins." *Crunchbase News*, September 14. https://news.crunchbase.com/news/theranos-elizabeth-holmes-trial-investors-board/.

Lacal-Arántegui, Roberto, José M. Yusta, and José A. Domínguez-Navarro. 2018. "Offshore Wind Installation: Analysing the Evidence Behind Improvements in Installation Time." *Renewable and Sustainable Energy Reviews* 92 (September): 133–45.

Lamb, William F. 1931. "The Empire State Building." *Architectural Forum* 54 (1): 1–7.
Larsen, Henning. 2009. *De skal sige tak! Kulturhistorisk testamente om Operaen.* Copenhagen: People's Press, 14.
Latour, Bruno. 1996. *Aramis; or, The Love of Technology.* Cambridge, MA: Harvard University Press.
Lauermann, John, and Anne Vogelpohl. 2017. "Fragile Growth Coalitions or Powerful Contestations? Cancelled Olympic Bids in Boston and Hamburg." *Environment and Planning A* 49 (8): 1887–904.
Lawson, Rebecca. 2006. "The Science of Cycology: Failures to Understand How Everyday Objects Work." *Memory & Cognition* 34 (8): 1667–75.
LeBlanc, Richard D. 2020. *Muskrat Falls: A Misguided Project,* vols. 1–6. Province of Newfoundland and Labrador, Canada: Commission of Inquiry Respecting the Muskrat Falls Project.
Lee, Douglass B., Jr. 1973. "Requiem for Large-Scale Models." *Journal of the American Institute of Planners* 39 (3): 163–78.
Lenfle, Sylvian, and Christoph Loch. 2010. "Lost Roots: How Project Management Came to Emphasize Control over Flexibility and Novelty." *California Management Review* 53 (1): 32–55.
Levinson, Marc. 2016. *The Box: How the Shipping Container Made the World Smaller and the World Economy Bigger.* Princeton, NJ: Princeton University Press.
Levy, Steven. 2017. "One More Thing." *Wired,* May 16.
Levy, Steven. 2020. "20 Years Ago, Steve Jobs Built the 'Coolest Computer Ever.' It Bombed." *Wired,* July 24.
Lia, Leif, Trond Jensen, Kjell E. Stensby, and Grethe H. Midttømme. 2015. "The Current Status of Hydropower Development and Dam Construction in Norway." *Hydropower & Dams* 22, no. 3.
Lieberman, Marvin. 2018. "First-Mover Advantage." In *Palgrave Encyclopedia of Strategic Management,* eds. Mie Augier and David J. Teece. London: Palgrave Macmillan.
Lieberman, Marvin B., and David B. Montgomery. 1988. "First-Mover Advantages." *Strategic Management Journal* 9 (51): 41–58.
Lindsey, Bruce. 2001. *Digital Gehry: Material Resistance, Digital Construction.* Basel: Birkhäuser.
Liou, Joanne. 2021. "What Are Small Modular Reactors (SMRs)?" International Atomic Energy Agency, November 4. https://www.iaea.org/newscenter/news/what-are-small-modular-reactors-smrs.
Little, Angela W. 2007. *Education for All and Multigrade Teaching: Challenges and Opportunities.* Dordrecht, Netherlands: Springer.
Liu, Li, and Zigrid Napier. 2010. "The Accuracy of Risk-Based Cost Estimation for Water Infrastructure Projects: Preliminary Evidence from Australian Projects." *Construction Management and Economics* 28 (1): 89–100.

Liu, Li, George Wehbe, and Jonathan Sisovic. 2010. "The Accuracy of Hybrid Estimating Approaches: A Case Study of an Australian State Road and Traffic Authority." *The Engineering Economist* 55 (3): 225–45.
Lopez, Oscar. 2021. "Faulty Studs Led to Mexico City Metro Collapse, Attorney General Says." *The New York Times*, October 14.
Lovallo, Dan, Carmine Clarke, and Colin Camerer. 2012. "Robust Analogizing and the Outside View: Two Empirical Tests of Case-Based Decision Making." *Strategic Management Journal* 33: 496–512.
Lovallo, Dan, Matteo Cristofaro, and Bent Flyvbjerg. 2022. "Addressing Governance Errors and Lies in Project Forecasting." *Academy of Management Perspectives*, forthcoming.
Lovallo, Dan, and Daniel Kahneman. 2003. "Delusions of Success: How Optimism Undermines Executives' Decisions." *Harvard Business Review* 81 (7): 56–63.
Lovering, Jessica R., Arthur Yip, and Ted Nordhaus. 2016. "Historical Construction Costs of Global Nuclear Power Reactors." *Energy Policy* 91: 371–82.
Luberoff, David, and Alan Altshuler. 1996. *Mega-Project: A Political History of Boston's Multibillion Dollar Central Artery/Third Harbor Tunnel Project*. Cambridge, MA: Taubman Center for State and Local Government, Kennedy School of Government, Harvard University.
Madsen, Heather L., and John P. Ulhøi. 2021. "Sustainable Visioning: Reframing Strategic Vision to Enable a Sustainable Corporation Transformation." *Journal of Cleaner Production* 288 (March): 125602.
Maillart, Thomas, and Didier Sornette. 2010. "Heavy-Tailed Distribution of Cyber-Risks." *The European Physical Journal B* 75 (3): 357–64.
Major Projects Association. 1994. *Beyond 2000: A Source Book for Major Projects*. Oxford, UK: Major Projects Association.
Makridakis, Spyros, and Nassim N. Taleb. 2009. "Living in a World of Low Levels of Predictability." *International Journal of Forecasting* 25 (4): 840–44.
Malamud, Bruce D., and Donald L. Turcotte. 2006. "The Applicability of Power-Law Frequency Statistics to Floods." *Journal of Hydrology* 322 (1–4): 168–80.
Manchester Evening News. 2007. "Timeline: The Woes of Wembley Stadium." *Manchester Evening News*, February 15.
Mandelbrot, Benoit B. 1960. "The Pareto-Lévy Law and the Distribution of Income." *International Economic Review* 1 (2): 79–106.
Mandelbrot, Benoit B. 1963. "New Methods in Statistical Economics." *Journal of Political Economy* 71 (5): 421–40.
Mandelbrot, Benoit B. 1963. "The Variation of Certain Speculative Prices." *The Journal of Business* 36 (4): 394–419; correction printed in Mandelbrot, Benoit B. 1972. *The Journal of Business* 45 (4): 542–43; revised version reprinted in Mandelbrot, Benoit B. 1997. *Fractals and Scaling in Finance*. New York: Springer, 371–418.

Mandelbrot, Benoit B. 1997. *Fractals and Scaling in Finance.* New York: Springer.
Mandelbrot, Benoit B., and Richard L. Hudson. 2008. *The (Mis)behavior of Markets.* London: Profile Books.
Mandelbrot, Benoit B., and James R. Wallis. 1968. "Noah, Joseph, and Operational Hydrology." *Water Resources Research* 4 (5): 909–18.
Mann, Michael E. 2021. *The New Climate War: The Fight to Take the Planet Back.* London: Scribe.
Marewski, Julian N., Wolfgang Gaissmaier, and Gerd Gigerenzer. 2010. "Good Judgments Do Not Require Complex Cognition." *Cognitive Processing* 11 (2): 103–21.
Marković, Dimitrije, and Claudius Gros. 2014. "Power Laws and Self-Organized Criticality in Theory and Nature." *Physics Reports* 536 (2): 41–74.
McAdam, Doug, Hilary S. Boudet, Jennifer Davis, Ryan J. Orr, W. Richard Scott, and Raymond E. Levitt. 2010. "Site Fights: Explaining Opposition to Pipeline Projects in the Developing World." *Sociological Forum* 25: 401–27.
McCormick, Iain A., Frank H. Walkey, and Dianne E. Green. 1986. "Comparative Perceptions of Driver Ability: A Confirmation and Expansion." *Accident Analysis & Prevention* 18 (3): 205–8.
McCully, Patrick. 2001. *Silenced Rivers: The Ecology and Politics of Large Dams.* London: Zed Books.
McCurdy, Howard E. 2001. *Faster, Better, Cheaper: Low-Cost Innovation in the U.S. Space Program.* Baltimore, MD: Johns Hopkins University Press.
Melis, Manuel. 2002. "Building a Metro: It's Easier Than You Think." *International Railway Journal,* April, 16–19.
Melis, Manuel. 2011. *Apuntes de introducción al Proyecto y Construcción de Túneles y Metros en suelos y rocas blandas o muy rotas: La construcción del Metro de Madrid y la M-30.* Madrid: Politécnica.
Merriam-Webster. "Your 'Deadline' Won't Kill You." Merriam-Webster. https://www.merriam-webster.com/words-at-play/your-deadline-wont-kill-you.
Merrow, Edward W. 2011. *Industrial Megaprojects: Concepts, Strategies, and Practices for Success.* Hoboken, NJ: Wiley.
Midler, Christophe. 1995. "Projectification of the Firm: The Renault Case." *Scandinavian Journal of Management* 11 (4): 363–75.
Miller, Roger, and Donald R. Lessard. 2000. *The Strategic Management of Large Engineering Projects: Shaping Institutions, Risks, and Governance.* Cambridge, MA: MIT Press.
MIT Energy Initiative. 2018. *The Future of Nuclear Energy in a Carbon-Constrained World.* Cambridge, MA: MIT.
Mitzenmacher, Michael. 2004. "A Brief History of Generative Models for Power Law and Lognormal Distributions." *Internet Mathematics* 1 (2): 226–51.
Mitzenmacher, Michael. 2005. "Editorial: The Future of Power Law Research." *Internet Mathematics* 2 (4): 525–34.

Molle, François, and Philippe Floch. 2008. "Megaprojects and Social and Environmental Changes: The Case of the Thai Water Grid." *AMBIO: A Journal of the Human Environment* 37 (3): 199–204.

Montealgre, Ramiro, and Mark Keil. 2000. "De-escalating Information Technology Projects: Lessons from the Denver International Airport." *MIS Quarterly* 24 (3): 417–47.

Moore, Don A., and Paul J. Healy. 2008. "The Trouble with Overconfidence." *Psychological Review* 115 (2): 502–17.

Morris, Peter W. G. 2013. *Reconstructing Project Management*. Oxford, UK: Wiley-Blackwell.

Morris, Peter W. G., and George H. Hough. 1987. *The Anatomy of Major Projects: A Study of the Reality of Project Management*. New York: John Wiley and Sons.

Morten, Alf, Yasutami Shimomure, and Annette Skovsted Hansen. 2008. *Aid Relationships in Asia: Exploring Ownership in Japanese and Nordic Aid*. London: Palgrave Macmillan.

Müller, Martin, and Chris Gaffney. 2018. "Comparing the Urban Impacts of the FIFA World Cup and the Olympic Games from 2010 to 2016." *Journal of Sport and Social Issues* 42 (4): 247–69.

Murray, Peter. 2003. *The Saga of the Sydney Opera House*. London: Routledge.

National Audit Office of Denmark, De af Folketinget Valgte Statsrevisorer. 1998. *Beretning om Storebæltsforbindelsens økonomi*. Beretning 4/97. Copenhagen: Statsrevisoratet.

Newby-Clark, Ian R., Michael Ross, Roger Buehler, Derek J. Koehler, and Dale W. Griffin. 2000. "People Focus on Optimistic and Disregard Pessimistic Scenarios While Predicting Task Completion Times." *Journal of Experimental Psychology: Applied* 6 (3): 171–82.

Newman, Alexander, Ross Donohue, and Nathan Eva. 2015. "Psychological Safety: A Systematic Review of the Literature." *Human Resource Management Review* 27 (3): 521–35.

Newman, Mark E. 2005. "Power Laws, Pareto Distributions and Zipf's Law." *Contemporary Physics* 46 (5): 323–51.

New Zealand Treasury. 2018. *Better Business Cases: Guide to Developing a Detailed Business Case*. Wellington, NZ: Crown.

Nouvel, Jean. 2009. "Interview About DR-Byen." *Weekendavisen*, Copenhagen, January 16.

O'Reilly, Charles, and Andrew J. M. Binns. 2019. "The Three Stages of Disruptive Innovation: Idea Generation, Incubation, and Scaling." *California Management Review* 61 (3): 49–71.

Orr, Ryan J., and W. Richard Scott. 2008. "Institutional Exceptions on Global Projects: A Process Model." *Journal of International Business Studies* 39 (4): 562–88.

Ørsted. 2020. "Making Green Energy Affordable: How the Offshore Wind Energy Industry Matured—and What We Can Learn from It." https://orsted.com/en/about-us/whitepapers/making-green-energy-affordable.
O'Sullivan, Owen P. 2015. "The Neural Basis of Always Looking on the Bright Side." *Dialogues in Philosophy, Mental and Neuro Sciences* 8 (1): 11–15.
Our World in Data. 2022. "Share of Electricity Production by Source, World." *Our World in Data.* https://ourworldindata.org/grapher/share-elec-by-source.
Pallier, Gerry, Rebecca Wilkinson, Vanessa Danthiir, Sabina Kleitman, Goran Knezevic, Lazar Stankov, and Richard D. Roberts. 2002. "The Role of Individual Differences in the Accuracy of Confidence Judgments." *The Journal of General Psychology* 129 (3): 257–99.
Park, Jung E. 2021. "Curbing Cost Overruns in Infrastructure Investment: Has Reference Class Forecasting Delivered Its Promised Success?" *European Journal of Transport and Infrastructure Research* 21 (2): 120–36.
Patanakul, Peerasit. 2014. "Managing Large-Scale IS/IT Projects in the Public Sector: Problems and Causes Leading to Poor Performance." *The Journal of High Technology Management Research* 25 (1): 21–35.
Patel, Ashish, Paul A. Bosela, and Norbert J. Delatte. 2013. "1976 Montreal Olympics: Case Study of Project Management Failure." *Journal of Performance of Constructed Facilities* 27 (3): 362–69.
PBS. 2015. "Looking Back at Frank Gehry's Building-Bending Feats." *PBS NewsHour,* September 15. https://www.pbs.org/newshour/show/frank-gehry.
Perrow, Charles. 1999. *Normal Accidents: Living with High-Risk Technologies,* updated ed. Princeton, NJ: Princeton University Press.
Phys.org. 2014. "Japan to Abandon Troubled Fast Breeder Reactor." Phys.org, February 7. https://phys.org/news/2014-02-japan-abandon-fast-breeder-reactor.html.
Pickrell, Don. 1985. "Estimates of Rail Transit Construction Costs." *Transportation Research Record* 1006: 54–60.
Pickrell, Don. 1985. "Rising Deficits and the Uses of Transit Subsidies in the United States." *Journal of Transport Economics and Policy* 19 (3): 281–98.
Pickrell, Don. 1990. *Urban Rail Transit Projects: Forecast Versus Actual Ridership and Cost.* Washington, DC: US Department of Transportation.
Pickrell, Don. 1992. "A Desire Named Streetcar: Fantasy and Fact in Rail Transit Planning." *Journal of the American Planning Association* 58 (2): 158–76.
Pisarenko, Valeriy F., and Didier Sornette. 2012. "Robust Statistical Tests of Dragon-Kings Beyond Power Law Distributions." *The European Physical Journal: Special Topics* 205: 95–115.
Pitsis, Tyrone S., Stewart R. Clegg, Marton Marosszeky, and Thekla Rura-Polley. 2003. "Constructing the Olympic Dream: A Future Perfect Strategy of Project Management." *Organization Science* 14 (5): 574–90.
Polanyi, Michael. 1966. *The Tacit Dimension.* Chicago: University of Chicago Press.

Popovich, Nadja, and Winston Choi-Schagrin. 2021. "Hidden Toll of the Northwest Heat Wave: Hundreds of Extra Deaths." *The New York Times,* August 11.

Priemus, Hugo. 2010. "Mega-Projects: Dealing with Pitfalls." *European Planning Studies* 18 (7): 1023–39.

Priemus, Hugo, Bent Flyvbjerg, and Bert van Wee, eds. 2008. *Decision-Making on Mega-Projects: Cost-Benefit Analysis, Planning and Innovation.* Cheltenham, UK: Edward Elgar.

Proeger, Till, and Lukas Meub. 2014. "Overconfidence as a Social Bias: Experimental Evidence." *Economics Letters* 122 (2): 203–7.

Public Accounts Committee. 2013. *The Dismantled National Programme for IT in the NHS: Nineteenth Report of Session 2013–14,* HC 294. London: House of Commons.

Qiu, Jane. 2011. "China Admits Problems with Three Gorges Dam." *Nature,* May 25. https://www.nature.com/articles/news.2011.315.

Quinn, Ben. 2008. "253m Legal Battle over Wembley Delays." *The Guardian,* March 16.

Ramirez, Joshua Elias. 2021. *Toward a Theory of Behavioral Project Management,* doctoral dissertation. Chicago: Chicago School of Professional Psychology.

Randall, Tom. 2017. "Tesla Flips the Switch on the Gigafactory." Bloomberg, January 4. https://www.bloomberg.com/news/articles/2017-01-04/tesla-flips-the-switch-on-the-gigafactory.

Reichold, Klaus, and Bernhard Graf. 2004. *Buildings That Changed the World.* London: Prestel.

Ren, Xuefei. 2008. "Architecture as Branding: Mega Project Developments in Beijing." *Built Environment* 34 (4): 517–31.

Ren, Xuefei. 2017. "Biggest Infrastructure Bubble Ever? City and Nation Building with Debt-Financed Megaprojects in China." In *The Oxford Handbook of Megaproject Management,* ed. Bent Flyvbjerg. Oxford, UK: Oxford University Press, 137–51.

Reuters. 2021. "Bill Gates and Warren Buffett to Build New Kind of Nuclear Reactor in Wyoming." *The Guardian,* June 3.

Rich, Motoko, Stanley Reed, and Jack Ewing. 2021. "Clearing the Suez Canal Took Days. Figuring Out the Costs May Take Years." *The New York Times,* March 31.

Richmond, Jonathan. 2005. *Transport of Delight: The Mythical Conception of Rail Transit in Los Angeles.* Akron, OH: University of Akron Press.

Ries, Eric. 2011. *The Lean Startup.* New York: Currency.

Riga, Andy. 2016. "Montreal Olympic Photo Flashback: Stadium Was Roofless at 1976 Games." *Montreal Gazette,* July 21.

Robinson, John B. 1990. "Futures Under Glass: A Recipe for People Who Hate to Predict." *Futures* 22 (8): 820–42.

Romzek, Barbara S., and Melvin J. Dubnick. 1987. "Accountability in the Public

Sector: Lessons from the Challenger Tragedy." *Public Administration Review* 47 (3): 227–38.

Roser, Christopher. 2017. *Faster, Better, Cheaper in the History of Manufacturing.* Boca Raton, FL: CRC Press.

Roser, Max, Cameron Appel, and Hannah Ritchie. 2013. "Human Height." *Our World in Data.* https://ourworldindata.org/human-height.

Ross, Jerry, and Barry M. Staw. 1986. "Expo 86: An Escalation Prototype." *Administrative Science Quarterly* 31 (2): 274–97.

Ross, Jerry, and Barry M. Staw. 1993. "Organizational Escalation and Exit: The Case of the Shoreham Nuclear Power Plant." *Academy of Management Journal* 36 (4): 701–32.

Rothengatter, Werner. 2008. "Innovations in the Planning of Mega-Projects." In *Decision-Making on Mega-Projects: Cost-Benefit Analysis, Planning, and Innovation,* eds. Hugo Priemus, Bent Flyvbjerg, and Bert van Wee. Cheltenham, UK: Edward Elgar, 215–38.

Royer, Isabelle. 2003. "Why Bad Projects Are So Hard to Kill." *Harvard Business Review* 81 (2): 48–56.

Rozenblit, Leonid, and Frank Keil. 2002. "The Misunderstood Limits of Folk Science: An Illusion of Explanatory Depth." *Cognitive Science* 26 (5): 521–62.

Rumsfeld, Donald. 2002. "DoD News Briefing: Secretary Rumsfeld and Gen. Myers." U.S. Department of Defense, February 12. https://archive.ph/20180320091111/http://archive.defense.gov/Transcripts/Transcript.aspx?TranscriptID=2636#selection-401.0-401.53.

Ryan, Richard M., and Edward L. Deci. 2017. *Self-Determination Theory: Basic Psychological Needs in Motivation, Development, and Wellness.* New York: Guilford Press.

Sacks, Rafael, and Rebecca Partouche. 2010. "Empire State Building Project: Archetype of 'Mass Construction.'" *Journal of Construction Engineering and Management* 136 (6): 702–10.

Sanders, Heywood T. 2014. *Convention Center Follies: Politics, Power, and Public Investment in American Cities.* Philadelphia: University of Pennsylvania Press.

Sapolsky, Harvey M. 1972. *The Polaris System Development.* Cambridge, MA: Harvard University Press.

Sawyer, John E. 1951. "Entrepreneurial Error and Economic Growth." *Explorations in Entrepreneurial History* 4 (4): 199–204.

Sayles, Leonard R., and Margaret K. Chandler. 1971. *Managing Large Systems: Organizations for the Future.* New York: Free Press.

Schmidt-Nielsen, Knut. 1984. *Scaling: Why Is Animal Size So Important?* Cambridge, UK: Cambridge University Press.

Schön, Donald A. 1994. "Hirschman's Elusive Theory of Social Learning." In *Rethinking the Development Experience: Essays Provoked by the Work of Albert O. Hirschman,* eds. Lloyd Rodwin and Donald A. Schön. Washington, DC: Brookings Institution and Lincoln Institute of Land Policy, 67–95.

Schumacher, Ernst F. 1973. *Small Is Beautiful: A Study of Economics as If People Mattered,* new ed. London: Vintage.

Scott, James C. 1999. *Seeing Like a State: How Certain Schemes to Improve the Human Condition Have Failed.* New Haven, CT: Yale University Press.

Scott, W. Richard. 2012. "The Institutional Environment of Global Project Organizations." *Engineering Project Organization Journal* 2 (1–2): 27–35.

Scott, W. Richard, Raymond E. Levitt, and Ryan J. Orr, eds. 2011. *Global Projects: Institutional and Political Challenges.* Cambridge, UK: Cambridge University Press.

Scudder, Thayer. 1973. "The Human Ecology of Big Projects: River Basin Development and Resettlement." *Annual Review of Anthropology* 2: 45–55.

Scudder, Thayer. 2005. *The Future of Large Dams: Dealing with Social, Environmental, Institutional and Political Costs.* London: Earthscan.

Scudder, Thayer. 2017. "The Good Megadam: Does It Exist, All Things Considered?" In *The Oxford Handbook of Megaproject Management,* ed. Bent Flyvbjerg. Oxford, UK: Oxford University Press, 428–50.

Selznick, Philip. 1949. *TVA and the Grass Roots: A Study in the Sociology of Formal Organization.* Berkeley: University of California Press.

Servranckx, Tom, Mario Vanhoucke, and Tarik Aouam. 2021. "Practical Application of Reference Class Forecasting for Cost and Time Estimations: Identifying the Properties of Similarity." *European Journal of Operational Research* 295 (3): 1161–79.

Shapira, Zur, and Donald J. Berndt. 1997. "Managing Grand Scale Construction Projects: A Risk Taking Perspective." *Research in Organizational Behavior* 19: 303–60.

Sharot, Tali. 2011. *The Optimism Bias: A Tour of the Irrationally Positive Brain.* New York: Pantheon.

Sharot, Tali, Alison M. Riccardi, Candace M. Raio, and Elizabeth A. Phelps. 2007. "Neural Mechanisms Mediating Optimism Bias." *Nature* 450 (7166): 102–5.

Shepperd, James A., Patrick Carroll, Jodi Grace, and Meredith Terry. 2002. "Exploring the Causes of Comparative Optimism." *Psychologica Belgica* 42 (1–2): 65–98.

Siemiatycki, Matti. 2009. "Delivering Transportation Infrastructure Through Public-Private Partnerships: Planning Concerns." *Journal of the American Planning Association* 76 (1): 43–58.

Siemiatycki, Matti, and Jonathan Friedman. 2012. "The Trade-Offs of Transferring Demand Risk on Urban Transit Public-Private Partnerships." *Public Works Management & Policy* 17 (3): 283–302.

Silberston, Aubrey 1972. "Economies of Scale in Theory and Practice." *The Economic Journal* 82 (325): 369–91.

Simmons, Joseph P., Robyn A. LeBoeuf, and Leif D. Nelson. 2010. "The Effect of Accuracy Motivation on Anchoring and Adjustment: Do People Adjust from Provided Anchors?" *Journal of Personality and Social Psychology* 99 (6): 917–32.

Simon, Herbert A. 1991. "The Architecture of Complexity." In *Facets of Systems Science*, ed. G. J. Klir. Boston: Springer, 457–76.

Singh, Satyajit. 2002. *Taming the Waters: The Political Economy of Large Dams in India*. New Delhi: Oxford University Press.

Sivaram, Varun. 2018. *Taming the Sun: Innovations to Harness Solar Energy and Power the Planet*. Cambridge, MA: MIT Press.

Skamris, Mette K., and Bent Flyvbjerg. 1997. "Inaccuracy of Traffic Forecasts and Cost Estimates on Large Transport Projects." *Transport Policy* 4 (3): 141–46.

Skar, Harald O., and Sven Cederroth. 1997. *Development Aid to Nepal: Issues and Options in Energy, Health, Education, Democracy, and Human Rights*. Abingdon-on-Thames, UK: Routledge.

Sleesman, Dustin J., Donald E. Conlon, Gerry McNamara, and Jonathan E. Miles. 2012. "Cleaning Up the Big Muddy: A Meta-analytic Review of the Determinants of Escalation of Commitment." *The Academy of Management Journal* 55 (3): 541–62.

Slovic, Paul. 2000. *The Perception of Risk*. Sterling, VA: EarthScan.

Smith, Stanley K. 1997. "Further Thoughts on Simplicity and Complexity in Population Projection Models." *International Journal of Forecasting* 13 (4): 557–65.

Sorkin, Andrew R. 2010. *Too Big to Fail: The Inside Story of How Wall Street and Washington Fought to Save the Financial System—and Themselves*. London: Penguin.

Sornette, Didier, and Guy Ouillon. 2012. "Dragon-Kings: Mechanisms, Statistical Methods and Empirical Evidence." *The European Physical Journal Special Topics* 205 (1): 1–26.

Sovacool, Benjamin K., and L. C. Bulan. 2011. "Behind an Ambitious Megaproject in Asia: The History and Implications of the Bakun Hydroelectric Dam in Borneo." *Energy Policy* 39 (9): 4842–59.

Sovacool, Benjamin K., and Christopher J. Cooper. 2013. *The Governance of Energy Megaprojects: Politics, Hubris and Energy Security*. Cheltenham, UK: Edward Elgar.

Sovacool, Benjamin K., Peter Enevoldsen, Christian Koch, and Rebecca J. Barthelmie. 2017. "Cost Performance and Risk in the Construction of Offshore and Onshore Wind Farms." *Wind Energy* 20 (5): 891–908.

Stanovich, Keith, and Richard West. 2000. "Individual Differences in Reasoning: Implications for the Rationality Debate." *Behavioral and Brain Sciences* 23 (5): 645–65.

Statens Offentlige Utredningar (SOU). 2004. *Betalningsansvaret för kärnavfallet*. Stockholm: Statens Offentlige Utredningar.

Staw, Barry M. 1976. "Knee-Deep in the Big Muddy: A Study of Escalating

Commitment to a Chosen Course of Action." *Organizational Behavior and Human Resources* 16 (1): 27–44.

Staw, Barry M. 1997. "The Escalation of Commitment: An Update and Appraisal." In *Organizational Decision Making*, ed. Zur Shapira. Cambridge, UK: Cambridge University Press, 191–215.

Steinberg, Marc. 2021. "From Automobile Capitalism to Platform Capitalism: Toyotism as a Prehistory of Digital Platforms." *Organization Studies* 43 (7): 1069–90.

Steinel, Wolfgang, and Carsten K. W. De Dreu. 2004. "Social Motives and Strategic Misrepresentation in Social Decision Making." *Journal of Personality and Social Psychology* 86 (3): 419–34.

Stevens, Joseph E. 1988. *Hoover Dam: An American Adventure*. Norman: University of Oklahoma Press.

Stigler, George J. 1958. "The Economies of Scale." *Journal of Law & Economics* 1 (1): 54.

Stinchcombe, Arthur L., and Carol A. Heimer. 1985. *Organization Theory and Project Management: Administering Uncertainty in Norwegian Offshore Oil*. Oslo: Norwegian University Press.

Stone, Brad. 2021. *Amazon Unbound: Jeff Bezos and the Invention of a Global Empire*. New York: Simon & Schuster.

Stone, Richard. 2008. "Three Gorges Dam: Into the Unknown." *Science* 321 (5889): 628–32.

Stone, Richard. 2011. "The Legacy of the Three Gorges Dam." *Science* 333 (6044): 817.

Suarez, Fernando, and Gianvito Lanzolla. 2005. "The Half-Truth of First-Mover Advantage." *Harvard Business Review* 83 (4): 121–27.

Suls, Jerry, and Choi K. Wan. 1987. "In Search of the False Uniqueness Phenomenon: Fear and Estimates of Social Consensus." *Journal of Personality and Social Psychology* 52 (1): 211–17.

Suls, Jerry, Choi K. Wan, and Glenn S. Sanders. 1988. "False Consensus and False Uniqueness in Estimating the Prevalence of Health-Protective Behaviors." *Journal of Applied Social Psychology* 18 (1): 66–79.

Sunstein, Cass R. 2002. "Probability Neglect: Emotions, Worst Cases, and Law." *Yale Law Review* 112 (1): 61–107.

Sunstein, Cass R. 2013. "An Original Thinker of Our Time." *The New York Review of Books*, May 23, 14–17.

Sutterfield, Scott J., Shawnta Friday-Stroud, and Sheryl Shivers-Blackwell. 2006. "A Case Study of Project and Stakeholder Management Failures: Lessons Learned." *Project Management Journal* 37 (5): 26–36.

Swiss Association of Road and Transportation Experts. 2006. *Kosten-Nutzen-Analysen im Strassenverkehr*, Grundnorm 641820, valid from August 1. Zürich: Swiss Association of Road and Transportation Experts.

Swyngedouw, Erik, Frank Moulaert, and Arantxa Rodriguez. 2002. "Neoliberal

Urbanization in Europe: Large-Scale Urban Development Projects and the New Urban Policy." *Antipode* 34 (3): 542–77.

Szyliowicz, Joseph S., and Andrew R. Goetz. 1995. "Getting Realistic About Megaproject Planning: The Case of the New Denver International Airport." *Policy Sciences* 28 (4): 347–67.

Taleb, Nassim N. 2004. *Fooled by Randomness: The Hidden Role of Chance in Life and in the Markets*. London: Penguin.

Taleb, Nassim N. 2007. *The Black Swan: The Impact of the Highly Improbable*. New York: Random House.

Taleb, Nassim N. 2012. *Antifragile: How to Live in a World We Don't Understand*. London: Allen Lane.

Taleb, Nassim N. 2018. *Skin in the Game: Hidden Asymmetries in Daily Life*. London: Penguin Random House.

Taleb, Nassim N. 2020. *Statistical Consequences of Fat Tails: Real World Preasymptotics, Epistemology, and Applications (Technical Incerto)*. New York: STEM Academic Press.

Taleb, Nassim N., Yaneer Bar-Yam, and Pasquale Cirillo. 2022. "On Single Point Forecasts for Fat-Tailed Variables." *International Journal of Forecasting* 38 (2): 413–22.

Tallman, Erin. 2020. "Behind the Scenes at China's Prefab Hospitals Against Coronavirus." *E-Magazine* by MedicalExpo, March 5. https://emag.medical expo.com/qa-behind-the-scenes-of-chinas-prefab-hospitals-against -coronavirus/.

Tauranac, John. 2014. *The Empire State Building: The Making of a Landmark*. Ithaca, NY: Cornell University Press.

Teigland, Jon. 1999. "Mega Events and Impacts on Tourism; the Predictions and Realities of the Lillehammer Olympics." *Impact Assessment and Project Appraisal* 17 (4): 305–17.

Tepper, Fitz. 2015. "Satellite Maker Planet Labs Acquires BlackBridge's Geospatial Business." *TechCrunch*, July 15. https://techcrunch.com/2015/07/15 /satellite-maker-planet-labs-acquires-blackbridges-geospatial-business/.

Tetlock, Philip E. 2005. *Expert Political Judgment: How Good Is It? How Can We Know?* Princeton, NJ: Princeton University Press.

Tetlock, Philip E., and Dan Gardner. 2015. *Superforecasting: The Art and Science of Prediction*. New York: Random House.

Thaler, Richard H. 2015. *Misbehaving: How Economics Became Behavioural*. London: Allen Lane.

Torrance, Morag I. 2008. "Forging Global Governance? Urban Infrastructures as Networked Financial Products." *International Journal of Urban and Regional Research* 32 (1): 1–21.

Turner, Barry A., and Nick F. Pidgeon. 1997. *Man-Made Disasters*. Oxford, UK: Butterworth-Heinemann.

Turner, Rodney, and Ralf Müller. 2003. "On the Nature of the Project as a Temporary Organization." *International Journal of Project Management* 21 (7): 1–8.

Tversky, Amos, and Daniel Kahneman. 1973. "Availability: A Heuristic for Judging Frequency and Probability." *Cognitive Psychology* 5 (2): 207–32.

Tversky, Amos, and Daniel Kahneman. 1974. "Judgment Under Uncertainty: Heuristics and Biases." *Science* 185 (4157): 1124–31.

Tversky, Amos, and Daniel Kahneman. 1981. "The Framing of Decisions and the Psychology of Choice." *Science* 211 (4481): 453–58.

Tversky, Amos, and Daniel Kahneman. 1982. "Evidential Impact of Base Rates." In *Judgment Under Uncertainty: Heuristics and Biases*, eds. Daniel Kahneman, Paul Slovic, and Amos Tversky. Cambridge, UK: Cambridge University Press, 153–62.

Tyrnauer, Matt. 2010. "Architecture in the Age of Gehry." *Vanity Fair,* June 30.

UK Department for Transport. 2006. *Changes to the Policy on Funding Major Projects.* London: Department for Transport.

UK Department for Transport. 2006. *The Estimation and Treatment of Scheme Costs: Transport Analysis Guidance.* London: Department for Transport. http://www.dft.gov.uk/webtag/documents/expert/unit3.5.9.php.

UK Department for Transport. 2015. *Optimism Bias Study: Recommended Adjustments to Optimism Bias Uplifts.* London: Department for Transport.

UK Department for Transport and Oxford Global Projects. 2020. *Updating the Evidence Behind the Optimism Bias Uplifts for Transport Appraisals: 2020 Data Update to the 2004 Guidance Document "Procedures for Dealing with Optimism Bias in Transport Planning."* London: Department for Transport.

UK Infrastructure and Projects Authority. 2016. *Improving Infrastructure Delivery: Project Initiation Routemap.* London: Crown Publishing.

UK National Audit Office. 2009. *Supplementary Memorandum by the National Audit Office on Optimism Bias.* London: UK Parliament.

UK National Audit Office. 2013. *Over-Optimism in Government Projects.* London: National Audit Office.

UK National Audit Office. 2014. *Lessons from Major Rail Infrastructure Programmes,* No. HC: 267, 14–15. London: National Audit Office, 40.

UNESCO World Heritage Convention. 2022. "Sydney Opera House." https://whc.unesco.org/en/list/166.

US Congress, House Committee on Science and Astronautics. 1973. *1974 NASA Authorization. Hearings, 93rd Congress, First Session, on H.R. 4567.* Washington, DC: US Government Printing Office.

US Department of Justice. 2021. *U.S. v. Elizabeth Holmes, et al.* US Attorney's Office, Northern District of California, August 3. Department of Justice. https://www.justice.gov/usao-ndca/us-v-elizabeth-holmes-et-al.

US Department of Justice. 2021. "Former SCANA CEO Sentenced to Two Years for Defrauding Ratepayers in Connection with Failed Nuclear Construction Program." Department of Justice, October 7. https://www.justice

.gov/usao-sc/pr/former-scana-ceo-sentenced-two-years-defrauding-ratepayers-connection-failed-nuclear.

US National Research Council. 2007. *Metropolitan Travel Forecasting: Current Practice and Future Direction.* Special report no. 288. Washington, DC: Committee for Determination of the State of the Practice in Metropolitan Area Travel Forecasting and Transportation Research Board.

US Office of the Inspector General. 2012. *NASA's Challenges to Meeting Cost, Schedule, and Performance Goals.* Report no. IG-12-021 (Assignment N. A-11-009-00). Washington, DC: NASA.

Van der Kraats, Marion. 2021. "BER Boss: New Berlin Airport Has Money Only Until Beginning of 2022." *Aviation Pros.* https://www.aviationpros.com/airports/news/21244678/ber-boss-new-berlin-airport-has-money-only-until-beginning-of-2022.

Van der Westhuizen, Janis. 2007. "Glitz, Glamour and the Gautrain: Mega-Projects as Political Symbols." *Politikon* 34 (3): 333–51.

Vanwynsberghe, Rob, Björn Surborg, and Elvin Wyly. 2013. "When the Games Come to Town: Neoliberalism, Mega-Events and Social Inclusion in the Vancouver 2010 Winter Olympic Games." *International Journal of Urban and Regional Research* 37 (6): 2074–93.

Véliz, Carissa. 2020. *Privacy Is Power: Why and How You Should Take Back Control of Your Data.* London: Bantam.

Vickerman, Roger. 2017. "Wider Impacts of Megaprojects: Curse or Cure?" In *The Oxford Handbook of Megaproject Management*, ed. Bent Flyvbjerg. Oxford, UK: Oxford University Press, 389–405.

Vining, Aiden R., and Anthony E. Boardman. 2008. "Public-Private Partnerships: Eight Rules for Governments." *Public Works Management & Policy* 13 (2): 149–61.

Vogel, Steve. 2007. *The Pentagon: A History.* New York: Random House.

Wachs, Martin. 1986. "Technique vs. Advocacy in Forecasting: A Study of Rail Rapid Transit." *Urban Resources* 4 (1): 23–30.

Wachs, Martin. 1989. "When Planners Lie with Numbers." *Journal of the American Planning Association* 55 (4): 476–79.

Wachs, Martin. 1990. "Ethics and Advocacy in Forecasting for Public Policy." *Business and Professional Ethics Journal* 9 (1): 141–57.

Wachs, Martin. 2013. "The Past, Present, and Future of Professional Ethics in Planning." In *Policy, Planning, and People: Promoting Justice in Urban Development*, eds. Naomi Carmon and Susan S. Fainstein. Philadelphia: University of Pennsylvania Press, 101–19.

Wal, S. 2006. *Education and Child Development.* Derby, UK: Sarup and Sons.

Wallis, Shane. 1993. "Storebaelt Calls on Project Moses for Support." *TunnelTalk*, April. https://www.tunneltalk.com/Denmark-Apr1993-Project-Moses-called-on-to-support-Storebaelt-undersea-rail-link.php.

Wallis, Shane. 1995. "Storebaelt: The Final Chapters." *TunnelTalk*, May. https://

www.tunneltalk.com/Denmark-May1995-Storebaelt-the-final-chapters.php.
Ward, William A. 2019. "Cost-Benefit Analysis: Theory Versus Practice at the World Bank, 1960 to 2015." *Journal of Benefit-Cost Analysis* 10 (1): 124–44.
Webb, James. 1969. *Space-Age Management: The Large-Scale Approach.* New York: McGraw-Hill.
Weick, Mario, and Ana Guinote. 2008. "When Subjective Experiences Matter: Power Increases Reliance on the Ease of Retrieval." *Journal of Personality and Social Psychology* 94 (6): 956–70.
Weinstein, Neil D., Stephen E. Marcus, and Richard P. Moser. 2005. "Smokers' Unrealistic Optimism About Their Risk." *Tobacco Control* 14 (1): 55–59.
Weintraub, Seth. 2016. "Tesla Gigafactory Tour Roundup and Tidbits: 'This Is the Coolest Factory in the World.'" *Electrek,* July 28. https://electrek.co/2016/07/28/tesla-gigafactory-tour-roundup-and-tidbits-this-is-the-coolest-factory-ever/.
Weinzierl, Matthew C., Kylie Lucas, and Mehak Sarang. 2021. *SpaceX, Economies of Scale, and a Revolution in Space Access.* Boston: Harvard Business School.
West, Geoffrey. 2017. *Scale: The Universal Laws of Life and Death in Organisms, Cities, and Companies.* London: Weidenfeld and Nicolson.
Whaley, Sean. 2016. "Tesla Officials Show Off Progress at Gigafactory in Northern Nevada." *Las Vegas Review-Journal,* March 20.
Williams, Terry M., and Knut Samset. 2010. "Issues in Front-End Decision Making on Projects." *Project Management Journal* 41 (2): 38–49.
Williams, Terry M., Knut Samset, and Kjell Sunnevåg, eds. 2009. *Making Essential Choices with Scant Information: Front-End Decision Making in Major Projects.* London: Palgrave Macmillan.
Williams, Walter. 1998. *Honest Numbers and Democracy.* Washington, DC: Georgetown University Press.
Willis, Carol. 1995. *Form Follows Finance: Skyscrapers and Skylines in New York and Chicago.* New York: Princeton Architectural Press.
Willis, Carol, ed. 1998. *Building the Empire State Building.* New York: Norton Architecture.
Wilson, Michael. 2002. "Study Finds Steady Overruns in Public Projects." *The New York Times,* July 11.
Wilson, Timothy D., Christopher E. Houston, Kathryn M. Etling, and Nancy Brekke. 1996. "A New Look at Anchoring Effects: Basic Anchoring and Its Antecedents." *Journal of Experimental Psychology: General* 125 (4): 387–402.
Winch, Graham M. 2010. *Managing Construction Projects: An Information Processing Approach,* 2nd ed. Oxford, UK: Wiley-Blackwell.
Woo, Andrea. 2021. "Nearly 600 People Died in BC Summer Heat Wave, Vast Majority Seniors: Coroner." *The Globe and Mail,* November 1.
World Bank. 2010. *Cost-Benefit Analysis in World Bank Projects.* Washington, DC: World Bank.

World Health Organization (WHO). "Climate Change." World Health Organization. https://www.who.int/health-topics/climate-change#tab=tab_1.

World Nuclear News. 2016. "Japanese Government Says Monju Will Be Scrapped." *World Nuclear News,* December 22. https://www.world-nuclear-news.org/NP-Japanese-government-says-Monju-will-be-scrapped-2212164.html.

Young, H. Kwak, John Waleski, Dana Sleeper, and Hessam Sadatsafavi. 2014. "What Can We Learn from the Hoover Dam Project That Influenced Modern Project Management?" *International Journal of Project Management* 32 (2): 256–64.

Zimbalist, Andrew. 2020. *Circus Maximus: The Economic Gamble Behind Hosting the Olympics and the World Cup,* 3rd ed. Washington, DC: Brookings Institution.

Zou, Patrick X., Guomin Zhang, and Jiayuan Wang. 2007. "Understanding the Key Risks in Construction Projects in China." *International Journal of Project Management* 25 (6): 601–14.

INDEX

AC/DC, 130
Academia, 193
Adele, 130
adjustments, 102, 103, 108, 110, 224
airports, 7, 22, 145–55, 165, 173, 187, 230, 231
Amazon, 34, 53–55
Amazon Fire Phone, 54–55
Amazon Prime, xiii
American Civil War, 146
American Institute of Architects, xvi
anchoring, 102–4, 108–10, 113, 114, 126, 221, 224, 237
Apple, xiii, 52–53, 85, 165, 167–68, 189
archaeology, 120, 121
Aristotle, 81, 94, 189, 216, 220
Arlington Farm, 23, 24, 30, 41
Arlington National Cemetery, 23–25
artificial intelligence, 125
arXiv, 193
Atomic Energy Agency, Japan, 157
Auken, Svend, 180
Aurora Place skyscraper, Australia, 138
Australia, 49, 60, 61, 63–65, 69, 73, 80–82, 93, 94, 109, 134, 135, 137–40, 138–39, 213–15, 214, 218, 220, 229, 232
availability bias, 34, 210–11, 237
averages, 9

Bach, Steven, 37
backcasting, 51–52
Bangladesh, 133
bankruptcy, 7, 11, 30

Barcelona Olympic Games (1992), 67
Barnard, Michael, 175
BART system, San Francisco, 6
base rates for cost risk, 191–92
Basic and Primary Education Project (BPEP), Nepal, x–xi, 204, 232
Basque Country, 48–49
behavioral bias, 110, 190
behavioral science, 27, 105, 138
bell curve, 9, 116
Bergendahl, Anders, 115–17
bespokeness, 87, 159, 160, 170
best-case scenario, 33, 107
Bezos, Jeff, 34, 53, 206
bias, 96
  for action, 33–34
  anchoring, 102–4, 108–10, 113, 114, 126, 221, 224, 237
  availability, 34, 210–11, 237
  base rate neglect, 191, 221
  behavioral, 110, 190
  cognitive, 74, 104, 111, 138, 209
  escalation of commitment, 38–40, 211–12
  optimism, xii, 28–31, 123, 138, 209, 224
  overconfidence, 28
  planning fallacy, 210
  planning fallacy writ large, 210
  power, xii–xiii, 208, 209
  survivorship, 136
  against thinking, 34
  strategic misrepresentation, 26–27, 35–36, 38, 104, 110, 208, 209
  uniqueness, 84, 105, 108, 111–12, 114–16, 121, 122, 216
"Big Dig," Boston, 11

Bilbao, Spain, 48–50, 60, 61, 65–70,
    77–79, 213, 219, 220
Bilbao effect, 213
Bill & Melinda Gates Foundation, xi
Birol, Fatih, 179
Biskind, Peter, 133
black swan management, 118–23
black swans, 11–14, 99, 155, 160
Blackberry, 85
Boeing, xiii
boring machines, 85, 97, 98, 124, 170,
    233
Bornu Railway, Nigeria, 228–29
Boston, Massachusetts, 11
Bowie, David, 130
Box, The: How the Shipping Container Made the World Smaller and the World Economy Bigger (Levinson), 171
Brandenburg Airport, Germany, 7
break-fix cycle, 19, 26
bridges, 3–4, 6, 10
British Airports Authority (BAA),
    145–50, 152–55
Brockner, Joel, 211
Brookings Institution, 132
Brown, Gordon, 104, 109, 111
Brown, Willie, 35–38, 40
Bryar, Colin, 54
budgets and cost overruns, 5, 7–13,
    27, 28, 35, 37, 38, 43, 45, 57–59,
    61, 64, 65, 69, 73, 84, 85, 87, 89,
    93, 95, 97–99, 104, 110, 111,
    116–18, 123, 124, 126, 129, 132,
    133, 137–39, 144, 146, 153–55,
    158, 162, 169, 170, 173, 174, 182,
    191–92, 205–6, 209, 219, 234, 235
Buehler, Roger, 210
Buffett, Warren, 177
building phase, 77

Caesar Augustus, Emperor, 19
Cahill, Joe, 64
California High-Speed Rail, ix–x, xi,
    xiii, 19, 40, 46, 82, 180, 203
California High-Speed Rail Peer
    Review Group, 19
Cambridge Analytica, 78

Canada, 11, 82–83
Capitol, Washington, D.C., 24, 78
carbon capture, 179
Caro, Ina, 100
Caro, Robert, 55, 99–104, 109, 113
Carr, Bill, 54
Carreyrou, John, 74, 78
cars, 167, 169
CATIA software, 67–68, 73, 214, 215
Catmull, Ed, 18, 75–76, 186
Chan, Edwin, 66
Channel Tunnel, 6
Chernobyl, 115
China, 97, 109, 126, 166, 174–76
Chrysler Building, New York City, xiv
Churchill, Winston, 208
Cimino, Michael, 37–38
Clapton, Eric, 130
Clash, 130
climate crisis, 21, 156, 177–83,
    189–90, 224, 235
cognitive bias, 74, 104, 111, 138, 209
Cohn, Harry, 37
Colosseum, Rome, 162
Columbia Pictures, 37
commitment, escalation of, 38–40,
    211–12
commitment fallacy, 26–42
containerization, 171, 187
contingency plans, 118, 122, 224, 228
    (*see also* schedules)
Cook, Tim, 168
Copenhagen Infrastructure Partners
    (CIP), 236
Copenhagen Opera House, 16
cost overruns, 191–92
    (*see also* budgets and cost overruns)
cost risk, 115
Covid-19 pandemic, 13, 166, 167,
    174
creativity, 130–33, 136, 140–41
Crowe, Frank, 144, 145
CubeSat modules, 169
Cupertino, California, 167

Daft Punk, 130
dams, xiii, 7, 10, 117, 144–45, 155,
    159, 168, 173, 227

Dassault Systèmes, 67, 215
data
  in reference class forecasting, 112–14
  vs. stories, 134–36
decision theory, 207
defense, 7, 173
Del Ray, Lana, 130
Denmark, x, 3–5, 16, 80, 81, 83–84, 109, 180–84
design for manufacture and assembly, 147, 165
Development Projects Observed (Hirschman), 132–33, 228
Digital Project, 215
digital simulation, 67–68, 73, 147
digitalization, 235
Disney, Lillian, 219
Disney, Walt, 70, 219
Disney Animation, 76
Disney (*see* Walt Disney Company, The)
Disney family, 93, 219
Docter, Pete, 69–73, 79, 86, 91, 92
Drapeau, Jean, 36, 38, 89
driving into the blizzard, 39, 42
droughts, 178
Drummond, Helga, 211

earthquakes, 118–19, 160, 161, 226, 227
Easy Rider (movie), 136
Easy Riders, Raging Bulls: How the Sex-Drugs-and-Rock'n'Roll Generation Saved Hollywood (Biskind), 133
Edison, Thomas, 62–63, 73
Edmondson, Amy, 153
education, x–xi, xiii, 119, 161–62, 164–65, 167, 203–4, 232
Egan, Sir John, 147
Eiffel Tower, Paris, 151
8 Spruce Street, New York City, 68
Eldrup, Anders, 181–83
Electric Lady Studios, New York City, 130–31, 134, 135, 137, 140, 141
Electric Ladyland (Hendrix), 130

electricity transmission, 62–63, 73, 155, 168–69, 171, 172, 175, 176, 179, 181, 182, 190, 235–36
electrification, 179, 235–36
electrolyzer capacity, 179
Elizabeth II, Queen of England, 65, 214
emotions, distinguished from intuitive judgments, 29
Empire State Building, New York City, xiii–xvi, 18, 23, 43, 90–91, 123, 144, 163–64, 172
Empire State Inc., xiv, xv
escalation of commitment, 38–40, 211–12
estimates, 31–33, 35–38, 99, 101–3, 106–7, 110, 111, 113–16, 138
European Union, 174
Ever Given (container ship), 14
experience, 109, 126, 143, 159, 160, 163
  being first and, 83–85
  Empire State Building example, 90–91
  frozen and unfrozen, 86–87, 95
  of Gehry and Utzon, 80–81, 92–94
  marginalizing, 81–83
  Olympic Games example, 87–90
  quest for superlatives, 85–86, 88
  tacit knowledge and, 91–92
experiential learning, 62
experimentation, 62–64, 73, 77, 143, 159, 160, 163
experiri, 62, 94–96, 159, 180

Facebook, 78
fat-tailed distribution, 10–13, 116–19, 155, 158, 171–73, 178, 206–7, 225, 234
fat-tailed projects, 172–73
feasibility studies, 35–36
Final Cut: Art, Money, and Ego in the Making of Heaven's Gate, the Film That Sank United Artists (Bach), 37
Finding Nemo (movie), 18
firearms registry, 11
first-mover advantage, 84–85
floods, 177, 178, 226, 227

flowcharts, 51, 53, 62
Flyvbjerg, Bent, further readings by, 193–96
Football Association (FA) Cup Final, United Kingdom, 154
forecasting, 20, 33, 99–104, 106–15, 117, 118, 123–25, 143, 225
foreign aid, x–xi
Forster, Danny, 167
fossil thermal power, 155, 171, 172
Foster, Norman, 167
France, 35, 82
Franklin, Benjamin, 15, 122
freight shipping, 171
frozen and unfrozen experience, 86–87, 95, 170
Fukushima disaster, 158, 160

Galton, Sir Francis, 225–26
Gates, Bill, 136, 177
Gaussian distribution, 206–7, 225
Gehry, Frank, 174
  8 Spruce Street, New York City, designed by, 68
  experience of, 80–81, 92–94
  Guggenheim Museum Bilbao designed by, 48–50, 60, 61, 66, 67–70, 77–81, 213, 219
  questioning by, 47–48, 50–51, 56
  Simpsons, guest appearance on, 68–69, 140
  simulation and models used by, 66–67, 73, 78, 79, 214
  teams led by, 144, 145, 214
  Walt Disney Concert Hall designed by, 93–94, 218–20
General Motors, 230
Generation nightclub, New York City, 127–28
Germany, 7, 174, 177, 182
Gigafactory 1 (Giga Nevada), 169
Gigerenzer, Gerd, 30, 236
Gino, Francesca, 34
Giroux, Yves, 83
Gladwell, Malcolm, 132, 134
goals, 49–53, 56–57
Goldberger, Paul, 66, 218
Google, 231

Google Scholar, 193
Grand Central Terminal, New York City, 151
Great Belt project, Denmark, 3–5
Great Chicago Fire Festival, 121–23, 190
Great Depression, 123
Great Wall of China, 60
Green, Mike, 164–65, 167
greenhouse gases, 178
Guangzhou, China, 97
Guardian, The, 154
Guggenheim Museum Bilbao, 48–50, 60, 61, 65–70, 77–81, 83, 94, 213, 219, 220

Hall, Peter, 214
Harper, Richard, 148–55
Harvard Business Review, 27
HealthCare.gov website, 6
heat waves, 177, 178
Heathrow Airport, United Kingdom, 145, 165, 187, 230, 231
Heaven's Gate (movie), 37–38
height, 10
Hendrix, Jimi, 127–31, 135, 137, 138, 141
Hero's Journey, 138
heuristics, 28, 185–90, 236–37
heuristics and biases school, 217–18
heuristics for better leadership, 185–90
Hiding (Hidden) Hand, 133, 228–29
High Speed 2 (HS2), United Kingdom, 119–20, 172
Hirschman, Albert O., 131–34, 136–38, 140, 142, 228–29
Hofstadter, Douglas, 31
Hofstadter's Law, 31
Holland Tunnel, New York, 5–6
Holm, Mette K. Skamris, 205
Holmes, Elizabeth, 74
home and kitchen renovations, 12–13, 43–47, 50, 53, 56–59, 106–10, 112–14, 116, 131, 135
honest numbers, 5
Hong Kong, 97–99, 103–4, 119, 123–26, 166

INDEX

Hoover, Herbert, xiv, xvi
Hoover Dam, xiii, 144, 145
Hopper, Dennis, 135–36
Hornsea Project, United Kingdom, 182
Hughes, Robert, 63
hurricanes, 178
hydroelectricity, 168–69

ice melt, 178
Ickes, Harold, 25
ignorance, 132
IKEA, 166
illusion of explanatory depth, 74
inchstone approach, 125
Incredibles, The (movie), 18
Infinite Jest (Wallace), 26
information technology (IT) projects, 6, 10–12, 76–77, 83–84, 117, 136, 143–44, 155, 159, 173, 189, 191, 207, 227, 235
(*see also* specific projects)
Inside Out (movie), 69, 72
inside view (detail), 105–6, 114, 190
Instagram, 78
International Energy Agency, 178, 179
International Olympic Committee (IOC), 87–88
International Renewable Energy Agency, 175
Internet, 183
intuitive judgments, 20, 29, 31, 93, 217–18
iPod, xiii
Ireland, 109
Iron Law of Megaprojects, 7, 8
iterations (*see* planning)
Ive, Jony, 167

James Webb Space Telescope, 11, 169
Japan, 13, 88, 157–58, 158, 160–61, 174, 231–32
Jaws (movie), 133–35, 137
Jay-Z, 130
Jobs, Steve, 52, 136, 167–68, 189, 213

Johnson, Lyndon B., 55
Jørgensen, Hans Lauritz, 161, 204
Judaism, 47
Justice, US Department of, 12

Kahneman, Daniel, 27–32, 102, 104–5, 109, 111, 138, 208–10, 217–18, 237
Kazan, Elia, 37, 38
Kennedy, John F., 24
King Kong, xvi
Kissinger, Henry, 74
Klein, Gary, 30, 217–18
Kmart, 11
Kramer, Eddie, 127–30, 134, 141
kurtosis, 206–7

LaGuardia Airport, New York, 22
Lamb, William, xiv–xvi, 90–91
large numbers, law of, 9
Larsen, Henning, 16
Lasko, Jim, 121–22, 190
Last Movie, The (movie), 136
Lawrence of Arabia (movie), 37
lean startup model, 76–78
Lean Startup, The (Ries), 76, 77
Led Zeppelin, 130
Lego, 158, 162–65, 167–71, 181, 184, 187, 233
Lennon, John, 130
Levi Strauss, 11–12
Levinson, Marc, 171
Levy, Steven, 168
lightbulbs, 62–63, 73
Lincoln, Abraham, 18, 208
Lincoln Center, New York City, 141
lock-in, 25–26, 38, 211
London, Olympic Games in, 88
Los Angeles, California, ix–x, 88, 93–94, 218–20
Lötschberg Base Tunnel, Switzerland, 7

Machiavelli factor, 208
Madrid Metro, 170, 174, 233
Maersk, 16
Mandelbrot, Benoit, 166, 206–7
Marriott hotel, New York City, 167

Mass Transit Railway (MTR), Hong Kong, 97–98, 102–4, 109, 123–26, 220
masterbuilders, 186
maximum virtual product model, 78–79, 95
McAllister, Ian, 53
McKinsey & Company, 6
McLean, Malcolm, 171
Mead, Margaret, 105
mean, regression to, 116–17
means and ends, 50, 208
megaprojects, xi–xiii, 5, 27
  adjustments and, 103, 108, 110, 224
  airports, 7, 22, 145–55, 165, 173, 187, 230, 231
  anchoring and, 102–4, 108–10, 113, 114, 126, 221, 224, 237
  budgets and cost overruns, 5, 7–13, 28, 35, 37, 38, 43, 45, 57–59, 61, 64, 65, 69, 73, 84, 85, 87, 89, 93, 95, 97–99, 104, 110, 111, 116–18, 123, 124, 126, 129, 132, 133, 137–39, 144, 146, 153–55, 158, 162, 169, 170, 173, 174, 182, 219
  commitment, escalation of, 38–40, 211–12
  ending world hunger, as a megaproject, 174, 234
  estimates and, 31–33, 35–38, 99, 101–3, 106–7, 110, 111, 113–16, 138
  experience and (*see* experience)
  fat-tailed distribution and, 10–13, 116–19, 155, 158, 171–73, 178, 206–7, 225, 234
  forecasting and, 20, 33, 99–104, 106–15, 117, 118, 123–25, 143, 225
  heuristics for better leadership, 185–90
  home and kitchen renovations, 12–13, 43–47, 50, 53, 56–59, 106–10, 112–14, 116, 131, 135
  information technology (IT) projects, 6, 10–12, 76–77, 83–84, 117, 136, 143–44, 155, 159, 173, 189, 191, 207, 227, 235
  inside view (detail) and, 105–6, 114, 190
  Lego and, 158, 162–65, 167–71, 181, 184, 187, 233
  modularity and, 20–21, 157, 162–64, 166–72, 175, 184, 187
  movie production, 18, 20, 37–38, 69–79, 133–35, 137
  normal distribution and, 116–18, 129–10, 206–7, 225
  outside view (accuracy) and, 106–9, 114, 188
  planning and, 17–20, 34, 36, 40–42, 44–47, 50–54, 58, 60–79, 93, 95–96, 103, 119, 131–33, 135, 137–42, 187–88
  rail projects, ix–x, xi, xiii, 6, 10, 19, 40, 46, 82, 97–99, 103–4, 109, 119–20, 123–26, 159, 173, 180, 203, 220, 228–29
  reference-class forecasting (RCF) and, 109–15, 117, 121, 124–26, 146, 188, 222–24
  right to left, thinking from, 51–53, 55, 56, 59, 60, 126
  risk mitigation and, 15, 99, 107, 117–24, 126, 143, 188
  schedules and, 7–9, 11–13, 27, 28, 37, 38, 43, 61, 64, 74, 85, 89, 93, 95, 97–99, 103, 110, 111, 120–21, 123–26, 129, 132, 133, 144, 146, 153–55, 173, 219, 235
  teams and, 20, 142–45, 147–55, 186, 214, 231
  think slow, act fast and, xiii, xvi, 3, 18–19, 22, 46, 64, 69, 119, 126, 142, 143, 185
  tunnels, 3–7, 10, 11, 85–86, 97, 98, 123–26, 155, 170, 173, 233
  uniqueness bias and, 84, 105, 108, 111–12, 114–16, 121, 122, 216
Mexico City, 16–17
Microsoft, 165
milestones, 125, 149
Miller, Diane Disney, 219
minimum viable product model, 78, 95
mining, 7, 10, 173

models, 66
models and simulation, 66–67, 73, 78, 79, 214
modularity, 20–21, 157, 162–64, 166–72, 175, 184, 187
Møller, Arnold Maersk Mc-Kinney, 16
Monju nuclear power plant, Japan, 157–59, 161, 180, 231–32
Montreal Gazette, 89
Montreal Olympic Games (1976), 36, 38, 87–89, 118
Moses, Robert, 55, 99–100
movie production, 18, 20, 37–38, 69–79, 133–35, 137
Museum of Modern Art, New York City, 130
Musk, Elon, 169

NASA (National Aeronautics and Space Administration), 11, 77–78, 169, 170
National Architectural Association, 91
National Health Service, United Kingdom, 6
National Museum of Qatar, 141
naturalistic decision making (NDM), 217–18
negative heuristics, 236–37
negative learning, 160
Nepal school project, x–xi, xiii, 119, 161–62, 164, 203–4, 232
Netherlands, 109, 182
New York Public Library, 101, 113
New York Review of Books, The, 132
New York Times, The, 6, 16, 17
New Yorker, The, 132
Newsday, 99
Newsom, Gavin, 40
Newton, Isaac, 7
NIMBY (not in my back yard), 175
No Time to Die (movie), 13
Nobel Prize in Economic Sciences, 105
normal distribution (Gaussian), 9–10, 116–18, 206–7, 225
Norway, 168–69, 174

Nouvel, Jean, 35
nuclear power, 7, 10, 12, 115–16, 117, 155, 157–61, 173, 175–76, 179, 191, 227, 231–32
Nuclear Regulation Authority, Japan, 158

Obamacare, 6
offshore wind farms, 180–81, 236
oil and gas projects, 7, 10, 173
old project data, 112–13
Olympic Fish, Barcelona, 67
Olympic Games, 7, 10, 13, 36, 38, 67, 87–90, 117, 118, 173, 191, 227
one-building architect, 139, 229
one of those, 97, 107, 108, 122, 188
OPEC (Organization of Petroleum Exporting Countries), 180
opportunity costs, 139
optimism, xii, 28–31, 123, 138, 209, 224
Organisation for Economic Co-operation and Development (OECD), 178
organization of the artist, 220
Ørsted, Hans Christian, 182
Ørsted (DONG Energy), Denmark, 180–83, 236
outside view (accuracy), 106–9, 114, 188
overconfidence, 28
overpass collapse, 16–17

Paralympic Games, 87
Parliament Building, Scotland, 11
past projects, 112–13
Paz del Río steel mill, Colombia, 228
Pearl River Delta Economic Zone, 97
PensionDanmark, 236
Pentagon, 22–26, 30–31, 40–41
Pentagon, The: A History (Vogel), 22, 40
Perrow, Charles, 15
phronesis, 81, 94, 116, 185, 186, 189, 220
Piano, Renzo, 138
pioneer companies, 84
pipelines, 173, 187

Pixar Animation Studios, 140
Pixar planning, 18, 20, 60, 69–79, 86, 93, 95, 126, 147
Planet (Planet Labs, Inc.), 169–70
Planet Dove satellite, 169–70
planning, 17–20, 34, 36, 40–42, 44–47, 50–54, 58, 60–79, 86, 93, 95–96, 103, 119, 126, 131–33, 135, 137–42, 187–88
planning fallacy, 31, 210
planning fallacy writ large, 210
Polanyi, Michael, 91–92, 94
politics, 27, 40–41, 50, 81–83, 85, 88
positive heuristics, 236, 237
positive learning curve, 63, 163
postpandemic investment, 174
Potomac River, 23, 24
Poulsen, Henrik, 181–83
power bias, 208, 209
Power Broker, The: Robert Moses and the Fall of New York (Caro), 100
Power Mac G4 Cube computer, 52–53
PR/FAQ (press release/frequently asked questions), 53–54
presidential election of 1928, xiv
"Principle of the Hiding Hand, The" (Hirschman), 131–33, 228
Pritzker Architecture Prize, 214
probability theory, 206
Project Apollo, 77–78
prospect theory, 105
providential ignorance, 132
psychological safety, 153, 231
psychology, xii–xiii, 27–30, 40–41, 50, 102, 110, 141, 147, 212, 216, 217, 230
Pulitzer Prize, 100

Quartermaster Depot site, 24–25, 41

R.J. Reynolds Tobacco Company, 90
rail projects, ix–x, xi, xiii, 6, 10, 19, 40, 46, 82, 97–99, 103–4, 109, 119–20, 123–26, 159, 173, 180, 203, 220, 228–29
Raskob, John J., xiv

Reed, Lou, 130
reference class, 105, 112–14
reference-class forecasting (RCF), 109–15, 117, 121, 124–26, 146, 188, 222–24
data for, 112–14
regression to the mean, 9, 225–27
regression to the tail, 117, 226–27
ResearchGate, 193
reversibility, 34
Reynolds Building, Winston-Salem, North Carolina, 90–91
Ries, Eric, 76, 77
right to left, thinking from, 51–53, 55, 56, 59, 60, 126
risk mitigation, 15, 99, 107, 117–24, 126, 143, 188
roads, 6, 11, 155, 171, 173, 187
Robinson, John B., 51
rockets, 7
Rolling Stones, 130
Roosevelt, Franklin Delano, 22, 23, 25, 41, 121
Rountree, Stephen, 218
Royal Danish Opera, 16
Rumsfeld, Donald, 107, 110, 222

sampling, 9
San Francisco, California, ix–x, 6
San Francisco Chronicle, 35
satellites, 169–70
scale-free scalability, 165–66
scaling up, 155–56
schedules, 7–9, 11–13, 27, 28, 37, 38, 43, 61, 64, 74, 85, 89, 93, 95, 97–99, 103, 110, 111, 120–21, 123–26, 129, 132, 133, 144, 146, 153–55, 157–58, 162, 169, 170, 173, 219, 235
Schelling, Friedrich von, 86
Scotland, 11
Sears Modern Homes, 166–67, 232–33
Seattle, Washington, 85–86
self-determination theory, 230
Serra, Richard, 60
settler companies, 84
747 aircraft, xiii

Shreve, Richmond, xvi
Shultz, George, 74
Silicon Valley, 52, 74, 76, 78, 163, 183
Simpsons, The (television show), 68–69, 140
simulation and iteration, 20, 62, 66–68, 78, 79, 95, 143, 147, 214
skilled intuition, 92
skyscrapers, xiii–xvi, 18, 23, 43, 90–91, 123, 138, 144, 159, 163–64, 172
Sleesman, Dustin J., 211
small-business owners, 29–30
small modular reactors (SMRs), 177
small-scale hydroelectric, 168
Smith, Al, xiv
Smith, Patti, 130
SMS texting app, xiii
snap judgments, 28–29, 31
SNCF, France, 82
Social Science Research Network (SSRN), 193
solar power, 77, 155–57, 171–73, 175–76, 179, 187, 191, 235
Solomon R. Guggenheim Foundation, 48
Somervell, Brehon B., 22–26, 30–31, 40–43
Sonning Prize, 214
Soul (movie), 18, 69
South Africa, 109
space, 11, 169
SpaceX, 169
Spain, 48–50, 60, 61, 65–70, 77–79, 213, 219, 220, 233
speed, 3, 15–19, 29, 33–34
Spielberg, Steven, 133–35, 137
Staats, Bradley, 34
standard deviations, 9
Stanovich, Keith, 29
Starrett Brothers and Eken, 90
start digging a hole strategy, 36–37, 64
State Route 99 tunnel, Seattle, 85–86
statistics, 9, 206–7, 226–27
Staw, Barry M., 211
Stone, Brad, 55
stories vs. data, 134–36

Storyk, John, 127–30, 134, 141–42
strategic misrepresentation, 26–27, 35–36, 38, 104, 110, 208, 209
subways, 170, 174, 233
Suez Canal, 14
sunk-cost fallacy, 39–40
Sunstein, Cass R., 31, 132, 135, 210
supply chains, 14
survival of the fittest, 163
survivorship bias, 136
Sweden, 115–16, 174
Swiss Parliament Building, 141
Switzerland, 7, 109
Sydney Opera House, Australia, 49, 60, 61, 63–65, 69, 73, 80–82, 93, 94, 134, 135, 137–40, 213–15, 218, 220, 229, 232

tacit knowledge, 91–92
Taillibert, Roger, 89
Taj Mahal, India, 60
Takemori, Tensho, 68
Taleb, Nassim Nicholas, 11, 225
Tali, Sharot, 209
Target, 11
team building, 148–50
teams, 20, 142–45, 147–55, 186, 214, 231
technology, 52, 86–87
Terminal 5 (T5), Heathrow Airport, United Kingdom, 145–55, 165, 187, 230, 231
Tesla, 169
testing, 77–78, 95, 109
Thames Barrier flood controls, United Kingdom, 151
theory of change, 52
Theranos, 74, 78
thin-tailed projects, 171–73, 206
think slow, act fast, xiii, xvi, 3, 18–19, 22, 46, 64, 69, 119, 126, 142, 143, 185
Thinking, Fast and Slow (Kahneman), 109, 208–9
Thompson, Louis, 19
Three-Mile Island, 115
Tokyo Olympic Games (2020), 13, 88
Toy Story (movie), 18, 70, 75

Toyota, 230
Transbay Terminal, San Francisco, 35
transportation projects, 5–7, 35,
    115–16, 171, 223
    (*see also* specific projects)
tsunamis, 118, 160
tunnels, 3–7, 10, 11, 85–86, 97, 98,
    123–26, 155, 170, 173, 233
Tversky, Amos, 27, 28, 30, 31, 102,
    104, 105, 210, 237
Twain, Mark, 208
Twitter, 78

U2, 130
underestimation, 103, 104, 132–33,
    137, 138, 210
UNESCO, 60
uniqueness bias, 84, 105, 108, 111–12,
    114–16, 121, 122, 216
United Artists, 37–38
United Kingdom, 6, 12, 88, 104,
    119–20, 145–55, 164–65, 167, 174,
    182, 187, 230, 231
United Nations, 178
unknown unknowns, 107, 110, 111,
    222, 224
Up (movie), 69
Utzon, Jan, 215
Utzon, Jørn, 140, 232
    experience of, 80, 81, 93, 94
    one-building architect, 139, 229
    Sydney Opera House designed by,
    61, 63–65, 73–74, 80, 93, 94, 134,
    139, 214–15, 218, 220, 229, 232

vaporware, 74
Vestas, Denmark, 183
vision, x, xi, xiii, 17, 19
Vitra Design Museum, Germany, 67
Vogel, Steve, 22, 40

Waldorf-Astoria hotel, New York
    City, xiv
Wall Street Journal, The, 74
Wallace, David Foster, 26
Walmart, 11
Walt Disney Company, 75

Walt Disney Concert Hall, Los
    Angeles, 93–94, 218–20
Walters-Storyk Design Group, 141
War Department, 22
Warner Bros., 130
Washington, DC, 23–24
Washington Monument, 24
water projects, 10, 173, 207
wealth, 10
weather events, 177
wedding cakes, 163, 187
Weil am Rhein, Germany, 67
Wembley Stadium, United Kingdom,
    154, 231
West, Richard, 29
What You See Is All There Is
    (WYSIATI), 29, 47, 50, 55
wildfires, 177, 178, 226, 227
Williams, Walter, 5
Willis, Carol, 90
wind power, 77, 155–56, 171–73,
    175–76, 179–84, 187, 235, 236
windmills, 172
window of time, window of doom,
    13–15
Winfrey, Oprah, 53
Winston-Salem, North Carolina,
    90–91
Winwood, Steve, 130
Wired magazine, 168
Wolf Prize, 214
Wolstenholme, Andrew, 146–48, 150,
    151, 153–55, 186–87
Wonder, Stevie, 130
Wood, Ron, 130
work backwards, 51–53
World Development journal, 137
World Health Organization, 177
world hunger, ending, 174, 234
World War II, 22, 24, 80, 123
WYSIATI (What You See Is All
    There Is), 29, 47, 50, 55

XRL project, Hong Kong, 97–99,
    103, 123–26, 220, 228

Zuckerberg, Mark, 136

ABOUT THE AUTHORS

BENT FLYVBJERG is a professor at the University of Oxford, an economic geographer, and "the world's leading megaproject expert," according to the global accounting network KPMG. He is also Villum Kann Rasmussen Professor and chair at the IT University of Copenhagen. He is principal author of *Megaprojects and Risk* and editor of *The Oxford Handbook of Megaproject Management*. He has consulted on over one hundred projects costing $1 billion or more and has been knighted by the Queen of Denmark.

DAN GARDNER is a journalist and the *New York Times* bestselling author of *Risk* and *Future Babble* and co-author of *Superforecasting* (with Philip E. Tetlock).

ABOUT THE TYPE

This book was set in Caslon, a typeface first designed in 1722 by William Caslon (1692–1766). Its widespread use by most English printers in the early eighteenth century soon supplanted the Dutch typefaces that had formerly prevailed. The roman is considered a "workhorse" typeface due to its pleasant, open appearance, while the italic is exceedingly decorative.